ELIZABETH OF YORK

QUEENSHIP AND POWER

Series Editors: Carole Levin and Charles Beem

This series brings together monographs and edited volumes from scholars specializing in gender analysis, women's studies, literary interpretation, and cultural, political, constitutional, and diplomatic history. It aims to broaden our understanding of the strategies that queens—both consorts and regnants, as well as female regents—pursued in order to wield political power within the structures of male-dominant societies. In addition to works describing European queenship, it includes books on queenship as it appeared in other parts of the world, such as East Asia, Sub-Saharan Africa, and Islamic civilization.

Editorial Board

Linda Darling, University of Arizona (Ottoman Empire)
Theresa Earenfight, Seattle University (Spain)
Dorothy Ko, Barnard College (China)
Nancy Kollman, Stanford University (Russia)
John Thornton, Boston University (Africa and the Atlantic World)
John Watkins (France and Italy)

Published by Palgrave Macmillan

The Lioness Roared: The Problems of Female Rule in English History
By Charles Beem

Elizabeth of York
By Arlene Naylor Okerlund

Learned Queen: The Imperial Image of Elizabeth I (forthcoming)
By Linda Shenk

Tudor Queenship: The Reigns of Mary and Elizabeth (forthcoming)
By Anna Whitelock and Alice Hunt

Elizabeth I's Amorous Discourse
By Ilona Bell

French Queen's Letters
By Erin Sadlack

The Face of Queenship: Early Modern Representations of Elizabeth I (forthcoming)
By Anna Riehl

Renaissance Queens of France (forthcoming)
By Glenn Richardson

ELIZABETH OF YORK

Arlene Naylor Okerlund

palgrave
macmillan

ELIZABETH OF YORK

First published in hardcover in 2009 by
PALGRAVE MACMILLAN®
in the United States—a division of St. Martin's Press LLC,
175 Fifth Avenue, New York, NY 10010.

Where this book is distributed in the UK, Europe and the rest of the world,
this is by Palgrave Macmillan, a division of Macmillan Publishers Limited,
registered in England, company number 785998, of Houndmills,
Basingstoke, Hampshire RG21 6XS.

Palgrave Macmillan is the global academic imprint of the above companies
and has companies and representatives throughout the world.

Palgrave® and Macmillan® are registered trademarks in the United States,
the United Kingdom, Europe and other countries.

ISBN: 978–0–230–12048–8

Library of Congress Cataloging-in-Publication Data

Okerlund, Arlene.
    Elizabeth of York / Arlene Naylor Okerlund.
        p. cm.
    Includes bibliographical references and index.
    ISBN 978–0–230–61827–5
        1. Elizabeth, Queen, consort of Henry VII, King of England,
    1465–1503. 2. Henry VII, King of England, 1457–1509. 3. Great Britain—
    History—Henry VII, 1485–1509. 4. Queens—Great Britain—Biography.
    I. Title.
DA330.8.E44O44 2009
942.05'1092—dc22
[B]   2009007703

A catalogue record of the book is available from the British Library.

Design by Newgen Imaging Systems (P) Ltd., Chennai, India.

First PALGRAVE MACMILLAN paperback edition: October 2011

Transferred to Digital Printing in 2011

To my students, who have kept me intellectually agile during all these years. May you thrive in carrying on our great tradition of learning, teaching, and writing.

"You have a daughter called Elizabeth,
Virtuous and fair, royal and gracious."

Richard III to Queen Elizabeth Wydeville in
Shakespeare, *The Tragedy of Richard III,* 4.4.204–5

CONTENTS

ILLUSTRATIONS

ABBREVIATIONS

CCR	*Calendar of the Close Rolls.*
Calendar Spain	*Calendar of Letters, Despatches, and State Papers, relating to the negotiations between England and Spain, preserved in the Archives at Simancas and elsewhere: Henry VII. 1485–1509.*
Calendar Papal	*Calendar of Papal Letters.*
Calendar Venice	*Calendar of State Papers and Manuscripts, relating to English Affairs, existing in the Archives and Collections of Venice, and in other Libraries of Northern Italy.*
CP	*Complete Peerage*
CPR	*Calendar of Patent Rolls.*
CL	*Chronicles of London.*
Crowland	*The Crowland Chronicle Continuations: 1459–1486*
GC	*The Great Chronicle of London.*
L & P, R III & H VII	*Letters and Papers Illustrative of the Reigns of Richard III and Henry VII.*
L & P, Henry VIII	*Letters and Papers, Foreign and Domestic, of the Reign of Henry VIII*
Mancini	Mancinus, Dominicus. *The Usurpation of Richard the Third.*
ODNB	*Oxford Dictionary of National Biography.*
PP	*Privy Purse Expenses of Elizabeth of York.*
RP	*Rotuli Parliamentorum.*
Rozmital	*The Travels of Leo of Rozmital.*

Other references appear in the bibliography under the last name of the author or first word of the title.

GENEALOGICAL CHARTS AND TABLES

1. Henry VII Ancestry

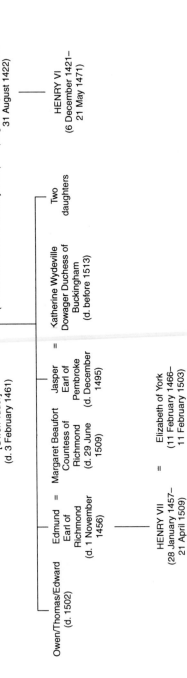

Tewdwr ap Goronwy = Margaret
(d. 1367)

Goronwy   Edward   Rhys   Gwilyn   Maredudd ap Tewdwr = Margaret
[Meredith]

Charles VI of France   =   Isabella of Bavaria
d. 21 October 1422   d. September 1435

Owain ap Maredudd ap Tewdwr   =   (2) Katherine of Valois (1)   =   HENRY V
[Owen Tudor]   (27 October 1401–3 January 1437)   (August/September 1387–
(d. 3 February 1461)   31 August 1422)

HENRY VI
(6 December 1421–
21 May 1471)

Katherine Wydeville
Dowager Duchess of
Buckingham
(d. before 1513)

Two
daughters

Owen/Thomas/Edward   Edmund   =   Margaret Beaufort   Jasper   =
(d. 1502)   Earl of   Countess of   Earl of
                      Richmond   Richmond   Pembroke
                      (d. 1 November (d. 29 June   (d. December
                      1456)   1509)   1495)

HENRY VII   =   Elizabeth of York
(28 January 1457–   (11 February 1466–
21 April 1509)   11 February 1503)

2. Elizabeth of York Ancestry

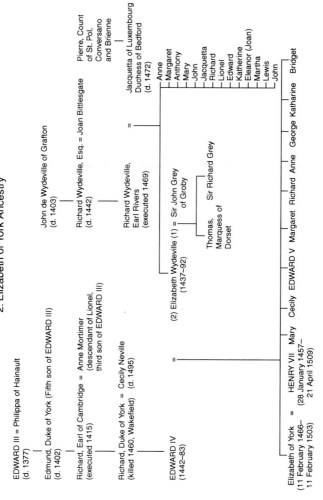

EDWARD III = Philippa of Hainault
(d. 1377)

Edmund, Duke of York (Fifth son of EDWARD III)
(d. 1402)

Richard, Earl of Cambridge = Anne Mortimer
(executed 1415)   (descendant of Lionel,
                                            third son of EDWARD III)

Richard, Duke of York = Cecily Neville
(killed 1460, Wakefield)   (d. 1495)

EDWARD IV
(1442–83)

John de Wydeville of Grafton
(d. 1403)

Richard Wydeville, Esq. = Joan Bittlesgate
(d. 1442)

Pierre, Count
of St. Pol,
Conversano
and Brienne

Richard Wydeville,
Earl Rivers
(executed 1469)

Jacquetta of Luxembourg
Duchess of Bedford
(d. 1472)

(2) Elizabeth Wydeville (1) = Sir John Grey
(1437–92)   of Groby

Thomas,   Sir Richard Grey
Marquess of
Dorset

Anne
Margaret
Anthony
Mary
John
Jacquetta
Richard
Lionel
Edward
Katherine
Eleanor (Joan)
Martha
Lewis
John

Elizabeth of York   =   HENRY VII   Mary   Cecily   EDWARD V   Margaret   Richard   Anne   George   Katharine   Bridget
(11 February 1466–   (28 January 1457–
11 February 1503)   21 April 1509)

3. Henry VII and Elizabeth of York Descendants

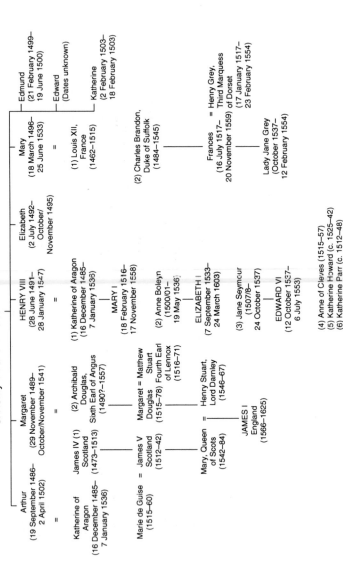

4. The Beauforts

EDWARD III (1312–77)

John of Gaunt (Fourth son of EDWARD III)
(1340–99)

married

(1) Blanche of Lancaster
(1345–69)

(2) Constance of Castile
(1354–94)

(3) Katherine Swynford
(1350–1403)

John Beaufort = Margaret Holland
Earl of Somerset
(d. 1410)

Henry
Bishop of Winchester,
Cardinal (d. 1447)

Thomas = Margaret Neville
Duke of Exeter
(d. 1426)

Joan (1379–1440)
= (1) Robert Ferrers
= (2) Ralph Neville, Earl
        of Westmorland

Thomas, Count of Perche
Edmund, Duke of Somerset (d. 1455)
Joan = James I of Scotland
Margaret = Thomas, Earl of Devon

Henry, Earl
of Somerset
(d. 1418)

John, Duke (2) = Margaret Beauchamp
of Somerset   of Bletsoe
(d. 1444)

Margaret Beaufort = (2) Edmund Tudor
(1443–1509)   (c. 1430–56)

John, Viscount Welles = Cecily of York (Sister of Elizabeth of York)
(d. 1499)   (1469–1507)

= (1) Oliver St. John
= (3) Lionel, Lord Welles
        (d. 1461)

John de la Pole (1) =
(annulled)

Henry Stafford (3) =
(d. 1471)

Thomas Stanley (4) =
Earl of Derby
(d. 1504)

HENRY VII = Elizabeth of York
(1457–1509)   (1466–1503)

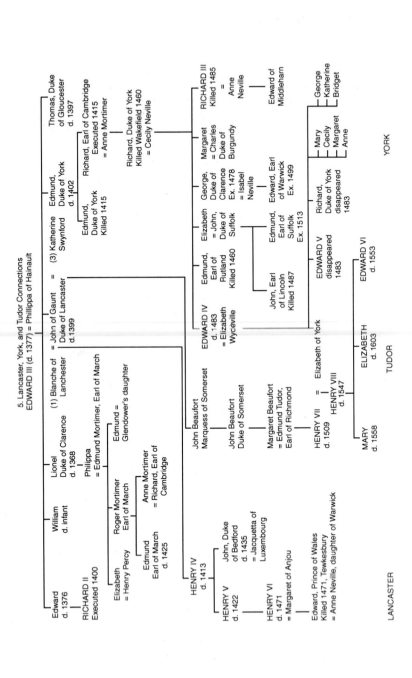

5. Lancaster, York, and Tudor Connections
EDWARD III (d. 1377) = Phillippa of Hainault

LANCASTER

TUDOR

YORK

6. Children of Henry VII and Elizabeth of York

Henry VII, born 28 January 1457 at Pembroke Castle, Wales. Died 21 April 1509.
>Father: Edmund Tudor, Earl of Richmond (son of Owen Tudor and Katherine of Valois).
>Mother: Margaret Beaufort, Countess of Richmond (daughter of John Beaufort, Duke of Somerset, and Margaret Beauchamp of Bletsoe).

Elizabeth of York, born at Westminster Palace, 11 February 1466. Died 11 February 1503.
>Father: King Edward IV (son of Richard, Duke of York, and Cecily Neville).
>Mother: Elizabeth Wydeville (daughter of Richard Wydeville, Earl Rivers, and Jacquetta of Luxembourg, Duchess of Bedford).

Children

1. Arthur, born 20 September 1486. Died 2 April 1502.
   Married Katherine of Aragon (by proxy Whitsunday 1499 and 19 May 1501; in person 14 November 1501).

2. Margaret, born 29 November 1489. Died 18 October 1541.
   Married (1) James IV of Scotland (by proxy 25 January 1502; in person 8 August 1503).
   Son James V of Scotland, born April 1512. Died 14 December 1542.
   Granddaughter Mary, Queen of Scots, born 8 December 1542. Executed 8 February 1587.
   Great-grandson James I of England (VI of Scotland), born 19 June 1566. Died 27 March 1625.
   Married (2) Archibald Douglas, Earl of Angus, August 1514. Divorced 11 March 1528.
   Married (3) Henry Stewart, Lord Methven, before 1 April 1528.

3. Henry VIII, born 28 June 1491. Died 28 January 1547.
   Married (1) Katherine of Aragon, 11 June 1509.
   Daughter Mary I, born 18 February 1516. Died 17 November 1558.
   Married (2) Anne Boleyn, 25 January 1533.
   Daughter Elizabeth I, born 7 September 1533. Died 24 March 1603.
   Married (3) Jane Seymour, 30 May 1536. Died 24 October 1537.
   Son Edward VI, born 12 October 1537. Died 6 July 1553.
   Married (4) Anne of Cleves, 6 January 1540. Marriage annulled 9 July 1540.

Married (5) Katherine Howard, 28 July 1540.
Married (6) Katherine Parr, 12 July 1543.

4. Elizabeth, born 2 July 1492. Died October/November 1495.

5. Mary, born 18 March 1496. Died 25 June 1533.
   Married (1) King Louis XII of France (by proxy 13 August 1514 at
       Greenwich and 2 September 1514 in Paris; in person 9 October
       1514).
   Married (2) Charles Brandon, Duke of Suffolk (in secret 3 March
       1515 in Paris, and in public 13 May 1515 at Greenwich).
   Daughter Frances, born 16 July 1517. Died 20/21 November
       1559.
   Granddaughter Lady Jane Grey, born October 1537. Executed
       12 February 1554.

6. Edmund, born 21 February 1499. Died 19 June 1500.

7. Edward, unknown dates of birth and death.

8. Katherine, born 2 February 1503. Died 20 February 1503.

ACKNOWLEDGMENTS

Writing historical biography is the ultimate collaborative enterprise. Since the genesis of *Elizabeth of York* lies in the scribes, archivists, antiquarians, and scholars who have recorded, preserved, transcribed, and analyzed documents created during the fascinating fifteenth century, I urge every reader to contemplate the bibliography and to recognize the individual and collective contributions of its authors and editors.

Books and archival materials are useless, however, unless they reach readers in this twenty-first century. Individuals who went out of their way to provide essential documents include Polly Armstrong and Mattie Taormina in Special Collections and Rare Books at Stanford University; Elisabeth Fairman, Curator, and Melissa Fournier, Associate Museum Registrar, Rare Books and Manuscripts, Yale Center for British Art, New Haven; Andrea Clarke, Curator of Early Modern Historical Manuscripts at the British Library; and Jan Graffius, Curator at Stonyhurst College, UK.

Specialists in local history added knowledge not always available in published texts: Geoffrey Wheeler, a colleague and friend in London, advised me on illustrative material; Sheila Gray, Winchester Cathedral Voluntary Guide, provided information about Queen Elizabeth's residency in Winchester Close; Chris Field and Angela Old described details of the Skenfrith Cope.

Equally important for a writer seeking information quite arcane to the Silicon Valley where I live are the dedicated staff of Interlibrary Loan Services at San José State University: Vicki Mercer, Shirley Miguel, Jamie Balderrama-Ratliff, and all student assistants. They are among the few individuals who understand my excitement at receiving a facsimile of *The Testament of Amyra Sultan Nichemedy* published in 1481, a book read by the young princesses Elizabeth of York and her sister Cecily.

Friends who suggested improvements to my manuscript include Helen Kuhn, Elsie Leach, and Judy Reynolds. Marianina Olcott untangled the syntax of my Latin translations, Sebastian Cassarino taught me lessons about Italian, and Jean Shiota in San José State's Instructional Resources calmed my nerves when overwhelmed by computers. Samantha Hasey and Christopher Chappell at Palgrave Macmillan provided helpful advice as they guided transformation of the manuscript into the present book. Throughout research, revisions, manuscript preparation, and production, my friend Cynthia Soyster and my daughter Linda Okerlund kept me sanely rooted in reality—or at least, they tried.

  Friends and colleagues, all, I thank you.

CHAPTER 1

THE GRACIOUS QUEEN: BEGINNINGS

The entire nation eagerly anticipated the birth. Edward IV, the 23-year old king of England, was awaiting the arrival of the first heir to his Yorkist throne. In five short years Edward IV had brought prosperity to England, after defeating the Lancastrian king Henry VI at the battle of Towton on March 29, 1461. Edward's victory ended 39 years of governance by the well meaning, but inept Henry VI who was now imprisoned in the Tower of London. The thriving merchants of London especially welcomed the vigor and intelligence of their young king, whose newborn heir would add stability to his reign and assure the future of the Yorkist dynasty.

Edward IV had secretly married his queen, Elizabeth née Wydeville, on May Day 1464,[1] a festive holiday that celebrated spring with joyous abandon. In many ways, May Day symbolized the king's somewhat reckless disregard of court politics in marrying a Lancastrian widow five years older than himself and already the mother of two small sons. Edward kept their marriage secret for more than four months—even while his unsuspecting advisors were negotiating a political marriage between him and Lady Bona, sister-in-law of the king of France. When Edward introduced Queen Elizabeth to his Council at Reading in September 1464, the surprise was universal. But if his advisors were publicly humiliated and politically embarrassed by their exclusion from the king's decision to marry, they hid their irritation as Edward proudly presented Elizabeth to his Council between the arms of his brother George, duke of Clarence, and his cousin Richard Neville, earl of Warwick. King Edward then staged an elaborate coronation procession through the streets of London on May 25, 1465, to display his beautiful, blonde queen to his subjects.

By February 1466, birth of the king's heir was imminent. Everyone expected a son. Dominic de Serigo, physician to Edward IV, had assured the king "that the queen was conceived with a prince."[2] The Court had prepared "great provision...for christening of the said prince," anticipating the heir who would extend England's stability, prosperity, and growth. When the queen's labor began, Master Dominic—who was banned from the birthing chamber where only women were allowed—hovered outside the door. He contemplated the reward that Edward, a generous monarch, would give his physician at news of his son's arrival. On February 11, 1466, when the first cries of the child were heard, Master Dominic

> knocked or called secretly at the chamber door, and frayned [asked] what the queen had. To whom it was answered by one of the ladies, "Whatsoever the queen's grace hath here within, sure it is that a fool stands there without," And so confused with this answer, he departed without seeing of the King for that time.[3]

Queen Elizabeth gave birth to a beautiful, golden daughter. Edward IV with his usual good humor showed no disappointment at the gender of his first legitimate heir and arranged a christening worthy of a Yorkist princess.

The Lady Princess, christened by George Neville, archbishop of York, was named Elizabeth. Her godfather was the powerful earl of Warwick ("the kingmaker"), and her godmothers were her grandmothers, Cecily Neville, duchess of York, and Jacquetta, duchess of Bedford, the two highest-ranking women in England after the queen. Edward's celebration of his healthy, beautiful daughter continued into March when he staged a churching ceremony for his queen that displayed the grand magnificence of his court to England and the world. Fortuitously, a group of Bohemian pilgrims visiting shrines throughout Europe were on hand to witness Queen Elizabeth's churching procession and banquet. Their travel diaries describe the world into which the Lady Princess Elizabeth of York was born:

> The queen left her childbed that morning and went to church in stately order, accompanied by many priests bearing relics and by many scholars singing and carrying lights. There followed a great company of ladies and maidens from the country and from London, who had been summoned. Then came a great company

of trumpeters, pipers, and players of stringed instruments. The king's choir followed, forty-two of them, who sang excellently. Then came twenty-four heralds and pursuivants, followed by sixty counts and knights. At last came the queen escorted by two dukes. Above her was a canopy. Behind her were her mother and maidens and ladies to the number of sixty. Then the queen heard the singing of an Office, and, having left the church, she returned to her palace in procession as before. Then all who had joined the procession remained to eat. They sat down, women and men, ecclesiastical and lay, each according to rank, and filled four great rooms.[4]

More important than such courtly ceremony for the newborn child was the churching ritual that "purified" her mother. Churching usually occurred 30–40 days after birth, timed to emulate the Virgin Mary's presentation of the Christchild at the Temple. The mother entered the church wearing a veil, knelt at the altar, and made an offering to God. After making penance for her sins and thanking God for her happy delivery, the mother asked God's grace in raising her child. For Queen Elizabeth, whose virtue and piety were renowned during her lifetime,[5] this churching ceremony was especially profound. On that day in late March 1466, Queen Elizabeth could not have known that her prayers for this baby would be answered—but only after years of trauma and tragedy for both mother and daughter. The newborn Elizabeth of York would grow up to become a monarch beloved by her subjects, who called her "the gracious queen."[6] The intervening years, however, would bring long periods of political ruin and personal pain.

As "the Lady Princess," Elizabeth was nurtured with exceptional care—as were all the children born to Edward IV and Queen Elizabeth. The children lived with the queen, who frequently included them as she carried out her duties as Edward IV's consort. She took the three-year-old Elizabeth and two-year-old Mary with her, for instance, when visiting Norwich in June 1469. Queen Elizabeth traveled alone since Edward IV was in the north fighting rebels. The glitter and pageantry of the holiday especially excited the children. As the queen's entourage entered Norwich through Westwick Gate, the full ceremony of the Corporate Body greeted her. A stage covered with red and green worsted fabric displayed figures of angels and giants whose crests glittered with gold and silver leaf. Banners and escutcheons powdered with crowns, roses, and fleurs-de-lys displayed the king and queen's arms. A pageant of the "Salutation of Mary and Elizabeth" included speeches, songs by clerks, and music from organs. A friar played the part of Gabriel, assisted by 2 patriarchs, 12 apostles, and 16 virgins. Perhaps this enchanting spectacle, seen through the eyes of a three-year-old child, inspired the love of pageantry that lasted throughout Elizabeth of York's life.

From Westwick Gate, the queen's party proceeded to the Friars Preachers where another stage had been constructed. The steps leading to the platform were covered with "Tapster work," and Queen Elizabeth watched the performance while sitting in the great chair of St. Luke's Guild. Rain, however, forced the queen and her party to scurry to their lodgings at the Friars Preachers—an early, if minor, lesson in exhibiting grace under pressure for Elizabeth of York.

Disastrous news interrupted the pleasantries of Norwich, however, and abruptly thrust the royal children into the political reality that would forever govern their lives. The rebellion that had caused the king to journey North turned out to be led by the earl of Warwick and the duke of Clarence—Edward's cousin and brother—who were disenchanted with the king's increasing independence and their own loss of power. They imprisoned Edward IV and captured Queen Elizabeth's father, earl Rivers, and her brother Sir John Wydeville. On August 12, 1469, the queen's father and brother were beheaded without trial at Coventry.[7] When Queen Elizabeth received the news, she fled Norwich for London where she lived the next months in "scant state."[8] The children, forced into hasty flight, found their privileged world of palaces and holidays replaced by scanty provisions in a secluded residence.

At age three, Elizabeth's secure, entitled world was shattered. As months passed, the situation deteriorated. Not satisfied with murdering the child's grandfather and uncle, the rebels accused her grandmother Jacquetta of witchcraft and sorcery. Whispers of sorcery had circulated through the Court in 1464 when Edward first revealed his marriage, suggesting that the king had been seduced by some strange power. Now the charge of witchcraft became explicit as the rebels attempted to discredit the family with whom Edward had aligned himself. Accusations of sorcery were not trivial in the fifteenth century. In 1441 Jacquetta's sister-in-law Eleanor Cobham, duchess of Gloucester, was convicted of necromancy, publicly humiliated, and imprisoned until death. Now Jacquetta, duchess of Bedford, faced similar accusations.

Queen Elizabeth's situation was terrifying: her father and brother were dead, her husband imprisoned, her mother accused of witchcraft, and her three tiny children vulnerable to the vicissitudes of power politics. How much the children sensed the fear and foreboding of the situation is difficult to assess, but the little princess Elizabeth was fast learning about death and experiencing her first personal peril.

Only after the citizens of England refused to support Warwick and Clarence did the rebels free Edward IV, who returned to London in late 1469. The king commissioned a Council that investigated the witchcraft charges against Jacquetta and exonerated her in January 1470. A forgiving man, Edward reconciled with Warwick and confirmed their accord by betrothing princess Elizabeth, now almost four years old, to George Neville, Warwick's nephew and male heir. Elizabeth of York was too young to comprehend the import of this betrothal, but she would have ample time to live through subsequent traumas inflicted by other political liaisons.

As her father regained control of the realm, a semblance of normal life returned to the royal family. In June, the king and queen made a pilgrimage to Canterbury to give thanks for their survival, taking the four-year-old Elizabeth with them.[9] A pattern was beginning to emerge that would define Elizabeth of York's life—a life that forever oscillated between moments of glory and months of despair.

To the degree that royal occasion permitted, Queen Elizabeth included her children in the rituals and revelries of the Court—introducing them to responsibilities they would encounter as heirs to the Yorkist dynasty. Such nurturing during childhood greatly influenced Elizabeth of York throughout her adult life. As queen consort to Henry VII, she surrounded herself with family—sisters, uncles, nieces, nephews—including them in her Court and generously paying their expenses from her privy purse.

Respite for the royal family in 1470 was short-lived. Warwick and Clarence began plotting with the Lancastrian queen Margaret of Anjou to attack England with an army funded by Louis XI of France. Their invasion in September forced Edward IV into exile in the Netherlands and caused Queen Elizabeth to flee with her children to Sanctuary at Westminster Abbey. On October 1, 1470, the royal children again found themselves in a world vastly different from the palaces they knew so well.

Exactly where the queen lived with her 3 children (Elizabeth, age 4; Mary, age 3; and Cecily, 18 months) during this first Sanctuary retreat is unknown, but the medieval Abbey that surrounded them was noisy and chaotic. The 50 or 60 tenements crammed into the Sanctuary grounds were dark, cramped, and smelly—filled with beggars, thieves, bankrupts, and heretics seeking refuge from the law.[10] Shops on the Abbey grounds served the needs of Sanctuary residents, the 100 or so monks, their servants, and hundreds of daily visitors. Every Friday, fishmongers arrived with mussels, oysters, and fresh fish for the Fast Day, their cries adding to the cacophony of brewers, bakers, barbers, butchers, carpenters, and smiths hawking their wares. This world differed drastically from the palaces where a plethora of attendants served the royal children in their private nursery.

Princess Elizabeth's mother was distracted by both personal needs and political responsibilities. Eight months pregnant with Edward's fourth child, Queen Elizabeth attempted to defend her husband's rights by sending Abbot Millyng to the Mayor of London to ask that the City take control of the Tower. No match for the invading army, the mayor and aldermen instead surrendered to the rebels, who released the Lancastrian king Henry VI from imprisonment, restored him to power, and ended the Yorkist reign. Elizabeth Wydeville was no longer queen. Elizabeth of York was no longer a princess. But that was the least of the family problems. Queen Elizabeth prepared to give birth—with scant time to prepare.

Normally, royal queens entered confinement approximately one month before an expected birth. "Taking to one's chambers" served both spiritual and physical needs. The expectant mother had time to reflect on her life—especially the sin she had committed in conceiving a child—and opportunity to ask God's succour for both body and soul. The period of repose allowed time to gather strength for the strenuous ordeal of childbirth, an extremely dangerous event in this era of rudimentary medical knowledge. Death often resulted from puerperal ("childbed") fever, a systemic disease caused by bacteria introduced into the womb by unclean hands and non-sterile clothing. The cause of childbed fever was unknown at the time, but the tradition of isolating the mother within her birthing chamber helped to reduce exposure to infection. Limiting the number of people with whom the mother came in contact and laying in supplies well before the birth decreased the sources of dangerous pathogens. A few female attendants received food and other necessary items through the carefully guarded door of the birthing chamber, where wall and ceiling tapestries provided warmth and window coverings shielded the mother from drafts and noise.

Queen Elizabeth was denied both this period of repose and the carefully prepared birthing chamber when she gave birth on November 2, 1470. Although she was attended by her trusted mid-wife, Marjory Cobbe, the makeshift, helter-skelter surroundings hardly offered solace to the expectant mother and her three tiny daughters. Uncertainty about the fate of Edward IV in exile added tension and terror. When the newborn turned out to be a healthy boy, joy and relief provided respite from a desperate situation. Christened "Edward" during a ceremony in Westminster Abbey, the baby received protection from his godfathers Abbot Millyng and the Abbey Prior and his godmother Lady Scrope.

Princess Elizabeth and her tiny siblings spent more than six months in Westminster Sanctuary. They may have been permitted to play in the Abbey Close, but the absence of playmates and the monastic environs hardly offered pleasures enticing to children. During those six months, her father (himself living in penurious exile in Holland) finally persuaded the duke of Burgundy to fund ships for an invasion of England. Edward IV landed at Ravenspur and marched through York to London, where he arrived on April 12, 1471. He immediately moved the queen and their four children from Westminster Sanctuary to Baynard's Castle, the residence of his mother, Cecily Neville, duchess of York. On Easter Sunday, April 14, Edward's troops killed the earl of Warwick at the battle of Barnet. Three weeks later on May 4, 1471, Edward IV defeated the remnant of the Lancastrian forces at Tewkesbury.

Her father's victory over the Lancastrians restored princess Elizabeth to her royal life, and the death of Warwick rendered her betrothal to George Neville moot. Once more, the splendour of palaces and parties surrounded Elizabeth of York. When Lord Gruuthuyse of Bruges visited England in September 1472 to be honored for his hospitality to Edward in exile, Bluemantle

Pursuivant described an evening in the Queen's chambers at Windsor:

> [The queen] sat playing with her ladies at the morteaulx [a game similar to bowls] and some of her ladies and gentlewomen at the Closheys of ivory [ninepins], and dancing... The king danced with my lady Elizabeth, his eldest daughter.[11]

The next evening, the queen feted Lord Gruuthuyse:

> The queen did order a great banquet in her own chamber. At the which banquet were the king, the queen, my lady Elizabeth the king's eldest daughter, the duchess of Exeter [the king's sister Anne], my lady Rivers [the queen's sister-in-law Elizabeth], and the lord Gruuthuyse, sitting at one mess; and at the same table sat the duke of Buckingham, my lady his wife [the queen's sister Katherine], with divers other ladies...
> ...
> And when they had supped, my lady Elizabeth the king's eldest daughter, danced with the duke of Buckingham, and divers other ladies also.[12]

Sophisticated company for a six-year-old girl! Her love of dancing, first evoked by these evenings in her mother's chambers, remained with the lady princess throughout her life, a love she transmitted to her own children. Twenty-nine years later when her son Arthur married Katherine of Aragon, Elizabeth of York's younger son Prince Henry doffed his jacket and danced with an abandon that delighted everyone who watched.

The traditional dancing witnessed by Lord Gruuthuyse at Windsor Castle in 1472 differed dramatically from the complex pageantry of the court over which Elizabeth of York presided as queen consort in 1501. During the intervening decades, Burgundian influences—introduced in part by the Wydeville relatives of Elizabeth of York—transformed drama, art, and architecture in England.[13] Elizabeth of York lived at the center of this transformation, but to arrive at the Tudor court of Henry VII, this queen had to travel a long, dangerous, and terrifying road.

CHAPTER 2

YOUTH AND TRAGEDY

G roomed from birth to become a royal consort, Princess Elizabeth's daily upbringing was supervised from age two by Margery, Lady Berners, mistress of her nursery.[1] Royal daughters were typically placed under the governance of a mature lady of the nobility until they reached early adulthood. Lady Berners was the wife of Sir John Bourchier (great-grandson of Edward III and brother of Thomas, archbishop of Canterbury, and Lord Treasurer Henry, earl of Essex). A long-time friend of the Wydevilles, Sir John Bouchier was knighted with Elizabeth's grandfather Richard Wydeville on Palm Sunday, May 19, 1426, and had married the daughter and heir of Sir Richard Berners, from whom he gained his baronage.[2] Lord Berners was constable of Windsor Castle during the years that Lady Berners served as governess. Although Princess Elizabeth was not subjected to the rigorous educational regimen of her brother Prince Edward,[3] she acquired knowledge and skills under Lady Berners' tutelage that later served her well as queen.

Elizabeth of York read and spoke both English and French, skills essential to enjoy the ever-popular historical romances of the era. Both Elizabeth and her sister Cecily inscribed a French prose manuscript of the *Romance of the Saint Graal* on folio 1, signing their names "Elysabeth, the kyngys dowther" and "Cecyl the kyngys dowther."[4] Other signatures on flyleaves of the *Romance* belong to members of the extended Wydeville family. "E Wydevyll" might be that of her mother Elizabeth Wydeville before she married Sir John Grey or it could belong to her uncle Edward Wydeville. The signature "Alyanor Haute" probably belongs to one of her Haute cousins descended from Joan Wydeville (sister of Elizabeth's grandfather Richard, first Earl Rivers). Another signature of "Jane Grey" may belong to her aunt Eleanor, sometimes called Joan, who married Anthony Grey of Ruthin, or to her distant cousin Lady Jane Grey born years after

Elizabeth of York's death. The many signatures indicate that reading was a family affair and that the Wydevilles shared books among relatives.

A particularly interesting manuscript owned by Elizabeth and her sister Cecily is the *Testament de Amyra Sultan Nichhemedy, Empereur des Turcs.*[5] The title page date is "12 Sept., 1481" and the fleur-de-lis stamped within lozenges on the dark leather binding suggests that their copy was bound before 1483 by John Guilebert, the first binder who worked for Caxton.[6] The two princesses wrote their names on the title page:

> Elysabeth the kyngys dowghter Boke
> Cecyl the kyngys dowghter

This French narrative of 45 pages describes the death and funeral of the Emperor of the Turks who set out to conquer Alleppo in Syria but instead became sick and died. The descriptions of the Emperor, his Janissary slaves, the Constantinople mosques, the prayers from the minarets ("Murmara"), the thousands of mourners, the funeral ceremonies, the fight between the deceased Sultan's sons, and the ultimate triumph of Sultan Ildrem Bayezid depict exotic settings and entrancing characters. This book suggests that Elizabeth and Cecily's reading taught them about the larger, unknown, intriguingly different world beyond the island where they lived.

Elizabeth also learned sufficient Latin to follow the rites of worship in her Book of Hours and psalters, but she was not conversant in that language. In 1498 as the future mother-in-law of Katherine of Aragon, Elizabeth requested that the Spanish princess learn to speak French before she came to England, where the "ladies do not understand Latin, and much less, Spanish."[7]

Writing was less valued than reading in the fifteenth century. While educated men and women could sign their names, they generally employed scribes for writing. Margaret Paston, matriarch of a prosperous Norfolk family, for instance, dictated to others the personal and intimate letters she sent to her husband and sons in London.[8] Princess Elizabeth, however, belonged to a family who valued writing more than most—in spite of readily available scribes and secretaries. Her uncle Anthony Wydeville's translations of philosophical and religious texts became bestsellers for the printer Caxton. The few official letters that survive from Elizabeth of York's reign as Queen were written by scribes, of course, but she carefully supervised the work of her staff, as indicated by her signatures on the pages of surviving Privy Purse accounts.

A contemporary ballad, though more fiction than fact, credits Elizabeth with considerable writing ability. In the popular "Song of Lady Bessie," which describes the lady Elizabeth in the desperate months before the battle of Bosworth, Thomas Stanley, earl of Derby, laments his inability to write to the earl of Richmond because he has no scribe he can trust. "Lady Bessie" readily solves the problem:

> Bessie said, "Father, it shall not need;
>   I am a clerk full good, I say."
>
> She drew a paper upon her knee,
>   pen and ink she had full ready,
> hands white & fingers long;
>   she dressed her to write speedily.
>
> "Father Stanley, now let me see,
>   for every word write shall I."
> "Bessie, make a letter to the Holt
>   there my brother Sir William doth lie." (1.195–204)[9]

Scribe Bessie proceeds to take dictation from the earl of Derby for five separate letters to his brother Sir William Stanley; his son George, lord Strange; his son Edward; Sir John Savage; and Sir Gilbert Talbot: "Bessie writeth, the lord [Derby] he sealeth." That task completed, the earl of Derby once more despairs because he has no messenger to deliver the letters. Bessie again saves the day:

> "Go to thy bed, father, & sleep,
>   & I shall work for thee & me,
> tomorrow by rising of the sun
>   Humphrey Bretton shall be with thee."
>
> She brought the lord to his bed,
>   All that night where he should lie;
> & Bessie worketh all the night;
>   there came no sleep in her eye. (1.243–60)[10]

Pure fiction though this ballad may be, it reflects the popular view of Elizabeth of York's abilities and the sentimental affection of her English subjects for their accomplished and beloved queen.

Singing, dancing, and music surrounded this lady princess in her youth. She herself learned to dance, to play instruments, and to love the music of the 13 minstrels retained by Edward IV for entertaining at court festivals.[11] The minstrels' trumpets, shawms, small pipes, and strings added a professional component to her early musical education and became a vital, ever-present part of Elizabeth of York's adult life. As queen, Elizabeth retained her own minstrels quite separate from those of Henry VII—and rewarded them generously. Her own children played the lute, virginal, clavichord, and organ,[12] while she herself played the clavichord (and perhaps other instruments).[13] Her son Henry VIII became renowned for his singing, dancing, and composing.

Princess Elizabeth loved horses and rode beside her mother in Garter parades and royal processions. Noble women enjoyed hunting and shooting, and among purchases during the last year of Elizabeth of York's life were a sheaf-and-an-half of broad arrows and a sheaf of broad heads.[14] Years after Elizabeth's death, her sister Katherine, countess of Devon, hunted well after age 40.[15] While only men engaged in rigorous equine activities such as jousting, women were important spectators at those sports. During Elizabeth's royal childhood, she watched her Wydeville uncles and cousins excel on the tilting fields, where they introduced the pageantry that later transformed English tournaments.

The princess learned the traditional feminine skills of needlework and sewing, crafts put to good use in 1502 when she made the Garter mantle of Henry VII (having purchased the lace and buttons from her own privy purse).[16] At the same time, parlor games of cards, dice, "tables" (backgammon), the *morteaulx* and *Closheys* developed sociability and ease in interacting with others. Combined with religious instruction emphasizing character, virtue, and morality, Elizabeth of York's early education produced a charming, accomplished lady: "the Gracious Queen," indeed.

The family in which Princess Elizabeth grew up was unusually inclined toward intellectual enterprises, despite the disdain of many peers for "clerkly" education. Both her mother and her uncle Anthony Wydeville patronized Caxton's printing press. Anthony, lord Rivers, translated philosophical treatises from French into

English, including the popular *Dictes or Sayengis of the Philosophers* published in three separate editions in 1477, 1479, and 1489.[17] His translations of *The Morale Proverbes of Christyne* (de Pisan) and the massive *Cordiale* (detailing the "four last things" essential for man's redemption) place Anthony Wydeville among the humanists who prefaced England's incipient literary Renaissance. Princess Elizabeth's grandfather, Richard Wydeville, first lord Rivers, commemorated the coronation of his daughter by purchasing a copy of *The Romance of Alexander,*[18] and he owned a copy of the *Codicile* of Jean de Meum, a sequence of devotional poems.[19]

Elizabeth's father, Edward IV, purchased illuminated manuscripts and collected histories, romances, and moral treatises,[20] although his interest in the content of his collection is uncertain. It is likely that Princess Elizabeth's intellectual accomplishments derived from her Wydeville relatives. Her grandmother Jacquetta, a princess of Luxembourg, grew up in the center of the Burgundian Renaissance, the source of the literature brought to England by Elizabeth's uncle Anthony. As queen, Elizabeth of York filled her court with Wydeville relatives who interlaced Burgundy pageantry with English tournaments and drama.[21]

Such a background prepared the lady princess Elizabeth for the role she was about to assume in fulfilling her father's ambitions. By 1474, Edward IV was preparing to invade France and regain the lands lost by Henry VI. Before departing England, Edward composed his Will and carefully provided for each of his children in case of his death: Elizabeth and Mary, his oldest daughters, were bequeathed 10,000 marks each as marriage dowry. Cecily, already betrothed at age five to Prince James of Scotland, received a dowry of 18,000 marks; Prince Richard inherited the traditional York lands and Prince Edward the realm of England.

Once in France, however, Edward avoided battle and negotiated a treaty with Louis XI that provided the king of England with a handsome annuity of £10,000. Equally significant, the treaty betrothed Princess Elizabeth to the heir of the French king. The marriage agreement was summarized:

> There shall be contracted and had a marriage between the right noble Prince Charles, the son of the said most excellent King of France, and the most benign princess my lady Elizabeth, daughter of the said most victorious King of England.[22]

This time Elizabeth, age nine, was old enough to comprehend—and to experience—the importance of betrothal. For the moment she would stay in England, but her future was determined. She was destined to become queen of France, the first time any English princess was deemed worthy of that honor. Louis XI agreed to pay expenses for Elizabeth's journey to France and to provide an annual dowry of £60,000 "as soon as she shall come to years of marriage."[23] From this moment on, Elizabeth of York was known in both England and France as "my lady the Dauphine," the name by which her father addressed her.[24] Immediately, her education in ritual and protocol became even more important as she prepared to join the magnificent French court.

At age ten, Princess Elizabeth, along with her sister Mary (age 8) participated in the ritualistic high mass when her grandfather, Richard, duke of York, was reburied at Fotheringhay in July 1476. The king first offered the Mass penny and "did his obeisance before the said body."

> Next the queen came to offer, dressed all in blue without a high headdress, and there she made a great obeisance and reverence to the said body, and next two of the king's daughters came to offer in the same way.[25]

Less than a year later at the Feast of St. George at Windsor Castle, the 10-year old princess Elizabeth rode with her mother in the Garter procession, wearing a robe that matched the queen's:

> To...Mass the queen came on horseback in a murrey [plum-colored] gown of Garters. *Item*: the lady Elizabeth, the King's eldest daughter, in a gown of the same livery.[26]

For the Garter ceremonies, the king presented the queen and the lady princess a gift of rich fabric for their gowns: 15 yards of green tissue cloth-of-gold and 40 yards of blue and purple velvet.[27]

In 1478, Princess Elizabeth attended the wedding of her 4-year old brother Richard and 5-year old Anne Mowbray in St. Stephen's Chapel, Westminster Palace, where she received an important lesson in canon law: the wedding party was stopped at the chapel door because the bride and groom were related within the prohibited degrees of consanguinity. Fortuitously, a Papal Bull appeared, dispensing their "nearness of blood" and allowing the marriage to proceed.[28] But the highlight of the wedding was the jousting.

Traditionally, tournaments celebrated weddings, festivals, and national holidays throughout medieval England. During the fifteenth century, Wydevilles dominated these contests. In 1440, Sir Richard Wydeville, Elizabeth's grandfather, defended England's honor against Pedro de Vasquez, chamberlain to the duke of Burgundy. In 1467, Anthony Wydeville, lord Scales, reprised his father's role against the Bastard of Burgundy in England's most famous tournament of the century.[29] The one-year-old Elizabeth was too young to appreciate the excitement that pervaded London for weeks before and during those tilts. She also missed the splendid pageantry of the 1468 tournaments in Burgundy when her aunt Margaret of York married Charles, duke of Burgundy. Again the Wydevilles dominated: Anthony, lord Scales, officially presented Margaret to the Burgundians, and Sir John Wydeville (another of Elizabeth's uncles) won honors as "Prince of the Tourney."[30]

On January 22, 1478, however, "my lady the Dauphine," an impressionable 11 year old, witnessed the spectacle and pageantry of the wedding tournaments held on Westminster's tilting fields to celebrate Prince Richard and Anne Mowbray.[31] Riding first into the lists for the "Jousts Royal" was Thomas, marquess of Dorset (half-brother of Princess Elizabeth by her mother's first husband, Sir John Grey). The duke of Buckingham (Elizabeth's paternal cousin and maternal uncle by marriage to Katherine Wydeville) carried Dorset's helmet onto the field. Buckingham was followed by knights and esquires dressed in livery of white and murrey and by six coursers trapped in cloth-of-gold and crimson velvet embroidered with gold. Second to enter the tilting field was Sir Richard Grey (half-brother of Princess Elizabeth), his helmet borne by Lord Maltravers (Elizabeth's uncle by marriage to her aunt Margaret Wydeville). Sir Richard's knights and esquires wore blue and tawny livery. What colorful excitement!

But the best was yet to come. The most celebrated jouster of England—her uncle Anthony Wydeville—next entered the field

> in the house of an Hermit, walled and covered with black velvet, windowed viiiiple [the number of windows in the hermitage.] in form of glass, a cross of Saint Anthony with a bell ringing and a pair of beads, upon the former end of the hermitage.[31]

Rivers himself was dressed as a White Hermit, wearing a habit of "pleasance" whose white color contrasted vividly against the black velvet hermitage. Mounted on a horse trapped in tawny satin and decorated with trees of gold, the White Hermit paid tribute to St. Anthony, the earl's patron saint whose ascetic life of prayer and penance inspired Rivers' vocation as moral philosopher and his practice of wearing a hair shirt.[32]

With this entrance of Anthony Wydeville into the lists, the Burgundian "pageant car" arrived in England. While English medieval tournaments always featured flamboyant displays of banners and badges, liveries and trappings, such spectacle merely highlighted the martial prowess and skills displayed by competing knights. Burgundian tournaments, on the other hand, featured costumed knights who entered the lists in pageant cars constructed as elaborate sets and painted with scenery "that transformed their combat into episodes from chivalric romances."[33] English jousters encountered such pageantry at the 1468 marriage tournament of Margaret of York and Charles, duke of Burgundy. Ten years later, Anthony Wydeville imported that tradition to England.

Although Anthony's hermitage was more symbol than allegory, it inaugurated the traditions that came to characterize Tudor pageantry, beginning with the allegories that celebrated the wedding of Prince Arthur to Katherine of Aragon in 1501. The merging of Burgundian spectacle with England's own dramatic traditions— the mystery and morality plays—inspired the blossoming of the nation's literary Renaissance. Anthony Wydeville's symbolic hermitage evolved into the sophisticated "disguisings" over which Elizabeth of York presided as queen consort. The music and allegory of those Tudor disguisings in turn inspired the literary pageantry of Sidney's *Arcadia*, Spenser's *Faerie Queene*, Shakespeare's *Tempest*, Jonson's *Masque of Blackness*, and Milton's *Comus*.

In 1478, the tournament reverted to its traditional medieval form as soon as Anthony removed his White Hermit's habit. Sir Edward Wydeville (uncle of Princess Elizabeth), Sir James Tyrell, and John Cheney, esquire for the King's body, joined Rivers, Dorset, and Sir Richard Grey to constitute a team of six ("the party within"). They competed with another team of six, "the party without," in the Jousts Royal and breaking of spears. After the competitions, the ladies of the court met to determine the winners. "The right high and excellent Princess Elizabeth, first daughter to the king our sovereign lord" received the great honor of awarding the prizes.[34] Although none of the three prizes went to the Wydeville team, Anthony, lord Rivers, generously rewarded the Kings of Arms and Heralds with 20 marks at the end of the matrimonial feast.[35]

As Princess Elizabeth grew older, her responsibilities increased. In 1480 when her youngest sister Bridget was christened, the 14-year-old Elizabeth stood as godmother, along with her grandmother Cecily Neville, duchess of York. But these heady and exciting days of privilege were about to change.

Problems with her betrothal to the Dauphin began when Princess Elizabeth reached the marriageable age of 12 and Edward IV demanded that Louis XI pay her £60,000 annual dowry.[36] Edward ought to have been forewarned by the duplicity of the French king in 1477 when Louis XI suddenly proposed that the Dauphin, then aged 7, marry the 20-year-old Mary, duchess of Burgundy. Louis acted as if the Dauphin's betrothal to Princess Elizabeth—made just two years earlier—did not exist! Fortunately, Mary of Burgundy married Maximilian of Hapsburg, and the English-French alliance continued. Edward IV chose to ignore what he did not want to know about the French king's perfidy.

Although Louis had faithfully paid Edward his £10,000 annuity since their 1475 treaty, he resisted the dowry demand. Edward sent ambassadors Richard Tunstall and Thomas Langton to deliver the message that the king of England greatly wished the marriage to occur as soon as possible and that the dowry was due because Elizabeth was now of age.[37] Louis, consummate diplomat, replied that he, too, desired the marriage as soon as possible, but there was some misunderstanding about the payment of the dowry: marriage contracts became due at the consummation of the marriage, not when the betrothed bride reached marriageable age. Louis had consulted with his advisors who had drawn up the 1475 Treaty, as well as with many other religious and legal experts, and received assurances that the contract required payment only after consummation. Even then, the husband received the dowry, which did not become property of the wife until the marriage was dissolved by death. In these negotiations, King Louis XI of France validated his popular nickname as "the universal spider."

Edward's advisors responded with indignation, and Edward began negotiations with Maximilian and with the dukes of Brittany and Burgundy aimed at threatening Louis into compliance. The standoff lasted several years, until Louis in 1480 offered to send a delegation to England to enact the formal betrothal and to accompany Princess Elizabeth to her new home in France. If Edward did not wish his daughter to marry so soon, Louis would contribute 20,000 crowns (£4,000 sterling) toward her annual expenses in England. That offer fell far short of the £60,000 pounds demanded by Edward.

The official documents record only the diplomatic shenanigans of the two kings. True to the times, no attention was paid to the feelings of the young princess being buffeted to and fro by her father's avarice and Louis' guile. Elizabeth was old enough to comprehend that she was a pawn in the larger game of posturing and power politics, knowledge that perhaps ameliorated any uncertainty she felt about her betrothal and future life. For the moment, Edward handled the situation by avoiding the French ambassadors and turning his attention to war with Scotland.

While Princess Elizabeth awaited her future fate, personal disasters struck the royal family. Anne Mowbray, the child bride of Prince Richard, died on November 19, 1481. Six months later, Elizabeth's sister Mary died on May 23, 1482. Elizabeth and Mary had grown up together in their mother's household, their joint expenses paid by a £400 annual grant from their father.[38] Born just 18 months apart, they had shared so many childhood experiences—the trip to Norwich, the months in Sanctuary, the reburial of their grandfather at Fotheringhay. The short life of Mary, recently betrothed to the king of Denmark, ended at age 14. Her death only added to the trauma hovering at the edge of Elizabeth of York's royal world.

Some news was hopeful. The Scots were defeated in August 1482 and peace was restored to England, although the conflict caused Edward IV to end the match made between his daughter Cecily and Prince James of Scotland. The royal family celebrated Christmas 1482 with a splendid display of grandeur. The king attracted attention with new fashions: his robes with full sleeves lined with costly furs and rolled over the shoulders gave him "a new and distinguished air." The Crowland Chronicler described the Court with unreserved pleasure and accolades:

> In those days you might have seen a royal Court such as befitted a mighty kingdom, filled with riches and men from almost every nation and (surpassing all else) with the handsome and most delightful children born of the marriage...to Queen Elizabeth.[39]

The joy did not last. On December 23, 1482, Louis XI signed the Treaty of Arras with Burgundy and married his son the Dauphin Charles to Margaret, daughter of Maximilian. The betrothal that had dominated Elizabeth's life for the past 7 years—the crucial, formative years from 9 to 16—abruptly ended.

The lady princess Elizabeth was jilted at age sixteen. But Elizabeth of York was still young and beautiful—and daughter of the king of England. If she thought that the new year would bring hope and promise of a better future, however, she was sorely disappointed. The year 1483 would be her *annus horribilis*.

CHAPTER 3

THE LADY PRINCESS DEPOSED

As long as Edward IV was king of England, Princess Elizabeth's prospects for another royal marriage were excellent. Her golden hair, lovely features, tall stature, and cultured charm—combined with the growing wealth and power of England—made her an attractive partner for any European prince. Thus, the year 1483 began well enough for the 16-year-old princess. Her father began to plot his revenge against Louis XI. With secure Scottish borders, England could concentrate its forces against its historic enemy across the Channel. When Parliament opened on January 20, Edward richly rewarded his brother, Richard, duke of Gloucester, for winning England's victory in the north. On Candlemas Day, February 2, King Edward and Queen Elizabeth led the Court in State procession from St. Stephen's Chapel to Westminster Hall. Everything seemed normal.

But around Easter (March 30), Edward suddenly fell ill:

> ...the king, though he was not affected by old age nor by any known type of disease which would not have seemed easy to cure in a lesser person, took to his bed about Easter-time and on 9 April gave up his spirit to his Maker at his palace of Westminster in the year 1483...[1]

The women of the Court did not participate in the public obsequies following Edward's death.[2] Lord Dacre, the queen's chamberlain, represented Queen Elizabeth at the mass of requiem where the earl of Lincoln (Edward IV's nephew) offered the traditional mass penny.[3] Among the courtiers paying their respects were Thomas, marquess of Dorset (son of Queen Elizabeth); Sirs Richard and Edward Wydeville (brothers to the queen); Thomas, lord Stanley; and William, lord Hastings. On his deathbed, the king had admonished the different factions of his Court to reconcile their differences and to support the young Edward V. The mourners seemed to have complied.

The royal women mourned in private as Queen Elizabeth—now queen dowager—helped plan her son Edward's move from Ludlow to London for his coronation. When the Council quarreled over the number of men to accompany the 12-year-old Edward V, queen dowager Elizabeth acted as peacemaker:

> the benevolent queen, desirous of extinguishing every spark of murmuring and unrest, wrote to her son that he should not have more than 2,000 men when he came to London.[4]

The compromise achieved a temporary harmony that would soon explode into rebellion.

Princess Elizabeth lost not only a dearly loved father, but also her prospects for marrying in the near future. Her 12-year-old brother and his Council had to stabilize the nation before they could think about brokering marriages for the new king's sisters. Little did Elizabeth suspect that her brother's youth, innocence, and political naïveté would be the least of her problems. Within weeks, her life would plunge to its nadir of despair.

On April 30, Richard, duke of Gloucester, took control of his nephew Edward V and arrested Anthony Wydeville, earl Rivers, brother of the queen dowager and governor of the young king for the past 10 years. Rivers was the male head of the Wydeville family—an erudite nobleman, skilled jouster, and successful businessman. He fatally misjudged Richard, duke of Gloucester, however, when he dined with him that fateful evening in Northampton. Trust of Gloucester—brother of Edward IV and uncle of the new King—cost Rivers his life and immersed England in two years of turmoil and rebellion. Gloucester arrested Rivers, the political and economic pillar of Wydeville power, leaving no doubt that he intended to undermine the queen dowager's influence over her son, King Edward V. Gloucester sent Rivers north to prison, along with Princess Elizabeth's half-brother Sir Richard Grey and Edward V's chamberlain, Sir Thomas Vaughan. Princess Elizabeth would never see them again.

The queen dowager immediately sought Sanctuary at Westminster Abbey with her five daughters and youngest son, Prince Richard. On May 1, she moved the family to the Abbot's manor of Cheneygates within Westminster Close. Princess Elizabeth was now 17 years old, an age when many royal women were already married and the mother of heirs. She would live the next 11 months in limbo at Westminster Sanctuary.

On May 7, Gloucester and his supporters turned the princess and her family into paupers by sequestering the property of the deceased Edward IV. During a meeting at Baynard's Castle (residence of Cecily Neville, duchess of York and grandmother of Edward IV's children), Gloucester and his adherents denied the queen dowager and Edward's daughters any access to his moveable goods.[5] Within days, Gloucester was declared the official "Protector" of King Edward V and effectively took control of all governing authority.

The Protector moved rapidly in executing his coup d'état. In a letter to the city of York on June 10, Gloucester accused queen dowager Elizabeth of plotting to murder him. He persuaded the king's Council and the archbishop of Canterbury to remove Prince Richard from his mother's protection in Westminster Sanctuary. The nine-year-old prince was sent to the Tower to join Edward V on June 16. On Sunday, June 22, Ralph Shaa, Doctor of Divinity and brother of London's mayor, preached a sermon at Paul's Cross declaring Edward IV's marriage to Elizabeth to be adulterous and their children "bastards." If Princess Elizabeth ever had hopes for a distinguished marriage—much less a royal one—it was dashed by Dr. Shaa's sermon, entitled "Bastard Slips Shall Never Take Deep Root." On Tuesday, June 24, the duke of Buckingham reiterated Shaa's claims of illegitimacy in a Guildhall speech.

Gossip swept through the rumor mill that was London. Edward IV was accused of bigamy based on an alleged precontract to marry another woman before his marriage to Elizabeth Wydeville. Only later was that woman identified as Eleanor Talbot Butler. Since she had been dead for 15 years, she could neither testify to clear her name nor verify the accusation. A second rumor suggested that Edward IV himself was illegitimate—born of an alleged liaison between his mother, Cecily Neville, duchess of York, and a French archer named Blaybourne. Cecily's adultery allegedly occurred in France while her husband was fighting the enemy. Never mind that Cecily Neville was alive and that her son Richard, duke of Gloucester, was using her London residence as the headquarters of his coup. Women were fair game in the propaganda wars that validated power. Slander was the weapon of choice.

The allegation of Edward IV's precontract to marry Eleanor Butler first surfaced after his death in 1483—19 years after the king's marriage to Elizabeth Wydeville. No mention of a precontract or the bastardy of the royal children had been voiced during those 19 years. Indeed, the nobles and citizenry of the kingdom had frequently sworn loyalty to Prince Edward as the heir to the English throne. The memoirs of Philippe de Commines, completed in 1498, ascribes the source of the precontract claim to Robert Stillington, bishop of Bath and Wells:

> This bishop discovered to the Duke of Gloucester that his brother King Edward had been formerly in love with a beautiful young lady and had promised her marriage, upon condition he might lie with her: the lady consented, and, as the bishop affirmed, he married them when nobody was present, but they two and himself. His fortune depending upon the court, he did not discover it, and persuaded the lady likewise to conceal it, which she did, and the matter remained a secret. After this King Edward married the daughter of an English gentleman, called the Lord Rivers: this lady was a widow, and had two sons.[6]

Stillington's word was sacrosanct because he was a bishop—though not a very good one. In 26 years, he visited his diocese only once.[7] He fathered several illegitimate children.[8] He flip-flopped his loyalties to the monarch of the moment. Having served the Lancastrian Henry VI as Keeper of the Privy Seal, he transferred his loyalty to Edward IV in 1461 after the decisive Yorkist victory at Towton. Many Lancastrians, of course, sought pardons from Edward IV after his accession to the throne. But that was only the beginning of Stillington's agile politics, whose shifting loyalties required several royal pardons: from Henry VI in October 1460 and again in January 1471; from Edward IV in February 1472.[9] Henry VI's pardon in 1460 suggests that the bishop had supported the duke of York during his 1459 rebellion, which could explain why Edward so readily awarded the bishop a position of trust when he became king. Henry VI's 1471 pardon suggests that Stillington switched his loyalties back to Lancaster during the readeption. Edward IV's pardon in 1472 after the Yorkist victory at Tewkesbury perhaps forgave the bishop for that Lancastrian lapse. In 1478 Stillington was imprisoned briefly during the period when George, duke of Clarence, was in conflict with Edward. The vacillating prelate secured yet a fourth pardon from Edward IV and restored himself to royal service.[10] His office as bishop conferred unassailable protection on the man.

If Stillington's testimony about the marital precontract of Edward with "a certain English lady" is true, he is surely damned as both man and prelate. For 19 years, the Bishop of Bath and Wells allowed his king to live in sin—endangering the mortal soul of Edward during every moment of his marriage to Elizabeth Wydeville. Surely as prelate the bishop had some responsibility to save the soul of the king—and thereby serve the moral weal of the nation. But he ignored the alleged precontract when Edward announced his marriage to Elizabeth Wydeville in 1464.

The good bishop further nullified any semblance of integrity in 1472 when he swore allegiance to Edward's son, Prince of Wales, as the king's legitimate heir. The bishop of Bath along with the archbishop of Canterbury and eight other "Lords Spiritual" and 36 "Lords Temporal" solemnly swore:

> I…take and repute You, Edward Prince of Wales, Duke of Cornwall and Earl of Chester, first begotten son of our Sovereign Lord Edward the IIIIth King of England and of France, and Lord of Ireland, to be very and undoubted Heir to our said Sovereign Lord, as to the Crowns and Realms of England and of France, and Lordship of Ireland, And promise and swear, that in case hereafter it happen You, by God's disposition, to outlive our said Sovereign Lord, I shall then take and accept You for true, very, and righteous King of England, &tc. And faith and truth to you shall bear. And in all things truly and faithfully behave me towards you, and your heirs, as a true and faithful subject oweth to behave him to his Sovereign Lord, and rightways King of England, &tc. So help me God and Holydom, and this holy Evangelist.[11]

The bishop confirmed his venality every time similar oaths were sworn across the nation: on May 3, 1474, for instance, the mayor and his brethren of Coventry assembled before the three-year-old Prince Edward to swear allegiance to the "first begotten son of our sovereign lord, Edward IV, King of England."[12]

Who, therefore, could possibly believe Bishop Stillington's word in 1483 about a "precontract"? The politically agile prelate now buttered his bread with Richard III's knife.

The second, equally nefarious rumor accused Cecily Neville of adultery in conceiving Edward. That accusation, if true, rendered Edward IV himself illegitimate. Rumors of Cecily's infidelity first surfaced in 1469 when Warwick and Clarence rebelled against Edward IV.[13] Such accusations were nothing new in Wars of the Roses propaganda, since bloodlines determined one's right to rule. The easiest way to the throne lay in bastardizing its occupant or heir. After the birth of Edward of Lancaster, for instance, rumors were rife that Margaret of Anjou had shared her bed with a partner more potent than Henry VI. Richard, duke of York, may have started that rumor—thereby teaching his son Clarence and nephew Warwick how to slander his own duchess less than a decade later.

Philippe de Commines records the gossip about Cecily Neville, delivered thirdhand to Louis XI of France, when England and Burgundy were fighting France in 1475. A messenger from the Constable of St. Pol entertained Louis XI by imitating the Duke of Burgundy. He stamped his feet, swore by St. George, and called the king of England "Blaybourne," the name of an archer's son who allegedly fathered Edward IV. King Louis, delighted with the calumny, asked that the story be repeated—and louder—so that Commines could hear it from behind the screen where he was hiding.[14]

Modern historians have disagreed about the credibility of stories regarding Cecily Neville's adultery. Based on the Duke of York's absence from Cicely's home in Rouen when Edward was conceived, Michael K. Jones argues that Edward IV's illegitimacy is probable.[15] York was maneuvering troops near Pontoise from mid-July to August 20, 1441, and Edward IV was born on April 28, 1442. Joanna Laynesmith responds that births may be premature or delayed—easily by a fortnight on either side of a projected birth date.[16] Calculating gestation periods is an inexact science and constitutes shaky grounds for accusations of adultery. There is also the possibility that York may have visited his wife during his month-long campaign just 50 miles away.

Most important, the charge of adultery was refuted clearly and explicitly by the only person who knew the truth. In her Will and Testament made in 1495, Cecily Neville wrote:

> I, Cecily, wife unto the right noble prince Richard, late Duke of York, *father unto the most Christian prince my Lord and son King Edward the iiith* the first day of April the year of our Lord 1495...make and ordain my testament in form and manner ensuing.[17] [Emphasis mine.]

Twice in her Will and Testament, Cecily Neville states firmly and unequivocally that Richard, duke of York, fathered their son Edward IV. Did she speak the truth? It is inconceivable to think that Cecily Neville would deceive her Lord at the very moment she was preparing to meet Him—the moment when she was seeking His final Grace.[18] In her last Testament, Cecily had nothing to gain and her eternal life to lose if she lied. The consequences argue compellingly for her truthfulness.

The rumors of illegitimacy that swept through London during the summer of 1483 rendered the future of Princess Elizabeth in Westminster Sanctuary bleaker with each passing day. Disinherited and bastardized, she received even more terrible news. On June 25, her uncle Anthony Wydeville, earl Rivers, and her half-brother Sir Richard Grey were executed at Gloucester's Pontefract estate in Yorkshire.[19] The next day, the duke of Gloucester assumed England's royal power by sitting in the royal chair in the Court of the King's Bench at Westminster Hall. Richard III dated his reign from June 26, 1483.

When Richard III was crowned king on July 6, Princess Elizabeth, her sisters, and her mother heard the joyful peal of the coronation bells ringing from the tower of Westminster Abbey—immediately next door to Chenygate mansion where the women lived. In announcing the anointment of King Richard III, the bells ironically sounded the death knell for Elizabeth's two little brothers. Each toll plumbed the depths of anguish felt by the six women, alone in their sanctuary.

The summer's news from the Tower brought only more despair. The two princes, once seen playing on the Tower green, were now immured—unseen and unattended—within its inner apartments.[20] Prince Richard had just turned 10. Crowland reports that public sentiment was growing to free the boys:

> In order to release them from such captivity, the people of the South and of the West of the kingdom began to murmur greatly, to form assemblies and to organize associations to this end—many were in secret, others quite open—especially those people who, because of fear, were scattered throughout franchises and sanctuaries.[21]

Already fearing the worst, some suggested that the daughters of Edward IV "leave Westminster in disguise and go overseas, so that if any human fate inside the Tower were to befall the male children, nevertheless through the saving of the persons of the daughters the kingdom might some day return to the rightful heirs."²² In response, Richard III surrounded Westminster Abbey with troops under the captaincy of John Nesfield: "no one inside could get out and no one from outside could get in without his permission."²³ Westminster Abbey was under siege.

To build support for his reign, Richard embarked on a progress through Windsor, Reading, Oxford, Gloucester, and Coventry on his way to York, where on September 8, 1483, he invested his son, Edward of Middleham, as Prince of Wales. That ceremony suggests that the former holder of the title, Edward V, was already dead. The king was beginning to alienate his subjects, even his loyal supporters. By late September, rebellion broke out, led by the duke of Buckingham and Henry Tudor, earl of Richmond.

No one has satisfactorily explained why Buckingham, Richard's most ardent adherent, abandoned the king. Some suggest that Buckingham himself sought the throne, a claim he could assert through his ancestor Thomas of Woodstock, youngest son of Edward III. Others believe that the death of the two princes transgressed the limits of the Buckingham's moral principles and political ambition. Yet others suggest pragmatically that Richard III's executions of Hastings, Rivers, Grey, and Vaughn caused Buckingham to fear for his own life. Whatever the reason, Buckingham retreated to his Welsh estates at Brecknock and joined with Henry Tudor and the remaining Wydevilles to fight Richard III.

The entry of Henry Tudor, earl of Richmond, into the fray reasserted the Lancastrian claim to England's throne. Richmond traced his lineage to Edward III through his mother, Margaret Beaufort, great-granddaughter of John of Gaunt. His father, Edmund Tudor, first earl of Richmond and half-brother to Henry VI, could claim the royal blood of France, but not of England. Following the 1471 victory of Edward IV at Tewkesbury, Henry Tudor had fled to exile in Brittany where he had spent the intervening years. At age 26, he was ready to claim the English crown.

Two strong women assisted the rebellion: queen dowager Elizabeth and her long-time friend, Margaret Beaufort, countess of Richmond. The two mothers plotted to marry Elizabeth of York, heir of Edward IV, to Henry Tudor, Lancastrian claimant

to England's throne. The go-between was Margaret's Welsh
physician Lewis Caerleon, who was permitted to visit the queen
dowager in Sanctuary. Without doubt, the marriage was politically motivated. No evidence indicates that Princess Elizabeth
and the earl of Richmond had ever met. Further, the documents
specified that in case of Elizabeth's death, Princess Cecily would
replace her. Polydore Vergil records the agreement:

> …[Queen Dowager Elizabeth] would do her endeavour to procure
> all her husband King Edward's friends to take part with Henry
> [Margaret's] son, so that he might be sworn to take in marriage
> Elizabeth her daughter after he shall have gotten the realm, or else
> Cecily the younger if the other should die before he enjoyed the
> same.[24]

Messengers sent to Brittany informed Richmond of the plan and
solicited financial support for invading England.

The rebellion launched by Buckingham in October 1483 failed
miserably. Ten days of storms had washed out bridges and made
roads impassable. Buckingham sought refuge in a cottage of one
of his tenants, Ralph Banaster, who turned him in to Richard's
men for a reward of £1,000 and land worth £100 a year.[25] The duke
of Buckingham—the uncle with whom the lady princess Elizabeth
had danced at age six—was beheaded by King Richard's men on
All Souls Day, November 2, 1483. The earl of Richmond, whose
ships were delayed by the storm, reached Plymouth on the day of
Buckingham's death. When Richmond heard the disastrous news,
he returned to Brittany to plan a second attack. By this time,
Richmond had been joined by Sir Edward Wydeville, naval commander and uncle to princess Elizabeth, and by Thomas, marquess of Dorset, half-brother to the princess.

Meanwhile, rumors about the fate of the two princes began to
sweep through London. Dominic Mancini, an Italian visiting
England to gather information for Angelo Cato, advisor to Louis
XI of France, feared the worst:

> The physician Argentine, the last of his attendants whose services
> the king [Edward V] enjoyed, reported that the young king, like a
> victim prepared for sacrifice, sought remission of his sins by daily
> confession and penance, because he believed that death was facing
> him.[26]

Contemporary chronicles report the boys dead by late summer 1483. Crowland writes:

> ...a rumor arose that King Edward's sons, by some unknown manner of violent destruction, had met their fate.[27]

Another London chronicle, the *Vitellius A XVI* manuscript, states:

> Anon as the said King Richard had put to death the lord chamberlain [Hastings] and other gentlemen, as before is said, he also put to death the two children of King Edward, for which cause he lost the hearts of the people.[28]

European sources repeat the accusation, many blaming King Richard for their deaths. Weinreich's Danzig *Chronicle* records in 1483:

> Item later this summer Richard, the king's [Edward IV] brother, had himself put in power and crowned in England and he had his brother's children killed, and the queen put away secretly also.[29]

Guillaume de Rochefort, the French chancellor, announced in a speech before the States General at Tours on January 15, 1484:

> Regard the events which have occurred in that land [England] since the death of King Edward. See how his children already quite old and brave have been murdered with impunity and the crown has been transferred to their assassin by the consent of the people.[30]

Commines, who completed his memoirs of the French court in 1498, remembers:

> The duke had his two nephews murdered and made himself king, with the title King Richard.[31]

As the Wydeville men gathered in Brittany to support Richmond, the women remained in Westminster Sanctuary, where Buckingham's widow, Katherine, sister of queen dowager Elizabeth, joined them. A glimmer of good news arrived when Henry Tudor, earl of Richmond, made a solemn oath of betrothal to Elizabeth of York at Rennes Cathedral in France on Christmas Day 1483. Sometime during this period, application was made to the Papal Penitentiary for a dispensation that would allow the couple to marry.[32] Although Princess Elizabeth was once again formally betrothed, she had been there twice before, and it is doubtful that her future seemed any less bleak. Richmond's prospects of gaining the throne were remote. His years of exile in Brittany meant that he was virtually unknown in England. He had no battle experience, no leadership background, no knowledge of royal administration, no army, no money. Life offered little hope for Princess Elizabeth. It soon grew worse.

On January 23, 1484, Richard III's Parliament began. Beyond attainting the Wydeville men, it issued the infamous *Titulus Regius: An Act for the Settlement of the Crown upon the King and his issue, with a recapitulation of his Title.* It is in the "recapitulation of his Title" that the bastard status of Princess Elizabeth and her sisters became the law of the land. The declaration was issued "in the name of the three Estates of this Realm of England, that is to wit, of the Lords Spiritual and Temporal, and of the Commons":

> ...the said pretended marriage betwixt the above named King Edward and Elizabeth [Wydeville] Grey, was made of great presumption, without the knowing and assent of the Lords of this Land, and also by Sorcery and Witchcraft, committed by the said Elizabeth, and her Mother Jacquetta, Duchess of Bedford....

> At the time of contract of the same pretended marriage, and before and long time after, the said King Edward was and stood married and troth plight to one Dame Eleanor Butler, daughter of the old Earl of Shrewsbury, with whom the same King Edward had made a precontract of matrimony, long time before he made the said pretended marriage with the said Elizabeth Grey, in manner and form abovesaid. Which premises being true, as in very truth they be true, it appears and follows evidently, that the said King Edward during his life, and the said Elizabeth, lived together sinfully and damnably in adultery, against the Law of God and of his Church;...

> Also it appears evidently and follows, that all the Issue and Children of the said King Edward, be Bastards, and unable to inherit or to claim any thing by inheritance, by the Law and Custom of England.[33]

Long deceased, the alleged first wife of Edward IV, Eleanor Butler, could not testify to the truth of the precontract. Bishop Stillington's word had become the law of the land.

The declaration of bastardy coincided with Princess Elizabeth's eighteenth birthday. She had been immured in Westminster Sanctuary 10 months. The happy days of her father's court were a nebulous memory. The future? What future?

CHAPTER 4

RESTORED TO COURT

The lady princess Elizabeth who once danced in castles was fast growing beyond marriageable age while confined in Westminster Sanctuary. She had no joy, no pleasure in life. Her male Wydeville relatives had joined Henry Tudor in his rebellion against Richard III and were either in exile or attainted by Richard III's Parliament of 1484. Her uncle Sir Edward Wydeville and her half-brother Thomas, marquess of Dorset, had sailed to Brittany. Her uncle Bishop Lionel Wydeville sought sanctuary at Beaulieu Abbey in south Hampshire. The whereabouts of Sir Richard Wydeville, third earl Rivers, during this period are unknown.

With the disappearance and rumored deaths of the two princes, Elizabeth of York, eldest daughter of Edward IV, was the legitimate heir of the house of York. As resistance to Richard III grew, she became a focal point for those plotting against the king. Her betrothal to Henry Tudor constituted a particular threat to the king's future. Richard turned Westminster Abbey into a prison for the queen dowager and her daughters, even as he urged them with "frequent intercessions and dire threats" to depart Sanctuary.[1] With no means of support and no future for her daughters, the queen dowager struck the best bargain she could manage. She agreed to leave Westminster Sanctuary after the king swore an oath before an assembly of the three Estates—clergy, nobles, and commons—pledging to protect her children. The vow made by Richard III on March 1, 1484 was extraordinary for a reigning monarch:

> I, Richard, by the Grace of God King of England and of France and Lord of Ireland, in the presence of you, my lords spiritual and temporal, and you, Mayor and Aldermen of my City of London, promise and swear *verbo regio* upon these holy Evangels of God by me personally touched, that if the daughters of dame Elizabeth

Grey, late calling herself Queen of England, that is to wit Elizabeth, Cecily, Anne, Katherine, and Bridget, will come unto me out of the Sanctuary of Westminster, and be guided, ruled and demeaned after me, then I shall see that they shall be in surety of their lives, and also not suffer any manner hurt by any manner person or persons to them or any of them or their bodies or persons, to be done by way of ravishment or defiling contrary their wills, nor them or any of them imprison within the Tower of London or other prison; but that I shall put them in honest places of good name and fame, and them honestly and courteously shall see to be found and entreated, and to have all things requisite and necessary for their exhibition and findings as my kinswomen; and that I shall marry such of them as now be marriageable to gentlemen born, and every of them give in marriage lands and tenements to the yearly value of two hundred marks for the term of their lives; and in likewise to the other daughters when they come to lawful age of marriage if they live. And such gentlemen as shall happen to marry with them I shall straitly charge, from time to time, lovingly to love and entreat them as their wives and my kinswomen, as they will avoid and eschew my displeasure.[2]

Trusting that the public ceremony and the powerful men before whom Richard swore his oath would force compliance, the queen dowager and her daughters left Sanctuary sometime in March 1484. Little is known about the fate of Elizabeth Wydeville and her four younger daughters during the next year, but Princess Elizabeth joined the court of King Richard and Queen Anne.

At court, Elizabeth's youth, tall stature, and golden beauty soon attracted attention. Queen Anne was ill with a lingering malaise, perhaps tuberculosis. Although she was relatively young at age 28, she could not compete with the 18-year-old beauty of Princess Elizabeth. Queen Anne had given birth to only one surviving son, Edward of Middleham, and her illness made it unlikely that she would bear further heirs. Within a month of Elizabeth's joining the court, Edward of Middleham died on April 9, 1484. Both Richard and Anne received the tragic news with searing pain:

You might have seen the father and mother, after hearing the news at Nottingham where they were then staying, almost out of their minds for a long time when faced with the sudden grief.[3]

The news may have exacerbated Queen Anne's illness, making her even less attractive to her husband. More important, her apparent infertility made her a problematic consort for a king who lacked a male heir.

Rumors began to link Richard with the beautiful princess Elizabeth of York. By Christmas 1485, the court was preoccupied with speculation:

> During this Christmas feast too much attention was paid to singing and dancing and to vain exchanges of clothing between Queen Anne and Lady Elizabeth, eldest daughter of the dead king, who were alike in complexion and figure. The people spoke against this, and the magnates and prelates were greatly astonished; and it was said by many that the king was applying his mind in every way to contracting a marriage with Elizabeth either after the death of the queen, or by means of a divorce for which he believed he had sufficient grounds. He saw no other way of confirming his crown and dispelling the hopes of his rival.
>
> A few days later the queen began to be seriously ill, and her sickness was then believed to have got worse and worse because the king himself was completely spurning his consort's bed. Therefore he judged it right to consult with doctors. What more is there to be said?[4]

Queen Anne died on March 16, 1485, after which rumors of a marriage between Richard and Elizabeth of York intensified. Under pressure, the king testified to his council that "such a thing had never entered his mind," but his denial was insufficient and unpersuasive to those "at that council who knew well enough that the contrary was true."[5] Sir Richard Ratcliffe and William Catesby, squire of the Body, warned the king that if he did not publicly deny his intent to marry his niece

> before the Mayor and commonalty of the City of London, the northerners, in whom he placed the greatest trust, would all rise against him, charging him with causing the death of the queen [Anne], the daughter and one of the heirs of the earl of Warwick, and through whom he had obtained his first honor, in order to complete his incestuous association with his near kinswoman, to the offence of God.[6]

"A dozen doctors of theology" further testified that the Pope could never grant a dispensation for a marriage between Richard and Elizabeth because of their degree of consanguinity (uncle and niece).

Crowland adds that Ratcliff and Catesby may have had their own motives for opposing the marriage because they feared "that if the said Elizabeth attained the rank and dignity of queen, it might be in her power, sometime, to avenge the death of her uncle, Earl Anthony, and of her brother, Richard, upon those who had been the principal counselors in the affair."[7] Whatever their motives, Ratcliff and Catesby prevailed:

> Shortly before Easter, therefore, the King took his stand in the great hall at St. John's [the Priory of the Knights Hospitaller in Clerkenwell] in the presence of the Mayor and citizens of London and in a clear, loud voice carried out fully the advice to make a denial of this kind—as many people believed, more by the will of these counselors than by his own.[8]

Shortly thereafter, Richard sent Elizabeth of York to Sheriff Hutton, his remote castle with towers and gatehouse that effectively imprisoned her in north Yorkshire. Elizabeth joined her cousin Edward, earl of Warwick, already immured there to prevent claims to the throne he might make as son of Clarence, elder brother of Richard III.

Elizabeth's own role—and emotions—regarding marriage to her uncle have generated much speculation and controversy. Polydore Vergil, recording the Tudor version of history, wrote 26 years later:

> Richard had kept [Elizabeth] unharmed with a view to marriage. To such a marriage the girl had a singular aversion. Weighed down for this reason by her great grief she would repeatedly exclaim, saying, "I will not thus be married, but, unhappy creature that I am, will rather suffer all the torments which St. Catherine is said to have endured for the love of Christ than be united with a man who is the enemy of my family."[9]

In 1619 the historian George Buck published a quite different perspective based on a letter then in the possession of Sir Thomas Howard, earl of Arundel and of Surrey. Elizabeth purportedly wrote the letter in February 1485 to Sir John Howard, duke of Norfolk, a man loved and trusted by her father and herself. Buck summarized the letter in his *History of King Richard the Third* (brackets within the text indicate emendations by

Buck's great-nephew in his attempts to make sense of the damaged manuscript):

> First she thanked him for his many courtesies and friendly [offices, an]d then she prayed him as before to be a mediator for her in the cause of [the marriage] to the k[i]ng, who, as she wrote, was her only joy and maker in [this] world, and that she was his in heart and in thoughts, in [body,] and in all. And then she intimated that the better half of Fe[bruary] was past, and that she feared the queen would nev[er die.] And all these be her own words, written with her own hand, and this is the sum of [her] letter, whereof I have seen the autograph or original d[raft] under her [own] hand.[10]

The letter has become infamous as proof of Elizabeth's desire to marry her uncle. Scholars have questioned, however, both the accuracy and historical objectivity of Buck, who was a vigorous apologist for Richard III. Most succinctly, Alison Hanham pointed to Buck's "cardinal sins of suppressing evidence and altering records" when he desired to prove a case.[11]

The fire-damaged manuscript from which editors have struggled to determine Buck's text complicates the case. Arthur Kincaid, Buck's modern editor, has meticulously transcribed the existing document, using "<" and ">" to indicate missing sections of the MS. (BL MS. Cotton Tiberius E. x. f. 238v).

>st she thanked him for his many Curtesies and friendly<	(1)
as before in the cause of<	(2)
>d then she prayed him ʌ to bee a mediator for her to the K<	(3)
>ge	(4)
whoe (as she wrote) was her onely ioye and her maker in <	(5)
in	(6)
Worlde, and that she was [in] his, harte, in thoughts in<	(7)
and \ in/ all, and then she intimated that the better halfe of Ffe<	(8)
was paste, and that she feared the Queene would neu<	(9)[12]

The words interpolated by editors drastically affect the letter's content. Buck's first editor, his great-nephew, chose "body" as the missing word at the end of line 7, a word that adds significant sexual intensity to the writer's feelings. The words "never die" at the end of line 9 depict a selfish, uncaring spirit, but again Buck's nephew inserted those words. Kincaid further explains the editor's dilemma: lines 3–4 can be read: "she prayed him as before to be a mediator for her to the K<inge> \ in the cause of <the marria>ge" *or* "she prayed him to bee as before a mediator for her to the K<ing> \ in the cause of <her marriage to the Kin>ge."[13] Livia Visser-Fuchs concludes: "...it is impossible to establish even Buck's paraphrase with any degree of accuracy, let alone certainty."[14]

Based on the letter's context within Buck's history, Kincaid has no doubt that Buck believed Elizabeth to be expressing her desire to marry Richard. Kincaid's own deduction is less certain: "Elizabeth in her letter was referring to a hoped-for marriage— though not necessarily with the king."[15] The letter could be as innocent as Elizabeth asking Norfolk for help in urging the king to arrange a marriage for her, as he had vowed before the assembled Estates. Such a request would be quite ordinary and innocent, especially since Richard arranged a marriage for her sister Cecily to Ralph, brother of the king's ally Lord Scrope of Upsall.[16]

On the other hand, Elizabeth may indeed have fallen in love with King Richard who had restored her to the gaiety, privileges, and prerogatives of his Court. After 11 months of immurement and deprivation in Sanctuary, what 19-year-old woman would not welcome the attentions of a rich, powerful, charming man? Although betrothed to Henry Tudor, Elizabeth may have regarded that agreement as a nebulous liaison negotiated by others to a man she had never met, a man whose future was as uncertain as any creature's on earth. Certainly two earlier betrothals had been broken without regard for her emotions or welfare. Elizabeth of York would not have been the first—or last—person to succumb to readily available pleasure and passion.

Further evidence of Elizabeth's feelings toward Richard may lie in her inscription in a copy of *De consolatione philosophiae* by Boethius, written on the last flyleaf following seven blank pages:

Loyalte me llye
Elyzabeth[17]

The motto is Richard III's well-known "Loyalty binds me." Because in other instances Elizabeth followed her signature with either "the King's daughter" or "the Queen," Visser-Fuchs suggests that the signature was written at a time when Elizabeth "was neither princess nor queen."[18] The likely period would be when she was in Richard's custody, a time when she might especially have sought consolation from her earthly misery in Boethius' popular *contempus mundi* philosophy. The combination of Richard's motto with Elizabeth's signature might indicate her desire for a bonding of their souls. But it could equally signal loyalty to some else. Her family? Henry Tudor?

In a second instance, Elizabeth wrote on a page of the French prose *Tristan* once owned by Richard, duke of Gloucester:

> sans re[mo]vyr
> elyzabeth[19]

The motto means "without changing" and appears at the foot of the page that has Richard's *ex libris*.[20] The question is: when she signs "sans removyr" is she expressing her feelings toward the King—or someone else? Speculation can never substitute for fact, and based on the available evidence, Elizabeth's feelings toward Richard III and their rumored marriage must remain purely speculative.

Henry Tudor in exile certainly took reports of a marriage between Richard III and Elizabeth of York quite seriously. When the rumors reached France, he immediately sought alignment with others who could support his invasion against Richard III and help him establish a foothold in England. Turning to the family with whom he had lived as a child, Richmond proposed to marry a daughter of William Herbert, earl of Pembroke, the Welsh landowner who had paid Edward IV £1,000 for Henry Tudor's wardship when the boy was six years old.[21] Lord Herbert had raised Henry on his extensive Welsh estates, educated him to become his future son-in-law, and contracted him to marry his daughter Maud. That contract ended during Henry's long exile when Maud married Henry Percy, earl of Northumberland. Now Richmond proposed to marry one of Maud's sisters—Jane, Cecily, and Katherine were still available.[22] Further, their brother Sir Walter Herbert was married to Anne, daughter of the duke of Buckingham who had led the rebellion against Richard in October 1483. Henry sent Christopher Urswick with a message to Northumberland proposing the marriage, but the message never reached its destination. Henry's preoccupation with invading England apparently preempted further efforts.

On Monday, August 1, 1485, Henry Tudor, Earl of Richmond, set sail with two thousand men and a few ships toward England. The fleet reached Milford Haven sometime before sunset on Sunday, August 7.

Within weeks, Elizabeth of York's future was determined forever.

CHAPTER 5

MARRIAGE TO A KING

Elizabeth of York faced a confused and uncertain future while Henry Tudor, earl of Richmond, marched his troops from Milford Haven toward King Richard's army. Richmond, her betrothed husband, was a "landless and penniless refugee," an exile for the past 14 years.[1] Victory by this man unknown to Elizabeth—and to all of England—seemed remote, improbable. Richmond had no experience in battle, no affinity with the English nobility, no connections with the commons. His stalwart advisor and uncle Jasper Tudor, earl of Pembroke and half-brother of Henry VI, was experienced as a warrior, but he, too, had lost touch with England's nobility during his exile. Richmond's mother, Margaret Beaufort, lived under suspicion in custody of her husband, Thomas, lord Stanley, steward of King's Richard's household.

Richmond's claim to the throne of England was dubious at best. His lineage to John of Gaunt through his mother, Margaret Beaufort, was problematic because Gaunt's Beaufort children were born to his mistress Katherine Swynford before the couple married. Pope Boniface IX declared the children legitimate in 1396—with secular legitimacy conferred by Richard II and Parliament in 1397—but Henry IV in 1407 added the phrase *excepta dignitate regale* [except the royal dignity] to his patent of legitimacy.[2] Henry IV thus excluded the Beauforts from claiming the crown, although the legality of his action has been questioned. While the Beaufort descendents rapidly gained enormous wealth through marriages with other rich, noble families and earned status through military and ecclesiastical service, whispers of their bastard origin still lingered.

Richmond's heritage on his father's side presented other complications. His Welsh ancestors had become substantial landowners through service to Llewyllyn the Great and his son David. When they supported Owen Glyndwr, however, they ended up on the wrong side of Henry IV. The family fortunes improved after Henry V took several of the young Welsh rebels into his service and made Owen Tudor his page. Some years later, Owen Tudor married Henry's widow, Katherine of Valois, a union that bore three sons and two daughters.[3] Unprecedented and scandalous, this marriage of a queen dowager to a Welsh retainer was not revealed until Katherine neared death. When she died on January 3, 1437, Katherine's first son by Henry V, King Henry VI, was just 16. He sent his half-brothers Edmund and Jasper Tudor to Catherine de la Pole, abbess of Barking and sister of the duke of Suffolk, for their upbringing.[4] Both boys were knighted on December 15, 1449. On November 23, 1452, Edmund Tudor was made earl of Richmond and Jasper Tudor earl of Pembroke. Their father Owen Tudor continued in the service of Henry VI until he was captured at the battle of Mortimer's Cross and beheaded by Yorkists in February 1461.[5]

Henry VI favored his Tudor half-brothers in 1452 by giving them the wardship and marriage of Margaret Beaufort, daughter and heiress of John Beaufort III, duke of Somerset. As a very rich great-granddaughter of John of Gaunt, Margaret Beaufort had been betrothed to John de la Pole as an infant. Henry VI dissolved that marriage in 1453 to permit marriage with the newly created earl of Richmond.[6] As soon as Margaret reached the legal age of 12, Edmund Tudor married and impregnated his ward before going off to fight for Lancaster. Captured and imprisoned by the Yorkist forces, Edmund Tudor died in prison on November 3, 1456. Three months later, his thirteen-year-old widow, Margaret, gave birth to Henry Tudor on January 28, 1457. Margaret Beaufort, countess of Richmond, bore no other children in two subsequent marriages, an indication perhaps that the birth was physically traumatic. Scars from the experience surfaced years later when she objected to the marriage of her granddaughter Margaret Tudor at age nine to James IV of Scotland: both the Countess of Richmond and Elizabeth of York withheld their approval for "fear the King of Scots would not wait, but injure her, and endanger her health."[7] The Countess was speaking from personal experience, painfully suffered when a child.

Margaret Beaufort idolized her only son, perhaps all the more because she had been deprived of a mother's role during his youth. Henry Tudor, ward of William, lord Herbert, lived a reasonably luxurious childhood in Wales, but he rarely saw his mother. After his exile in 1471, Henry and his mother communicated only through messengers during the next 14 years. Now, the Countess of Richmond was ready to devote the rest of her life to her son's success.

Henry Tudor, earl of Richmond, should have lost the battle at Bosworth. He had no war experience, while King Richard was a brilliant commander who had fought with distinction at Barnet, at Tewkesbury, and more recently in Scotland. Richmond marched across unfamiliar terrain, while Richard III stationed his troops on familiar territory where they occupied the high ground. Richard's soldiers, all defending their homeland, far outnumbered Richmond's 2,000 French mercenaries and Welsh recruits. Although the earl of Oxford, ever loyal to the Lancastrian cause, fought on Richmond's side, the English nobility supporting Richard far exceeded the invaders in puissance and numbers.

Volumes have been written about the battle at Bosworth and the shifting loyalties of its leaders, but only two men in the entire conflagration counted—Richard III and Henry Tudor. As the battle began on August 22, 1485, Richard watched as several of his commanders held their troops in reserve, then made a heroic, but foolhardy, decision to charge directly at the one man he had to eliminate. King Richard's personal attack almost worked. He came close enough to slay Richmond's standard bearer, Sir William Brandon, but in the crush of fighting men, Richard III himself was killed.

Henry, earl of Richmond, became King Henry VII of England—his crown won in battle. From the moment of victory, he showed the savvy intelligence that helped him establish the Tudor dynasty and quell the rebellions that would bedevil his first decade as king. First, Henry VII dated his reign from August 21, a ruling that allowed Parliament to attaint those who fought against him at Bosworth. Then he won popular support by forbidding the pillaging and robbery that frequently follows victory by battle:

Henry, by the grace of God, king of England and of France, Prince of Wales and Lord of Ireland, strictly chargeth and commendeth, upon pain of death, that no manner of man rob or spoil no manner of commons coming from the field; but suffer them to pass home to their countries and dwelling places, with their horses and harness. And moreover, that no manner of man take upon him to go to no gentleman's place, neither in the country, nor within cities nor boroughs, nor pick no quarrels for old or new matters; but keep the king's peace, upon pain of hanging, etc.[8]

Henry immediately sent Sir Robert Willoughby to Sheriff Hutton to escort Elizabeth of York, "attended by noble ladies," to London to live with her mother, the queen dowager.[9] Many regarded Elizabeth of York's claim to England's throne to be superior to Henry's. Even if his Lancastrian heritage were legitimate, Henry's mother, Margaret Beaufort, took precedence over him. But England was not ready for a female monarch, and Henry's victory in battle had proved his worth—indeed, his selection by God—to become England's king.

Henry Tudor—unknown and untested—had his work cut out for him. First, he had to establish his personal authority over a nation plagued by civil war and discord. Before he could marry Elizabeth, Parliament had to rescind her bastardy. And before Parliament could meet, the king had to be anointed and crowned, so that he could preside over it as England's sovereign. The timing was tricky and shrewdly political. On September 15, 1485, Parliament was summoned to meet at Westminster on November 7.[10] Henry's coronation was scheduled for Sunday, October 30. Henry would be crowned in his own right, quite independent of the heritage of Elizabeth of York. He would reign as a Tudor—not as an adjunct of the house of York.

Nevertheless, Henry courted Yorkist sympathizers, numerous and powerful after 24 years of rule by Edward IV and Richard III. With marriage to Elizabeth of York imminent, propaganda began disseminating the message that this king would end the fractious fighting afflicting England since the 1450s. A Lancastrian king chosen by God (victory at Bosworth!) had chosen a daughter of York as his wife. The resulting house of Tudor would unify England. If Elizabeth of York reigned as queen consort (rather than queen regnant), God's order, after all, placed women subordinate to men. In a brilliant political maneuver, Henry arranged the endorsement of his marriage by Parliament. Before that could happen, however, the king had to prove his legitimacy by displaying his regal magnificence to his nation and the world.

Henry's coronation replicated that of his predecessor just two years earlier, adopting the protocol book known as the "Little Device" compiled for the coronation of Richard III and Queen

Anne.[11] Matching the extravagance of Richard's coronation was important because kings created public confidence in their authority by displaying wealth and grandeur that differentiated them from their nobles and subjects. Over 496 yards of scarlet (fine wool cloth) decorated Westminster Hall, the Abbey, and the Tower with hangings;[12] 10 yards of purple cloth-of-gold tissue made one gown for the king, while 10 ¾ yards of crimson cloth-of-gold provided another.[13] The king's Parliament gown required 44 ¾ yards of crimson velvet, although another long gown used only 18 ¾ yards of crimson velvet-upon-velvet. Another gown consumed 12 yards of purple velvet, a shirt 3 yards of crimson sarcenet (fine, soft silk), and gloves ¾ ell of Holland cloth (one ell equals 45 inches). His stomachers and doublets were made of satin. Ermine, powdered (decorated with sewn pieces of black fur), for his mantle cost £30 6s 8d, while another 248 ermine backs cost just £6 4s.[14] Furring the robes of the king and his Master of Rolls required 12,820 miniver pure (white belly skins of the Baltic squirrel). One jacket of black velvet was furred with 16 skins of black bogy (lamb skins). A trapper for the king's horse required 12 yards of crimson damask cloth-of-gold, while another used 10 yards of crimson cloth-of-gold.

Gifts to the king's prelates, lords, henchmen, heralds, and footmen provided similarly luxuriant livery. "My lord of Buckingham" received 11 yards of crimson velvet, 8 yards of red sarcenet, 18 ells of Flemish cloth, 3 ells canvass for lining his doublets, and 5 ¼ yards of crimson velvet for covering two saddles, two harnesses, and two bits for horse bridles.[15] Henry VII provided this son of the duke who first rebelled against Richard III with a horse, saddle, sword, featherbed, bolster, pillow, celour, tester, blankets, sheets, mantle, and seven yards of red worsted.[16]

At his coronation, Henry set the standard for magnificence that famously came to characterize the entire Tudor dynasty. Most of his subjects saw King Henry for the first time as his coronation procession moved from the Tower to Westminster. Preceded by heralds, sergeants-of-arms, trumpeters, esquires, court attendants, the mayor and aldermen of London, and England's nobility—all dressed in their best livery—the king rode bareheaded under a canopy decorated with 28 ounces of gold and silk fringe. Henry wore his long gown of purple velvet furred with ermine and rode a horse trapped with cloth-of-gold trimmed with ermine. Twenty-four yards of crimson velvet covered the king's saddle, stirrups, and stirrup leaders. Banners of blue sarcenet fringed with silk decorated the trumpets. Behind the king rode Jasper Tudor, newly created as duke of Bedford, and John de la Pole, duke of Suffolk, followed by six henchmen on horses trapped with the arms and badges of the king.[17]

On Sunday, October 30, Henry VII was anointed and crowned at Westminster Abbey by Thomas Bourchier, the 80-year-old cardinal archbishop of Canterbury. A sumptuous coronation banquet followed, but the celebratory tournament was postponed until November 13—perhaps to allow the opening of Parliament on November 7 without the distractions of the jousting competitions.

Parliament began with an oration by Lord Chancellor Alcock, bishop of Worcester, followed by the first order of business, Parliament's affirmation of the king's lawful rule:

> by authority of this present Parliament...the Inheritance of the Crowns of the Realmes of England and of France...rest, remain, and abide in the most Royale person of our now Souveraign Lord King Harry the VIIth, and in the heirs of his body lawfully come perpetually with the grace of God so to endure, and in no other.[18]

Attainders against Henry VI, Margaret of Anjou, and Jasper Tudor were reversed and the "estate, dignity, preeminence, and name" of queen dowager Elizabeth, mother of Henry's betrothed, was reestablished.[19] Parliament restored the queen dowager's possessions and rescinded Richard III's *Titulus Regius* that had invalidated the marriage of Edward IV and Elizabeth Wydeville and bastardized their children. Determined to avoid any word that might suggest a tainted heritage for their next queen, Parliament never named the document, but acted against the "false and seditious bill of false and malicious imaginations, against all good and true disposition" demanding that

> The said bill be cancelled, destroyed, and that the said act, record, and enrolling shall be taken and avoided out of the roll and records of the said Parliament of the said late king [Richard III] and burnt, and utterly destroyed.[20]

Persons with copies of the bill were ordered to deliver them to the Chancellor of England or to "utterly destroy them, afore the feast of Easter next..., upon pain of imprisonment and making fine and ransom to the King at his will."

Before Parliament was prorogued, its speaker Sir Thomas Lovell endorsed Henry's plans to marry in his address on December 10, 1485:

> …quod hereditates regnorum Angliae & Franciae, cum preemenencia & potestate regali, sint, restent, remaneant & permaneant in persona ejusdem Domini Regis, & heredibus de corpore suo legitime exeuntibus, eadem Regalis Sublimatas vellet sibi illam preclaram Dominam Elizabeth, Regis Edwardi quarti filiam, in uxorem & conthoralem assumere; unde per Dei gratiam sobolum propagacio de stripe regum a multis speratur, in totius regni consolacionem. Consequenterque, Domini Spirituales & Temporales in eodem Parliamento existentes, a sedibus suis surgentes, & ante Regem in regali solio residentem stantes, capitibus suis inclinantes, eandem requestam fecerunt voce dimissa: quibus quidem respondebat ore proprio, Se juxta eorum desideria & requestus procedere fuisse contentum.[21]

> [… because the hereditary succession of the crowns of England & France, together with the superiority and regal power, is, remains, continues, and endures in the person of the same Lord King, & in the heirs legitimately issuing from his body, this same royal authority wishes to take for himself as wife & consort the noble Lady Elizabeth, daughter of King Edward the fourth; from whence through the grace of God, it is hoped by many the continuation of offspring by a race of kings, as consolation to the entire kingdom.

> Thereupon, the Lords Spiritual and Temporal in that same Parliament, rising from their seats, & standing before the King seated on his royal throne, bowed their heads, made the same request with lowered voice: to whom the King indeed responded with his own voice, "According to their desires and requests, he himself equally was pleased to proceed."][22]

This exchange has caused some to speculate that Henry deliberately delayed his marriage to Elizabeth of York until he was forced to act by Parliament. The tone of the Speaker's statement, however, sounds not at all confrontational. Further, Lovell was a friend who had spent time in exile with Henry. Now a member of the king's council, he served as chancellor of the Exchequer, treasurer of the Household, and esquire of the body.[23] The *Crowland Chronicle* confirms that the discussion was held "with the king's consent" after Henry's right to rule had already been established "not only by right of blood but of victory in battle and of conquest."

Marriage to "the lady Elizabeth, King Edward's eldest daughter" merely provided "whatever appeared to be missing in the king's title elsewhere."[24]

A literal translation of the king's response, "Se juxta eorum desideria & requestus procedere fuisse contentum" confirms that Henry had already determined to act, since the perfect infinitive *fuisse* indicates that his agreement preceded his response. Henry orchestrated Parliament's endorsement of his marriage as a shrewd political move to emphasize that king and Parliament were acting together in joining the divided houses of Lancaster and York and assuring England's future peace.

The practical demands during the five months between Henry's August 22 victory at Bosworth and his January 18 wedding to Elizabeth were so intense that it is difficult to accuse the king of procrastination. After Bosworth, Henry had to regroup his troops, meet the English nobility for the first time, march to London, secure the peace, summon his first Parliament, be crowned king, preside over Parliament, establish his government—and meet his future wife.

Henry and Elizabeth probably saw each other for the first time in London after Bosworth. If they had met before Henry's exile in 1471, he would have been 14 years old at most and Elizabeth no more than 5. Time to become acquainted was essential to establish a mutually respectful relationship. Sometime before their marriage, Henry moved Elizabeth to his mother's London mansion of Coldharbor where they could meet privately.[25] A more cynical perspective, of course, might regard the five-month delay as essential assurance that children born of this union were Henry's—and not the result of rumored escapades between Elizabeth and Richard III. If that pragmatic view undercuts romantic sentiment, the delay certainly eliminated nagging doubts of the sort that afflict many, more idyllic liaisons.

During this "delay," Henry also applied for a second Papal dispensation to marry Elizabeth, to whom he was related by blood in the double fourth degree of consanguinity. The Papal Penitentiary had issued an earlier dispensation for their marriage before March 27, 1484—soon after Henry in exile made his oath to marry Elizabeth in the Cathedral at Rennes on Christmas Day 1483.[26]

Rome (apud sanctum Petrum), vi kal. Aprilis. Henricus Richemont, laicus Eboracensis dioceses, et Elisabet Plantageneta, mulier

Londonensis dioceses, petunt similem gratiam (dispensari de cont-
rahendo in duplici quarto consanguinitatis cum legitimatione pro-
lis etc.) Fiat de speciali Iul. episcopus Brethonoriensis regens.[27]

[In Rome (at Saint Peter's) 6 kalends April. Henry Richmond, layman of the York diocese, and Elizabeth Plantagenet, woman of
the London diocese, request similar favor (dispensation from the
relationship in double fourth degree of consanguinity along with
their legitimate descendants, etc.) Let it occur by the specific ruling of Julius, Bishop of Brethonoriensis.]

Identifying the petitioners as "Henry Richmond, layman from
the York district" and "Elizabeth Plantagenet, woman of the
London district," suggests a deliberate attempt to preserve ano-
nymity and to avoid attracting attention from the Italian curates
who ruled on requests from England. Secrecy was essential in
1484, since Richard III would surely have intervened to prevent
any dispensation for these two to marry. When this dispensation
was being recorded in Rome, Elizabeth was joining Richard's
court. The titillating gossip about Richard's attentions to her
began soon after.

Since this March 1484 dispensation could have been challenged
as insufficient, Henry VII with his customary caution made sure
that no one could ever question the legitimacy of his marriage—or
any children resulting from it. A second dispensation issued on
January 16, 1486, by James, bishop of Imola and papal legate to
England and Scotland, conferred irrefutable legal and religious
authority on their union. In securing it, prominent witnesses testified to the lineage of both Henry and Elizabeth. John, bishop of
Worcester, and Thomas, bishop of London, gave depositions in
the presence of Richard Spencer and John Reed, notaries public.[28]
Thomas, earl of Derby and lord Stanley, swore that his wife,
Margaret, countess of Richmond, and the earl of Salisbury had
discussed issues of lineage "long before communing was had
between the said… Henry and Lady Elizabeth about contracting
marriage."[29] Master Christopher Urswick, archdeacon of North
Wiltshire, testified that he had heard the lineages recited and
declared by the archbishop of York, the bishop of Worcester, and
Master Richard Lessy, a chamberlain of the Pope.[30] Subsequent
challenges would be impossible.

Two days after this second dispensation, Henry married Elizabeth
of York at Westminster Abbey on January 18. The wedding ring,

Photo 1   Henry VII (1457–1509, reigned 1485–1509). Dressed
simply, but elegantly, Henry wears a robe with slashed
sleeves to reveal an underlying cloth-of-gold gown. His
only jewelry is a cap badge with three pearl pendants.
Henry holds the Tudor rose with outer petals of red
surrounding the white rose of York. *English School*,
1510–20. Berger Collection at the Denver Art Museum.
Photograph courtesy of the Denver Art Museum.

Photo 2   Elizabeth of York (1466–1503; queen consort 1486–1503).
In this portrait by an unknown artist, a gabled veil
frames the queen's face. Both veil and dress are
decorated with a lavishly embroidered border studded
with pearls. A descendant of the house of York, the
queen holds the red rose of Lancaster, a motif replicated
in her heavy, jeweled necklace. *English School*. Courtesy
of Sotheby's Picture Library, London.

which cost 23*s* 4*d*, was one of 15 "parcels delivered to the King's good grace at New Year's Tide."[31] If the sum seems less than princely, the cost of gold items was determined by weight. Among the other "parcels" delivered—all gold or gilt (and perhaps intended for use at the wedding banquet)—the price was consistent: gold cost 35*s* per ounce and gilt 5*s*. Presuming that the wedding ring was gold, it weighed 0.666 of an ounce. In the words of a modern jeweler, the ring was "huge—quite hefty," compared to today's "average" wedding band weighing from 0.13 to 0.18 ounce (recognizing that "average" wedding bands do not exist).

Almost all that is known about the marriage ceremony is that the venerable Thomas Bourchier, Cardinal Archbishop of Canterbury, conducted it "in the sight of the Church on 18 January 1486."[32] At age 80, archbishop Bourchier, had lived through decades of battles and bloodshed that nearly annihilated the houses of Lancaster and York. He had crowned Elizabeth's father, Edward IV, and her mother, Queen Elizabeth Wydeville. He had persuaded that first Queen Elizabeth to give up her youngest son Prince Richard to the "Protector" in 1483. He subsequently placed England's crown on the head of Richard III. The Cardinal Archbishop anointed and crowned Henry VII. Now in marrying this Lancastrian heir to Elizabeth of York, he was unifying those two warring families. The prelate perhaps marveled at God's patience and plans in dealing with the self-destructive passions of men seeking power. When Thomas Bouchier died just months later during Easter week, he could greet his maker with a sense of wonder and awe and relief.

Their subjects greeted the wedding of Henry and Elizabeth with joy and magnificent commendations. Bernard André, a historian employed by Henry VII, lauded the union in his *De Vita Atque Gestis Henrici Septimi Historia*, a work of encomiastic zeal.[33] The Papal Collector, Giovanni de Giglis, wrote a similarly panegyric *Epithalamium de nuptiis*.[34] An unfinished oration intended for delivery before the Pope and cardinals by Henry's ambassador suggests that Henry deliberately chose Elizabeth, rather than a more politically profitable foreign bride, to end England's civil conflicts—more evidence of Tudor propaganda at work. Other than a few dissident Yorkists, all of England welcomed the union that promised to end decades of civil war.

Henry celebrated their marriage by purchasing new furs for Elizabeth's Easter gown. He paid £44 2*s* to Hillebrand Vain for 49 timbers (40 skins each timber) of ermines "for the furring of one gown of the Lady Elizabeth, queen of England."[35] Another £10 went to Gerard Venmeer for 15 timbers of ermines for the gown, and £31 14*s* to Richard Story, the queen's skinner, for powdering the ermines. Ten verges (yards) of crimson velvet were delivered to the queen under authority of the Privy Seal.[36]

Determined to make his marriage legally unassailable, Henry VII acquired yet a third dispensation from Pope Innocent VIII on March 2, 1486, that removed the impediment of a possible fourth degree of affinity (i.e., relation through marriage), in addition to the double fourth degree of consanguinity (relation by blood). On March 27, 1486, the Pope further affirmed the right of succession of Henry's heirs with the threat to excommunicate any challengers.[37] A Papal Bull on July 23, 1486 publicly proclaimed the legitimacy of the marriage.[38]

Symbolizing the idea that God had intervened to end England's civil strife by uniting the houses of Lancaster and York, the Tudor rose began to appear in art and architecture. Its outer red petals surrounded the inner white rose of York to create the "union rose." The symbol was wholly contrived. Although Edward IV frequently displayed the white rose as his Yorkist badge, the Lancastrians never used the red rose as a comparable sign until Henry VII popularized it. The red rose contrasted with the well-known Yorkist badge, and its color replicated that of the red dragon of Cadwalader, Henry's personal standard. (The myth of a "Lancastrian red rose" was enshrined a century later by Shakespeare in *I Henry VI* when the fictionalized Duke of Somerset picked a red rose to differentiate himself from York)[39] Henry VII, who understood symbolism better than anyone, surrounded the white rose of York with outer petals of "Lancastrian red" to create the Tudor rose, which became an icon of the dynasty that ended England's decades of bloodshed known today as the "Wars of the Roses."

Under Henry VII and Elizabeth of York, the nation of England did, indeed, prosper. The new Queen Elizabeth immediately set about her task of furthering that goal. Eight months after their marriage, she gave birth to the first Tudor heir.

CHAPTER 6

BIRTH OF A PRINCE

On the night of September 19/20, 1486—eight months after her marriage--Elizabeth of York gave birth to a son. The baby may have been premature, or the couple may have consummated their relationship before the formal church ceremony. The church accepted marriage as legitimate if a couple privately exchanged words of commitment in each other's presence: "I take you as my wife... I take you as my husband."[1] The vows had to be stated in the present tense and could not be merely an expression of intent. Alternatively, betrothal (a promise to marry) followed by sexual consummation also became a legal and binding marriage. Henry's public betrothal in 1483, the Pope's dispensation in March 1484, and Parliament's endorsement of the marriage on December 10, 1485, provided every incentive for the couple to consummate their marriage before the public ceremony conducted by Archbishop Bourchier on January 18, 1486, a formality that made the union legally unassailable.

Anticipating the birth of his heir, Henry moved the queen and her family to Winchester, the site carefully chosen to recall the glory of early Celtic kings and the capital of Anglo-Saxon England. Fifteenth-century historians associated Winchester with the court of King Arthur, whose knights putatively gathered around the large round table displayed in the great hall of Winchester castle.[2] Henry VII traced his ancestry to those early heroes, a heritage emphasized when he first entered London and offered his red dragon standard at the rood by the north door of St. Paul's Cathedral.[3] The "red fiery dragon painted upon white and green sarcenet," symbol of the ancient Britains, was displayed by Owen Glyndwr, who claimed descent from Brutus, and by Jasper Tudor, whose father Owen was Glyndwr's cousin.[4] Henry VII's red dragon badge recalled the prophecy of the angel who told Cadwalader, the last British king, that his people would one day again rule the nation. That day had arrived. As Bernard

André stated in his history, the Tudors descended from Cadwalader.[5]

Queen Elizabeth settled in St. Swithin's Priory (now the Deanery) within Winchester Close, where the prior's great hall served as the queen's great chamber.[6] While Elizabeth awaited the birth of their first child, Henry tended to routine business of the kingdom. On March 4, 1486, he restored to queen dowager Elizabeth "the lordship and manors" of six properties in the county of Essex. The next day he added her dower property from the duchy of Lancaster.[7]

The king then set out to establish his authority in the north, a region where some subjects remained loyal to the Yorkist dynasty. Henry spent Easter at Lincoln, where he learned of the death of Archbishop Bourchier.[8] Traveling on to York, he received word that rebellion had broken out in Yorkshire, led by Francis, viscount Lovell, and in Gloucester, led by Sir Humphrey Stafford.[9] The plot collapsed when Henry promised a pardon to all who laid down their arms. The soldiers in the field accepted the king's offer, causing Lovell to flee to Flanders. Sir Humphrey was caught and executed, but his brother Thomas was pardoned. Henry returned to London before joining Elizabeth at Winchester.

Elizabeth—as she would throughout her life—surrounded herself with family. Her mother, queen dowager Elizabeth, and the king's mother, Margaret Beaufort, attended her, along with the queen's sisters. As Elizabeth prepared to give birth, her mother began to prepare for a new phase in her own life. On July 10, 1486, queen dowager Elizabeth obtained a lease from the Abbot of Westminster for "a mansion within the said Abbey called Cheyne gate ... with all the houses, chambers, aislement and other."[10] The queen dowager was preparing to enter a life of seclusion and religious contemplation.

During the two years of 1483 and 1484, queen dowager Elizabeth had suffered extraordinary traumas: the unexpected death of her husband Edward IV, the disappearance of her sons Edward V and Prince Richard, the executions of her son Sir Richard Grey and her brother Lord Anthony Wydeville, Parliament's negation of her marriage to Edward IV, the declaration that her children were "bastards," and 11 months in Sanctuary. Elizabeth Wydeville was planning a retreat from the murderous world of court politics. In February 1487, she entered Bermondsey Abbey, where she lived the rest of her life in contemplative seclusion—except for a visit to her daughter Elizabeth during her second confinement. Now, however, the queen dowager stayed with her daughter to await the birth of her first grandchild.

Elizabeth's mother-in-law, Margaret Beaufort, countess of Richmond, began to take an increasingly dominant role in the royal household. In preparation for the first Tudor heir, Margaret issued a series of *Ordinances* specifying exact requirements for the queen's birthing chamber, its furnishings, the christening ceremony, and the newborn's nursery. Few details escaped the wonderfully organized supervision of the king's mother, who specified that the queen's chamber would have rich cloth of arras covering the sides, roof, and windows—except for one window that could be uncovered to provide light when desired. The furnishings included

> 2 pair of sheets of Rennes [fine linen from Rheims, France], every of them 4 yards broad and 5 yards long; 2 head sheets of like Rennes, 3 yards broad and 4 yards long; 2 long and 2 square pillows of fustian [cotton and flax] stuffed with fine down...; a pane of scarlet furred with ermine and embroidered with crimson velvet-upon-velvet or rich cloth of gold; and a head sheet of like cloth-of-gold furred with ermine; a coverture of fine lawn of 5 breadths and 6 yards long; and a head sheet of 4 breadths and 5 yards long; a mattress stuffed with wool, a feather bed with a bolster of down, a sparver [canopy] of crimson satin embroidered with crowns of gold, the King's and Queen's arms, and other device, lined with double Tarterin [imported silk] garnished with fringes of silk, blue russet, and gold, with a round bolle [post to support canopy] of gold or silver and gilt; 4 cushions of crimson Damask cloth-of-gold [figured silk]; a round mantle of crimson velvet plain furred throughout with ermine, backed for the Queen to wear about her in her pallet. The pallet at the bed's feet must be arrayed according as the bed is, with sheets and panes, &c. except the cloth-of-gold of the panes that belong to the pallet to be of another colour than that of the bed.[11]

Margaret's *Ordinances* perhaps forewarned Queen Elizabeth (presumably grateful that someone cared enough to measure her bed sheets) that her future life would not always be her own to manage. The king's mother was on her way to becoming a dominant presence in the royal household.

Excitement built throughout Winchester as everyone anticipated the birth of the first Tudor heir. When the baby arrived on
that September night in 1486, the entire town celebrated. Bonfires
burned in the streets, bells rang in the churches, and *Te Deum
Laudamus* resonated throughout the Cathedral. Messengers rode
to "all the Estates and Cities of the Realm" announcing the birth
of a great, new dynasty. God was praised, and "every true
Englishman" rejoiced.[12]

Thanks to Margaret's *Ordinances*, Winchester Cathedral was
ready for the child's christening. Its walls were covered with "rich
arras" and its floors with layers of carpets. The font of silver gilt
brought from Canterbury was lined "with soft Rennes [linen] laid
in divers folds." Elevated on a stage of seven steps built in the middle of the church, the font allowed "the people [to] see the christening without pressing too nigh."[13] A great gilt canopy, fringed
but without curtains, was placed above the font, next to which
was a high cross covered with red worsted. Nearby, a "fair pan of
coals, well burnt," warmed and freshened the atmosphere as sweet
perfumes were cast on it.[14] Barriers of "good timber" surrounded
the font to protect the celebrants from the press of people.

Bad weather delayed the ceremony more than three hours while
the king awaited the earl of Oxford, the designated godfather for
the christening. Finally, Henry ordered the ceremony to proceed
with the earl of Derby and lord Maltravers serving as godfathers.
The christening procession began in the queen's great chamber
and proceeded to the Cathedral led by henchmen and gentlemen
of the Court walking two-by-two and carrying 120 unlighted
torches. Members of the Chapel followed, along with knights,
esquires, kings of arms, heralds, and pursuivants. The earl of
Derby and lord Maltravers preceded the men carrying the basins.
Lord Neville carried the taper, and the earl of Essex the covered
Salt of gold.

The queen's sister Anne bore the christening robe pinned to
her right breast and hanging over her left arm. Cecily, the queen's
eldest sister, followed with the prince wrapped in a mantle of
crimson cloth-of-gold furred with ermine, the train of which was
held by the marchioness of Dorset and supported in the middle by
Sir John Cheney. Thomas, marquess of Dorset, and John de la
Pole, earl of Lincoln, assisted Cecily, who walked beneath a canopy of Estate, one of whose bearers was Sir Edward Wydeville.
The procession moved through the cloister of the Abbey to the

south part of the Church where a rich Cloth of Estate hung: "the weather was too cold and too foul to have been at the West end of the Church," the normal baptism site.[15]

John Alcock, bishop of Worcester, baptized the baby, first placing a pinch of salt (preservative of both body and soul) into its mouth. He then wetted the baby's ears and nostrils with the salted saliva to prevent destructive forces from entering those orifices. Oil was rubbed on the baby's breast and back before he was immersed into the font three times—on the right side, the left side, and face downward. This child was then gloriously named Arthur, after that greatest of ancient Britains.

Just as the torches were lighted to conclude the christening, the earl of Oxford arrived—in time to serve as godfather at Prince Arthur's confirmation. Queen dowager Elizabeth, distinctly honored by her selection as Arthur's godmother, carried the christened child to the high altar where she laid him as offering. After the Gospel and the singing of *Veni Creator Spiritus* and *Te Deum*, the earl of Oxford took the prince in his right arm for confirmation by the bishop of Exeter. Queen dowager Elizabeth presented her godson with a "rich cup of gold, covered" set with stones, the earl of Oxford gave a pair of gilt basins with a cup of assay, the earl of Derby a "rich Salt of gold, covered," and lord Maltravers a coffer of gold set with stones.[16]

Following the offering at St. Swithin's shrine, everyone celebrated with spices, hippocras, and sweet wine. Then lady Cecily carried the baby home to the queen's chamber where he was blessed by his father and mother. The procession left the church with all torches burning, the king's trumpets sounding, and the minstrels playing their instruments. "In the church yard was set two pipes of wine, that every man might drink enough."[17]

The baby returned to a nursery appropriate for a prince. Among the "necessaries" specified by Margaret's *Ordinances* were

> 12 yards of scarlet; 24 yards of fine blanket; and 24 ells of fine Rennes; an ell of bauldkin of gold [embroidered silk] lined with buckram, fringed by the valence with silk to hang over the Prince by his chimney; a mantel of scarlet furred with miniver; 2 pallets of canvas; 2 mattresses; 2 pair of blankets; 4 pair of sheets; 2 tappets of red worsted; 2 cushions covered with crimson damask; a cushion of leather, made like a carving cushion for the nurse; a great pot of leather for water; a great chafer; a basin of latten [brass-like metal]; 2 great basins of pewter for the laundry in the

Photo 3 *The Procession at the Christening of Prince Arthur. Son*
torches, followed by knights, esquires, heralds, nobles,
marquess of Dorset and the earl of Lincoln under a canopy
to Arthur, followed with her train carried by an unknown
Courtesy of Department of Special Collections, Stanford

Arthur Son of Henry VII.

of Henry VII. Henchmen led the procession carrying 120
and prelates. Lady Cecily carried the baby assisted by the
of Estate. Queen dowager Elizabeth Wydeville, godmother
noblewoman. Engraving, *Antiquarian Repertory*, 1:353.
University Libraries.

nursery; 8 large carpets to cover the floors of the chambers, &c.;
also a traverse of red double Tartaron with a celle [canopy] to hang
in the chamber.[18]

The child was provided with two cradles, their designs meticulously specified by Margaret's *Ordinances*:

> ...A little Cradle of Tree [wood] of a yard and a quarter long and 22
> inches broad, in a frame fair set forth by painter's craft; the cradle
> shall have 4 pommels of silver and gilt, 2 like pommels of the same
> frame, five buckles of silver on either side the cradle without
> tongues for the swathing band, whose furniture of bedding and
> linen is above written; 2 panes of scarlet, the one furred with
> ermine and the other with grey, and both bordered with cloth-of-
> gold, the one crimson and the other blue; 2 head sheets of like
> cloth-of-gold, furred according to the panes, a Sparner [canopy?]
> of linen cloth for the same cradle, a baylle [hoop to support can-
> opy] covered with Reynes [fine linen], 2 cradle bands of crimson
> velvet.

> Also there must be ordained a great Cradle of Estate, containing
> in length 5 foot and an half and in breadth 2 foot and an half, cov-
> ered with crimson cloth-of-gold, having a case of Tree covered
> with buckram, a fair rich sparner of crimson cloth-of-gold lined
> with red double Tartaron, and garnished with fringes of silk and
> gold to hang over the same cradle, and the cradle must have five
> Stulpes [posts] of silver and gilt, whereof the cradle shall have
> 3,... one at the head and 2 at the feet, and the cradle case shall have
> other 2 like pommels at the head. The middle most Stulpe that
> standeth at the head of the cradle shall be graven with the King's
> Arms, and all the other Stulpes with other Armes, and the ground
> all about the cradle must be well carpeted. And the cradle must
> have 8 buckles of silver without tongues on either side thereof, a
> mattress, 2 pillows, with 4 beers [pillowcases?] of Reynes, a pair of
> fustians, a pane of scarlet furred with ermines, bordered with blue
> velvet upon velvet, cloth-of-gold furred with ermine, a bayle cov-
> ered with Reynes for the same cradle, a boole [post to support
> canopy] of silver and gilt for the abovesaid sparner, 2 swaddle
> bands, the one blue velvet and the other blue cloth-of-gold, with all
> other necessary furniture thereunto appertaining, like as the
> Prince or Princess...were laying therein.[19]

A Lady Governess of the Nursery, assisted by a dry nurse, supervised the child's upbringing. Both took oaths administered by the

chamberlain, as did the yeomen, grooms, and others who served the child. The food of the wet nurse was assayed, and a physician supervised her every meal so that "she giveth the child seasonable meat and drink."[20]

Queen Elizabeth apparently suffered an ague after giving birth, causing the court to remain at Winchester for her recovery and churching. Margaret's protocol for the queen's purification specified that a duchess or countess help her from her bed of state and lead her to the chamber door where two duchesses received her.[21] A traverse was drawn from a second chamber where a duke received her and led her to the church. "A great burning taper" preceded her in the procession. Following the ceremony of purification and offering, the queen sat in the great chamber under the king's cloth of Estate.

By the feast of All Hallows, the court had moved to Greenwich to begin life as a royal family.[22] On November 19, 1486, the king, stating his "desire of dignifying" the queen's half-brother, Thomas Grey, marquess of Dorset, confirmed his title "with succession in tail male" and granted him an annuity of £35.[23] On January 7, 1487, Henry assigned to Queen Elizabeth's uncle Sir Richard Wydeville £33 6s 8d as a special reward "for his counsel."[24] The queen's adventurous uncle Sir Edward Wydeville became the seventh Knight of the Garter elected during Henry's reign.[25]

As his Council prepared to meet on February 2, 1487, Henry began organizing the royal households. Arthur's nursery was established in the town of Farnham in Surrey, whose 2,000 inhabitants were under the constabulary of Thomas, lord Maltravers, uncle of the queen. On February 1, 1487, the king rewarded the people of Farnham for their hospitality to the prince by granting a license to found a perpetual chantry of one chaplain, with a mortmain license to acquire lands in the annual value of 12 marks.[26] Henry also assigned 1,000 marks to pay the expenses of Arthur, levied from the lands of the duke of Buckingham.[27]

Henry also needed to provide a permanent and separate income for his queen consort, a problem he solved by progressively transferring property to Elizabeth of York from her mother's dower restored during the Parliament of 1485. Traditionally, expenses for the queen's household were paid from duchy of Lancaster income. When Henry restored that property to the queen dowager, he severely limited resources available for his own consort. Gradually, Henry rectified that situation. At his Council meeting on

February 2, 1487, Henry vacated the rights of queen dowager Elizabeth to her dower property in preparation for transferring them to her daughter. On February 3, he granted Queen Elizabeth an annuity of £100, perhaps to provide a small income until she received her duchy of Lancaster property.[28] On February 20, 1487, Henry transferred "the lordships and manors of Waltham Magna, Badewe, Masshbury, Dunmowe, Lighes, and Farnham" in County Essex to his queen.[29]

During Easter term 1487, Henry ordered that payment be made to Queen Elizabeth of "all profits and issues of all lands, honours, and castles lately belonging to Elizabeth, late wife of Edward the Fourth."[30] As late as April 13, 1487, Henry was still paying expenses normally charged to the queen's household accounts, such as an annuity of £40 to Roger Cotton, Master of the Queen's horses.[31] On May 1, 1487, the king officially notified the treasurer and chamberlain of the Exchequer that he had granted

> ...all honors, castles, manors, lordships, knight's fees, advowsons, and all other lands and tenements, with their appurtenances and all manner fee farms and annuities by us late assigned unto Queen Elizabeth, late wife to the full noble prince of famous memory Edward the Fourth,...unto our dearest wife the Queen...And from henceforth yearly...we will and charge you that all the issues, profits, and revenues that hereafter shall grow of the premises and every of them ye pay and deliver to our said wife and to her receivers.[32]

In addition, Henry granted Elizabeth an annuity of £100 from the manors, lands, and tenements of William Trussell, knight, during the minority of his son.[33]

As Henry was establishing the royal households, problems surfaced that endangered his reign. Euphoria at the birth of Arthur was cut short when another rebellion threatened both the king's crown and his family. This rebellion, which began in early 1487, did not dissipate with an offer of amnesty, but ended only after a bloody battle with rebels led by the queen's first cousin—the very earl of Lincoln (son of Edward IV's sister Elizabeth) who had helped Princess Cecily carry Prince Arthur at his baptism.

The wars between the houses of Lancaster and York were not yet over.

CHAPTER 7

REBELLION IN THE REALM

I f Queen Elizabeth looked forward to a happy and peaceful year with her newborn son and family, she was sorely disappointed. The year 1487 brought military and political crises that forced the king to array his troops and fight an invading army. Ominously reminiscent of the last months of Richard III's reign, an invading army threatened the crown. Unlike the minor uprising led by Lovell in 1486, this rebellion was fomented and funded by Yorkist descendants. Subsequently named after the 10-year-old boy exploited by adults to front their attacks, the hostilities have become known as the Lambert Simnel rebellion.

The origins of the plot are murky, but the principal players are clear. Francis, viscount Lovell, who fled to Flanders after his failed effort to unseat Henry, may have been the instigator. Lovell's tenacity in opposing Henry VII originated in his loyalty to Richard III, whom he served during the Scottish campaign of 1480. After Richard was crowned king, Lovell became Chief Butler of England, gained control of lands he had been disputing with Sir Richard Grey (Elizabeth of York's half-brother), and served as chamberlain to the King.[1] His losses under Henry VII made him an irreconcilable enemy.

Lovell solicited the support of Margaret, dowager duchess of Burgundy and sister of Edward IV, Richard III, and George, duke of Clarence. Margaret, apparently caring not a whit for the welfare of her niece Elizabeth of York, directed her powerful passions and considerable resources toward unseating Henry VII. The 12-year-old son of Clarence—Edward, earl of Warwick—became the focal point around whom the plot coalesced. A Yorkist descendant whose lineage placed him one step farther from the throne than Queen Elizabeth, Warwick was an unlikely candidate on whom to hang a rebellion. Accusations that he was simpleminded are unproved, but certainly, he was socially and politically naive. After the death of Clarence, the custody and marriage of

the 3-year-old Warwick had been assigned to Thomas, marquess
of Dorset, but when Richard III became king, the boy was placed
first in the court of Queen Anne, then sequestered at Sheriff
Hutton (where Elizabeth of York joined her cousin during the last
months of Richard's reign). Immediately after Bosworth, Henry
VII imprisoned Warwick in the Tower of London, where he still
remained. As a male Yorkist heir, the boy represented a distinct
threat to the Tudor king: even his name "Warwick" stirred passions among those who fondly remembered his grandfather, the
"kingmaker."

The rebels selected a boy around age 10 to impersonate
Warwick, whom they claimed they had rescued from the Tower.
The impostor was taught courtly manners by "a lowborn priest" in
Oxford, a scholar "as cunning as he was corrupt" according to
Vergil's Tudor history.[2] The priest has been variously identified as
William Simonds or as Richard Simons, both Oxonians.[3] On
February 17, 1487, William Simonds confessed to the Convocation
of Canterbury:

> ...he himself abducted and carried across to places in Ireland the
> son of a certain organ-maker of the university of Oxford; and this
> boy was there reputed to be the earl of Warwick; and that after-
> wards he himself was with Lord Lovell in Furness fells.[4]

Simonds, who was sent to the Tower after his confession, may
have been a minor collaborator, since Henry seems to have learned
little from him in February when the rebellion was just getting
underway. The Richard Simons captured later at the battle of
Stoke may have been his brother engaged in the same plot, since
surnames were notoriously variant. The boy impostor, now infamous as Lambert Simnel, was identified as the son of a baker or a
shoemaker in André's history.[5]

Whether Lambert Simnel ever traveled to Burgundy, as Henry
VII believed, is unclear, but if he did, the dowager duchess
Margaret could have provided information about the royal family
that further abetted the pretense. Certainly, Henry VII blamed
Margaret as a central provocateur of the rebellion in his letter to
Sir Gilbert Talbot:

> ...the great malice that the Lady Margaret of Burgundy beareth
> continually against us, as she showed lately in sending hither of a

feigned boy, surmising him to have been the son of the duke of Clarence, and caused him to be accompanied with the earl of Lincoln, the lord Lovell, and with great multitude of Irishmen and of Almains [Germans]...[6]

Whoever provided Lambert Simnel's education in courtly manners and knowledge, the boy became sufficiently adept to deceive the Irish—and anyone else who needed an excuse to rebel—into believing that he was of royal descent.

Dowager duchess Margaret had loved Clarence and obviously preferred his son Warwick on England's throne to the daughter of Edward IV. By March 1487, the dowager duchess was assembling ships and men to invade England.[7] Under the leadership of Martin Schwartz, a captain from Augsburg, an army of 1,500–2,000 German and Swiss mercenaries set sail in Dutch and Flemish ships sometime in late April and landed in Ireland on May 5, 1487.[8]

In Dublin, the rebellion gathered dangerous momentum. John de la Pole, earl of Lincoln and son of Elizabeth, duchess of Suffolk (sister of Edward IV, Richard III, Clarence, and dowager duchess Margaret) had joined the growing army. Lincoln at age 24 was a more threatening opponent than Warwick. Many regarded him as the designated heir of Richard III, who on August 21, 1484, had appointed Lincoln to the lieutenancy of Ireland.[9] Lincoln also served as president of Richard III's Council of the North, the governing body that administered justice in that vast region, and he possessed experience and knowledge that the boy Warwick lacked.[10] Many expected Lincoln to claim the crown for himself if the rebels succeeded. Lincoln had professed allegiance to Henry VII, had participated in the baptism of Prince Arthur, and attended Henry's Council at Sheen on February 2, 1487.[11] Sometime in mid-February, however, Lincoln, perhaps involved in the insurrection as early as Christmas 1486,[12] fled to Flanders where he joined viscount Lovell and Margaret's mercenaries.

Dubliners welcomed the Yorkist rebels. Ever since 1447 when Richard, duke of York, was appointed Henry VI's lieutenant in Ireland, the Irish had viewed Yorkists favorably. The duke and his duchess Cecily had lived in Dublin Castle and brought stability to the unruly Pale. Clarence was born in Dublin in 1449, and its residents regarded his son almost as a native. They were delighted to support "Warwick's" bid to become the next king of England, and on May 24, 1487, the Irish lords gathered in Christchurch Cathedral where the archbishop of Dublin crowned Lambert Simnel as "King Edward VI."[13]

* * *

Henry VII had been following the growing conspiracy since the beginning of the year when his Council at Sheen on February 2, 1487, discussed how to deal with the rebels. To discourage others from joining the rebellion, he proclaimed a general pardon for those accused of treason and displayed the real earl of Warwick to the populace to disprove claims of the Dublin impostor. On February 29, Henry ordered Clarence's son, Edward, earl of Warwick, to be released from the Tower and paraded through London to St. Paul's. Vergil describes the scene at the Cathedral:

> Here the boy (as he had been instructed) showing himself to everyone, fell to prayer and took part in worship, and then spoke with many important people and especially with those of whom the king was suspicious, so that they might the more readily understand that the Irish had based their new rebellion on an empty and spurious cause. But this medicine was of no avail for diseased minds.[14]

The real Warwick then returned to the Tower while England prepared for war. The rebels in Ireland were not deterred.

Subsequent historians have implicated queen dowager Elizabeth in the rebellion. Vergil pointed to Henry's transfer of dower from Elizabeth Wydeville to Queen Elizabeth as evidence that the king suspected his mother-in-law of complicity with the rebels. Vergil summarized Henry's reasons: the queen dowager had collaborated with Richard III, had impeded Henry's marriage with Elizabeth, and had broken her promise to the English nobles in Brittany by leaving Sanctuary in March 1484.[15] Vergil's allegations do not ring true. For Henry to have waited three years to exact punishment for those deeds seems unlikely, especially since the king had consistently honored his mother-in-law during that interim. In July 1486, Henry proposed marriage between the queen dowager and James III of Scotland, an offer the king of England would never have made to his troublesome northern neighbor if he suspected his mother-in-law of treason.[16] Subsequently, Henry chose the queen dowager as godmother to his first-born son. When he vacated her dower five months later in February 1487, that action was taken to establish the royal households of Queen Elizabeth and Prince Arthur. In compensation, Henry granted the queen dowager an immediate payment of 200 marks[17] and subsequently an annuity of 400 marks.[18] If that sum seems paltry in exchange for her duchy of Lancaster property, it more than met her needs at Bermondsey Abbey, where she moved in mid-February.

The queen dowager's move to Bermondsey itself added fuel to the fires lit by historians. Francis Bacon claims she was "banished the world into a nunnery; where it was almost thought dangerous to visit her or see her."[19] Bacon, writing a century after Vergil, amplified upon his predecessor, but even he found Vergil's rationale insufficient to justify forcibly cloistering the queen dowager: the inequity between crime and punishment "makes it very probable there was some greater matter against her."[20] That "greater matter," Bacon surmises without evidence, was Elizabeth Wydeville's role as "the principal source and motion" of the Simnel plot. Bacon believed that her motivation derived from a belief that her daughter was "not advanced, but depressed" by Henry VII.[21] Assigning motives to a queen who lived 130 years earlier rather exceeds the historian's purview, but Bacon writes with a certitude that subsequent readers have found compelling. David Baldwin, for instance, agrees that the queen dowager "was undoubtedly being punished for something," but suggests she resented "Margaret Beaufort's influence over Henry" and thus attempted to remove both "the King and his overbearing mother" in order to marry Elizabeth of York to her cousin Warwick: "it seems certain that [the queen dowager] was actively working for Henry's overthrow and would surely have expected a large dividend in the new world she had helped to create."[22]

Not a shred of evidence links queen dowager Elizabeth Wydeville to the Lambert Simnel rebellion. Neither is there any indication that her long friendship with Margaret Beaufort had ended. Margaret had carried Elizabeth Wydeville's last baby, Bridget, at her christening, her family members had intermarried with several Wydevilles, and she had helped plan the marriage of Henry VII and Elizabeth of York. Further, the idea that queen dowager Elizabeth would support Warwick, the son of Clarence, is hardly credible. Clarence had tried to usurp the throne of her husband Edward IV. Clarence and the earl of Warwick had murdered the queen dowager's father and brother, had accused her mother of witchcraft, had forced her husband Edward IV into exile, and had caused herself, eight months pregnant, to seek sanctuary at Westminster Abbey with three small daughters. Neither would Elizabeth Wydeville have assisted a rebellion that included among its conspirators Robert Stillington, bishop of Bath and Wells, the man who invalidated her marriage to Edward IV and bastardized their 10 children!

More probably, queen dowager Elizabeth chose to retreat into a contemplative, religious life, a decision made by many noble ladies of the era. The lease signed at Westminster Abbey in July 1486 indicates her desire to live separately from the Court long before Lambert Simnel entered the picture. Such a choice seems almost inevitable, given Elizabeth Wydeville's lifetime of pious and benevolent acts.[23] That she ultimately moved to the relatively secluded Bermondsey Abbey, where royal women traditionally resided in the Clare guest suite, rather than Westminster Abbey's Cheynegate mansion may reflect her determination to avoid the distractions of bustling Westminster, the center of government and official residence of the king. Nineteen years as queen had cost her three sons, a father, and two brothers sacrificed to the Court's bloody politics. Elizabeth Wydeville now sought solace and peace in service to her God.

In fact, when Henry began the transfer of dower from mother to daughter on February 2, 1487, the Simnel rebellion was still quite nascent, little more than intelligence reports about the imposter in Dublin. The earl of Lincoln was still at court and the atmosphere at Sheen seemed relaxed at the beginning of Lent.[24] Henry's continuing grants to the queen dowager in subsequent years further argue against any alienation between the two. Instead, they reflect the king's genuine concern—even warm affection—for her welfare. While the pro forma language of official documents does not reveal Henry's personal feelings toward "the king's right dear mother Queen Elizabeth," his order to the Exchequer in 1488 to pay the queen dowager £6 "by way of reward for a tun of wine" demonstrates that he paid attention to little things in her daily life.[25] A gift of 50 marks in December 1490 "by way of reward against the feast of Christmas next coming" similarly suggests the king's personal interest in his mother-in-law's welfare.

By mid-March 1487, reports of the growing rebellion required action from the king. Since East Anglia seemed the probable point for an invasion from Flanders, Henry embarked on a progress through that region. On his way through Bury St. Edmunds, the king took into custody Thomas, marquess of Dorset, eldest son of the queen dowager by her first marriage, and sent him to the Tower. Dorset had purchased the wardship of the young Warwick under Edward IV, and perhaps Henry suspected that his sympathies for the boy still persisted. Dorset's arrest does not indicate the king's general distrust of the queen dowager's family because he displayed continued confidence in Sir Edward Wydeville. On March 13, 1487, the king granted to Sir Edward the property Dorset had held during the minority of Warwick: the manors of Swanston, Thorley, Welowe, and Brexton in the Isle of Wight.²⁶ Sir Edward Wydeville also led 2,000 men at Stoke, an array the king would never have permitted if he doubted Wydeville loyalty. The king further rewarded Sir Edward's support by electing him a Knight of the Garter.

While the rebellion was growing on the Continent, Henry attended Easter Sunday services at the Cathedral in Norwich, followed by a pilgrimage to the shrine at Walsingham on Monday, April 16.²⁷ He then visited Thetford and spent two nights in Cambridge before suddenly departing for Coventry—riding two full days to arrive by nightfall on April 22.²⁸ Perhaps information that Margaret's ships had sailed from Flanders caused his rapid return to Warwickshire where Kenilworth Castle became his central headquarters for monitoring both coasts against invasion. Here Henry planned his defense. On May 13, Henry wrote to Queen Elizabeth's chamberlain, the earl of Ormond, with news that "our rebels landed the fifth day of this month in our land of Ireland." Henry had already sent for "our dearest wife and for our dearest mother to come unto us" and asked Ormond to attend them.²⁹

That Henry wished his wife and mother to be with him during this crisis is both touching and typical. The royal family spent much time together, and Kenilworth, the strongest of the castles in the Midlands, offered a safe, pleasant, and strategically situated residence for Henry to prepare for battle. The fortified feudal palace of Kenilworth had been greatly enhanced by John of Gaunt, who added a magnificent Great Hall, and by Henry V, who constructed a "pleasance in the Marsh" about a half-mile to the west of the palace across the "Great Pool."³⁰ Surrounded by a moat, the Pleasance included a hall and chambers with extensive gardens—a setting that would appeal to Elizabeth of York's love of the outdoors.

To this site came Queen Elizabeth, the king's mother, and the queen's chamberlain Thomas Butler, seventh earl of Ormond. Her chamberlain was responsible for the queen's comfort and welfare, both private and public. He controlled access for all visitors and assured that her daily array of clothing was appropriate and ready for each occasion. He appointed carvers and cupbearers to serve at meals and supervised the almoners, knights, and attendants in her service. To adapt a phrase from *The Household Book* of Edward IV, the chamberlain was "the chief head of rulers in the [queen's] chambers."[31] Thomas, lord Ormond, was the third of three brothers who inherited the earldom successively from their father, the fourth earl of Ormond, whose landed wealth lay in Ireland. The family had been stalwart Lancastrians throughout the Wars of the Roses, but Ormond received a general pardon from Edward IV in 1471 and was restored to the family inheritance in England.[32] Henry VII rewarded the seventh earl for his family's long and loyal service to Lancaster by appointing him chamberlain to Queen Elizabeth in August 1486. Now Ormond's Irish connections might prove useful during Lambert Simnel's invasion.

* * *

The rebels set sail from Ireland and landed on a barren, windswept beachhead off the Cumbrian coast on June 4, 1487, to begin their march across England.[33] As the king prepared to leave Kenilworth and head north to meet the enemy, his mind was very much on family. He issued an order on June 8, to pay £46 for the wages of the lady mistress, nurses, and gentlewomen who cared for Prince Arthur.[34] Until receipts from Elizabeth's dower were available, Henry provided livery for her attendants. Deliveries from the Great Wardrobe in 1487 included

> to William Betell, Hamlett Clegge, Richard Smyth, and their 26 companions, servants of the lady queen, cloth of russet, as a gift from the King, for an allowance of their watches.[35]

For the queen's footman, Lewis Gough and John Rede, the king provided cloaks, cloth of velvet, sarcenet, Holland cloth, high boots, shoes, hats, and bonnets.[36]

By June 14, the king and his troops were just west and south of Nottingham. Fighting with him were Jasper Tudor, duke of Bedford; the earls of Oxford and Derby; and Sir Edward Wydeville commanding 2,000 cavalry on the right wing of the vanguard.[37] On June 16, 1487, the king's army clashed with an army of foreign mercenaries, supplemented by brave, but largely unarmored, Irish fighters. In a fiercely fought three-hour battle at Stoke, Henry's troops decimated the rebels.[38]

Killed in battle were the earl of Lincoln and Martin Schwartz. Viscount Lovell disappeared. While his body may have been lost among the thousands of unidentified dead, rumors proliferated. To this day, it is unknown whether he drowned while crossing the Trent, escaped to the Continent, or survived to live incognito at Minster Lovell.[39] Richard Simons and his protégé Lambert Simnel were captured. They received extraordinary leniency at the hands of Henry VII. Because Simons was a priest, he was not executed. Simnel, a mere boy manipulated by powerful, venal men, was assigned to the royal kitchens as a turnspit. Perhaps Henry VII had learned from the experience of Richard III that kings who fail to protect 10-year-old boys suffer dire consequences. Lambert Simnel prospered in later life and became the king's falconer.[40]

The Lambert Simnel rebellion consumed the energies and resources of both king and country during most of 1487. Even after his victory at Stoke, Henry had to deal with residual sympathy for the rebels. At the end of July, he advanced north into Yorkshire, where he spent almost a month in York exacting justice before moving on to Newcastle. Finally returning to London, Henry's second Parliament convened on November 9 and attainted 28 rebels. By the time Parliament dissolved on December 18, the king had made great progress in solidifying his governing power.[41]

As this year of peril and challenge drew to its end, the mood of the nation became distinctly optimistic. Indeed, Henry's successful handling of the political and military crises of 1487 amplified the hope and anticipation of this year's particularly triumphal conclusion. By September, planning for Queen Elizabeth's coronation had begun. Rapidly becoming a master of ceremony, Henry orchestrated his queen's coronation into a magnificent approbation of his reign. On St. Katherine's Day, November 25, 1487, all of England celebrated Elizabeth of York.

CHAPTER 8

THE CROWNING OF A QUEEN

Henry VII's first Parliament in November 1485 had witnessed his own magnificent coronation as king. His second Parliament in November 1487 reveled in an equally splendid crowning of his queen—not just any queen, but Elizabeth of York, whose subjects fondly remembered her father, Edward IV, for the peace and prosperity he had brought to England. She had already produced a male heir to the throne, a good omen for both king and nation, and her manners and actions charmed everyone—from foreign ambassadors to English commoners. Elizabeth of York was fast becoming the eponymous "Gracious Queen."[1]

If Elizabeth's coronation was delayed longer than her supporters may have wished, its timing at the end of 1487 was brilliant in focusing national attention on the thriving Tudor dynasty. Henry VII had earned respect through two victories on the battlefield—at Bosworth fighting against a crowned king and at Stoke against the resources and power of prominent Yorkists. The king now staged his queen's coronation during Parliament—when the maximum number of clergy, nobles, and commoners were in London to witness Tudor magnificence and the merging of Lancaster and York. The ceremonies celebrated peace, deepened English pride, and forged national unity. Gaily decorated streets promised even better times ahead. The optimism was not misplaced.

On Saturday before the feast of All Hallows, the king and queen left Warwick to travel to London. They stopped at St. Albans to keep the Feast of All Hallows and to hear the divine service on All Soul's Day. The Abbey, one of the best known in England, was built on the site where St. Albans was believed to have been martyred around the year 304.[2] The shrine of St. Albans had attracted relics of other saints, carefully preserved in the Benedictine monastery founded in 793 by King Offa of Mercia. Construction of a great Norman church began in 1077, and from the twelfth to the fourteenth centuries, the Abbot at St. Albans was the most prominent in England. The monks were famous for their literary and artistic works. While half of the monks died during the Black Death, about 50 resided at this sacred and historical site during this fifteenth-century visit of Henry VII and Elizabeth of York.

The king and queen left St. Albans after dinner on All Soul's Day and spent the night at Barnet, departing for London the next morning. On the way they were met by the mayor, sheriffs, aldermen, and selected craftsmen of London—all on horseback and dressed in livery—waiting to escort the king into the city. The royal procession rode through freshly cleaned streets. From Bishop's Gate (one of seven original gates in London's wall) to St. Paul's Cathedral, the streets were lined on both sides with "Citizens of every craft," dressed in livery and organized in rows according to "due order."[3] At the west door of St. Paul's, the choir in habits and copes greeted the king. The archbishop of Canterbury and other prelates escorted Henry into the church where he was "sensed with the great senser of Paul's by an Angel coming out of the roof," while the choir sang a solemn anthem.[4] *Te Deum Laudamus* celebrated the king's victory over rebels and his arrival in London.

The queen, "my lady the king's mother," and their attendants secretly stayed in a house outside Bishops Gate beside St. Mary Spital until the king's procession passed, then they went on to Greenwich to prepare for the coronation ceremonies. The ladies of the Court anticipated three exciting and busy weeks of fitting gowns, dressing hair, choosing makeup, and planning their official entry into the City of London. On November 7, the Common Council voted to present Queen Elizabeth with a gift of 1,000 marks.[5] On November 9, the official commission for conducting the coronation was appointed, headed by the king's uncle, Jasper Tudor, duke of Bedford; Thomas Stanley, earl of Derby; and William, earl of Nottingham.[6]

> On Friday next before Saint Katherine's Day [November 25], the Queen's good Grace, royally appareled and accompanied with my Lady the King's mother and many other great Estates, both Lords and Ladies richly beseen, came forward to the Coronation.[7]

The queen's procession departed Greenwich by water, proceeding up the Thames with a dramatic flair that excited those watching on both shores. The mayor, sheriffs, and aldermen of London, along with prominent commoners from the guilds, joined the procession dressed in their best livery. All sailed on personal barges flying vividly colored banners and silk streamers displaying their arms. *The Bachelor's Barge* excelled all others with a "great red Dragon spouting flames of fire into the Thames."[8] The red dragon reminded all viewers that this queen was married to the man prophesized by Cadwalader to restore England's glory. Pageants provided sport and pleasure along the way. Trumpets, clarions, and minstrels accompanied the procession from Greenwich and announced the queen's landing at Tower Wharf. Inside the Tower, the king waited to greet her.

As was the tradition, the king commemorated the coronation by creating 14 new Knights of the Bath, a highly honorific appointment that rewarded—and cemented the loyalty of—selected men of his realm. The ceremony began that evening with a ritualistic cleansing of body and soul. Each initiate's beard was shaved and hair cut before immersion in a bath. During the night of watch, two esquires and a governor supervised each initiate while he received instruction in the mysteries of knighthood. The ritual concluded with the garbing of each new knight in a blue robe with straight sleeves and a white lace of silk on his left shoulder.[9] The proud "new made Knights of Bath" constituted one of the most honored and colorful units in the next day's coronation procession from the Tower to Westminster.

For the Saturday procession, the queen wore a kirtle of white cloth-of-gold of damask and an ermine-furred mantle, fastened in front with a gold and silk lace ending in knots of gold and tassels. A net-like headdress covered her "fair yellow hair hanging down plain behind her back."[10] On her head, she wore a circlet of gold with precious stones. With her sister Cecily bearing her train, she entered her litter that was covered with cloth-of-gold of damask and filled with large pillows of down covered with the same cloth-of-gold. A cloth-of-gold canopy covered the litter, fringed with valences and supported by four gilt poles each carried by a Knight of the Body. The heavy canopy required three teams, each with four Knights of the Body, who took turns in carrying it from the Tower to Westminster.

The freshly cleaned streets of London were decorated with tapestries and arrases. Cloths of gold velvet and silks displayed the wealth of Cheapstreet. From the Tower to St. Paul's, members of the crafts, all dressed in their liveries, lined the streets. People hung out of windows to see their queen. Along the way, groups of children—some dressed as angels and others as virgins—sang "sweet songs as Her Grace passed by." Officers of the Marshall, dressed in red gowns of livery and carrying tipped staves, walked alongside the procession to force back the press of people and open a way for the queen.

Esquires, knights, and bannerets rode in front of the procession, followed by the "new-made Knights of Bath" in their blue gowns and white lace scarves. Behind them came the pursuivants, heralds, and kings of arms, followed by the duke of Suffolk and other nobility. The mayor of London with two esquires of Honor followed in gowns of crimson velvet and mantels of ermine, wearing hats of red cloth-of-gold with beaks pointing forward. Next came the Garter King, followed by the earl of Nottingham, Marshall of England; Thomas Stanley, earl of Derby and Constable of England; and the earl of Oxford, Great Chamberlain. Immediately before the queen's litter rode Jasper Tudor, duke of Bedford and Great Steward of England for the coronation.

Following the queen, Sir Roger Cotton, Master of the Queen's Horse, led the horse of Estate with a woman's saddle of red cloth-of-gold tissue. The henchmen followed next, creating a controversial point of protocol among the heralds, some of whom thought that the horse of Estate " should have followed... after the Henchmen."[11] Instead, the queen's horse preceded the six henchmen who rode on white mounts harnessed with cloth-of-gold embroidered with white roses and suns, badges of the house of York.

Next came horse-borne chairs covered with cloth-of-gold to carry Katherine Wydeville, duchess of Bedford (the queen's aunt who had married Jasper Tudor) and Cecily, the queen's sister. The second chair bore the duchess of Suffolk (the queen's paternal aunt), the duchess of Norfolk, and the countess of Oxford. Six baronesses, all gowned in crimson velvet, followed on horses with saddles of Estate. Two chairs followed them, carrying the queen's ladies and gentlewomen. Then rode the gentlewomen of the lady Bedford and lady Cecily, followed by gentlewomen who waited on the queen. The magnificent procession excited all who saw and participated in it, building anticipation for the next day's crowning.

For her coronation on Sunday, Queen Elizabeth wore a kirtle and a mantle of purple velvet furred with ermine and fronted by lace. On her hair rested a circlet of gold garnished with pearl and other precious stones. Her sister Cecily bore her train as she entered Westminster Hall, where she waited under a cloth of Estate until the procession began.

At the head of the coronation procession were the esquires and knights, followed by the Knights of Bath, the barons, and other nobility in order of ascending rank. Heralds and sergeants of arms walked on each side to make room for the procession. The monks of Westminster and the King's Chapel in white tunics led the procession of abbots and bishops, one of whom carried the Chalice of St. Edward and another the Patent. The archbishop of York preceded the Garter King of Arms, the mayor of London, the Constable, and the Marshall of England. The earl of Arundel next carried the Verge of Ivory with a dove on its top, followed by the duke of Suffolk bearing the Scepter. The earl of Oxford, Great Chamberlain, wore his Parliament robes and carried his staff of office. The duke of Bedford in his robes of Estate, but bareheaded, carried a "rich crown of gold."

Finally, the queen! Her path from Westminster Hall to the pulpit of Westminster Abbey was carefully covered with new ray cloth (striped wool) on which she walked beneath a canopy of Estate carried by barons of the Cinque Ports. Walking on either side of Elizabeth were the bishop of Winchester and the bishop of Ely. Lady Cecily carried her train. Following the queen were the duchess of Bedford, another unnamed duchess, and a countess—all wearing mantles and surcoats of scarlet, furred and powdered. The two duchesses wore coronets of gold garnished with pearls and other stones, and the countess a circlet of gold with pearls and stones.

Tradition allowed those watching the procession to claim the ray cloth upon which the queen walked. The popularity of Elizabeth of York made this cloth particularly desirable:

> ...the more pity, there was so huge a people inordinately pressing to cut the ray cloth that the Queen's Grace went upon, so that in the Presence certain persons were slain, and the order of the ladies following the Queen was broken and distroubled.[12]

Queen Elizabeth entered Westminster Abbey through the west door where she paused for the prayer *Omnipotens sempiterne Deus* before proceeding through the choir to the pulpit, where an elevated seat of Estate had been constructed, covered with cloth of gold and cushions. King Henry and "my Lady his Mother" watched the ceremony from an elevated stage, concealed by lattice and cloth of arras, built on the right side of the Church between the pulpit and high altar. With the king's mother were her attendants, including Lady Margaret Pole, daughter of the duke of Clarence. Queen Elizabeth's mother did not attend the coronation, but remained in religious retreat at Bermondsey Abbey.

Inside Westminster Abbey on November 25, 1487, the archbishop of Canterbury received Elizabeth of York before the high altar, around which lay carpets and cushions of Estate. The queen prostrated herself before the archbishop while he said the prayer *Deus qui solus habes*. Elizabeth then arose and kneeled, the archbishop opened her gown over the breast and anointed her twice— first on the forehead and second on the breast, intoning *In nomine Patris & Filii,.. profit tibi hec unctio* and praying *Omnipotens sempiterne Deus*. The queen closed her gown, the archbishop blessed her ring and cast holy water on it. He put the ring on the fourth finger of the queen's right hand while saying *Accipe annulum* and *Dominus vobiscum* He then blessed the queen's crown, *Oremus Deus tuorum*, and set it on her head. The archbishop delivered to the queen a Scepter in her right hand and a Rod of Gold in her left, while praying *Omnipotens Domine*. The crowned queen was then led to her seat of Estate by the bishops of Winchester and Ely, followed by her ladies. As the organs played the offertory, Elizabeth approached the high altar with Scepter and Rod of Gold borne before her. She then returned to her royal seat of Estate for the *Agnus Dei*, during which the Pax was brought for her to kiss. The archbishop blessed the queen with a prayer to which she answered, "Amen." Elizabeth then rose and walked to the high altar where two bishops held a towel before her as she inclined low to the ground and said her *Confiteor*. The archbishop gave the *Absolution* and the queen received the Blessed Sacrament before returning to her seat for the conclusion of the Mass.

The queen next accompanied the archbishop, prelates, and nobles to the shrine of Saint Edward where the archbishop took the crown from her head and placed it on the altar. At the conclusion of the divine service, Queen Elizabeth returned to her chambers through the White Hall before going on to Westminster Palace. The events of the day, along with the heavy robes and crown, had been exhausting, but she needed to prepare for the coronation banquet.

* * *

Clearing the press of people from Westminster Hall to make way for the banquet was the responsibility of the Stewards of the Coronation—the duke of Bedford, the earl of Derby, and the earl of Nottingham. Mounted on horses, "the three Estates" rode around the hall accompanied by servants carrying tipped staves. The magnificence of the Stewards' dress added to their authority: the duke of Bedford wore a furred cloth-of-gold gown with a rich chain around his neck, carried a white rod in his hand, and presided from a horse with a gold-bordered trapper embroidered with red roses and red dragons. The earl of Derby's gown was furred with sable and his chain lay in "many folds about his neck." Carrying his staff of office as Constable of England, he rode a horse with trapper "right curiously wrought with the needle," showing arms with a man's visage "very well favored." The earl of Nottingham, seated on a horse elegantly trapped with cloth-of-gold, carried the gilt staff of the Marshal of England.[13]

After the hall was cleared, the queen returned, refreshed for the banquet where she sat at the center of a table on the dais. The archbishop of Canterbury said Grace, after which "Dame Katherine Gray and Mistress Ditton went under the table, where they sat on either side the Queen's feet all the dinner time."[14] The archbishop of Canterbury sat on the queen's right, while the duchess of Bedford and Lady Cecily sat on her left. The countess of Oxford and the countess of Rivers (widow of the queen's executed uncle, Anthony Wydeville) kneeled on either side of the queen and held a kerchief before her when she ate.

Seated at the table next to the right wall were the barons of the Cinque Ports and the members of the Chancery. At the table next to the left wall were the mayor and aldermen of London and distinguished merchants and citizens. Two tables were placed in the middle of the hall. At the middle table on the right were the bishops and abbots on one side, and the Lords Temporal on the other; at the lower end sat the judges, barons of the Exchequer, knights and other nobles. The middle table on the left was reserved for duchesses, countesses, baronesses, and the wives of bannerets and bachelors—80 in number.

Photo 4   The Royal Arms of Elizabeth of York, impaling
Mortimer and Ulster, quarterly. Queen Elizabeth
adopted the motto "Humble & Reverence." From
Nicholas Harris Nicolas, *Privy Purse Expenses of
Elizabeth of York: Wardrobe Accounts of Edward IV.*
London: 1830. Geoffrey Wheeler, London.

A stage constructed in a window on the left side of the hall
allowed King Henry and his mother to observe the feast from
behind a lattice and cloths of arras, unseen by the revelers. On the
right was another stage where the kings of arms, heralds, pursuiv-
aunts, and selected "strangers" viewed the banquet.

The serving of the food was a ceremony unto itself. At the end of
the hall, a stage constructed high above the diners held trumpeters
and minstrels who announced each course. The food arrived via a
procession led by the sergeants of arms, the Controller, and the

Treasurer, followed by the duke of Bedford and earls of Derby and Nottingham on horseback. Next entered Lord Fitzwater, sewer, in surcoat with tabard sleeves and hood about his neck, carrying his signature towel. The sewer was in charge of the entire banquet— the arranging of tables, the seating of the guests, the tasting and serving of the dishes. As the trumpets sounded, the first course arrived—carried high on the shoulders of knights.

A herald carefully recorded the dishes served during each of two courses. The menu indicates that presentation and embellished descriptions were as important in 1487 as they are today:

Furst, a Warner byfor the Course. [Trumpets sounded as an elaborate decoration made of spun sugar, pastry, or marzipan was paraded through the hall][15]
Sheldes of Brawne in Armor. [Flesh of boar, perhaps decorated with the queen's heraldic arms]
Frumetye with Veneson. [Wheat porridge with venison]
Bruet riche. [Rich broth]
Hart powderd graunt Chars. [Ground deer meat mixed with spices, raisins, and dates]
Fesaunt intramde Royall. [Pheasant]
Swan with Chawdron. [Swan with sauce of chopped entrails and spices]
Capons of high Goe. [Castrated rooster]
Lampervey in Galantine. [Eel-like fish in spiced wine and vinegar sauce]
Crane with Cretney. [Crane with seasoned soup]
Pik in Latymer Sawce. [Pike in sauce]
Heronufew with his Sique. [Young heron—with his beak?]
Carpe in Foile. [Carp in thin pastry]
Kid reversed. [Baby goat with flesh turned out]
Perche in Jeloy depte. [Perch in gelatin]
Conys of high Grece. [Fatted rabbits]
Moten Roiall richely garnysshed. [Mutton]
Valance baked. [Valencia almonds or oranges?]
Custarde Royall. [Egg and cream dessert]
Tarte Poleyn. [Tart of chicken]
Leyse Damask. [Damask prunes]
Frutt Synoper. [Fruit dessert]
Frutt Formage. [Fruit dessert of another type]
A Soteltie, with Writing of Balads, whiche as yet I have not.[16]

A "Soteltie" or Subtlety was a spectacular dessert designed to surprise and amaze the guests—to leave a lasting impression of the splendor and magnificence of the dinner. Spun sugar, pastry, or marzipan was molded into fantastic ornamental shapes, such as St. George on horseback slaying a dragon, St. Paul's Cathedral with its spires, or a castle with parapets. The Subtlety was sometimes eaten, but at other times it functioned as a gigantic decoration. Many Subtleties were accompanied by verses to explain the intricacies of the decoration. At the coronation of the seven-year-old King Henry VI, the Subtlety depicted the Virgin Mary with Jesus on her lap holding out a crown to Henry, who was flanked on one side by St. Denis of France and on the other by St. George of England. The poet Lydgate composed verses to explain the tableau and bless the king. Unfortunately, the herald recording the banquet menu for Elizabeth of York's coronation did not receive copies of the ballads in time to include them. A woeful loss for us!

During the lull between courses, tables were cleared and the knights prepared for the next procession of food. Guests conversed, caught up on gossip, and observed the surrounding fashions. Noise and bustle prevailed until the trumpets blared, the marshals entered the hall on horseback, and the knights presented the next dishes for the hundreds of diners. Each "mess," a serving of food for two to four guests, was placed on the long tables. Individuals served themselves with a spoon or with their hands. Forks were unknown, but sometimes guests brought personal knives to cut and spear pieces of meat and to transfer salt from the shared saltcellar to their trenchers. At formal banquets, professional carvers presided to cut the meat for distinguished guests.

At Queen Elizabeth's banquet, the second course was as daunting as the first:

A Warner byfor the Course.

Joly Ypocras. [Spiced wine]

Mamane with Lozengs of Golde. ["Mawmenny" or "maumenye" was a broth of ground capon, pork, or beef thickened with flour or breadcrumbs in a wine sauce. This broth was decorated with diamond-shaped pieces of gold foil]

Pekok in Hakell. [Roasted peacock, re-dressed with its plumage and tail feathers]

Bittowre. [Bittern, a small bird, similar to heron]
Fesawnte. [Pheasant]
Browes. [Brewes—a small bird]
Egrets in Beorwetye. [Egrets]
Cokkes. [Cocks]
Partricche. [Partridge]
Sturgyn fresshe Fenell. [Sturgeon with fresh fennel]
Plovers. [Wading bird]
Rabett Sowker. [Suckling rabbit]
Seyle in Fenyn entierly served richely. [Seal]
Red Shankks. [Game bird]
Snytes. [Snipe-like bird]
Quayles. [Quails]
Larkes ingraylede. [Larks]
Creves de Endence. [Crayfish]
Venesone in Paste Royall. [Venison in pastry]
Quince Baked. [Quince]
Marche Payne Royall. [Marzipan]
A cold Bake Mete flourishede. [Cold meat, baked]
Lethe Ciprus. [Slices of a jellied dessert, perhaps with fruits
    from Cyprus]
Lethe Rube. [Another jellied dessert, sliced]
Fruter Augeo. [Fritters—fried egg and flour dough, sweetened
    and sometimes filled with apples or other fruit]
Fruter Mouniteyne. [Fritters of another type]
Castells of Jely in Temple wise made. [Jelly or gelatin, shaped
    into castles]
A Soteltie. [Subtlety]

After the service, the Garter King of Arms, accompanied by other kings of arms, heralds, and pursuivants made their obeisance to the queen. In the name of all officers, the Garter King addressed Elizabeth with thanks:

Right high and mighty Prince, most noble and excellent Princess, most Christian Queen, and all our most dread and Sovereign liege Lady, We the Officers of Arms, and servants to all nobles, beseech Almighty God to thank you for the great and abundant largesse which your Grace hath given us in the honor of your most honorable and right wise Coronation, and to send your Grace to live in honor and virtue.[17]

The queen was then "cried" at five places throughout the hall, as the Garter King loudly proclaimed:

> De la tres hault, tres puissaunt, tres excellent Princesse, la tres noble Reigne d'Engleter, et de Fraunce, et Dame d'Irland, *Largesse.*
>
> [From the most high, most mighty, most excellent Princess, the most noble Queen of England, and of France, and Lady of Ireland, *Largesse.*][18]

The officers then drank, and the minstrels—king's, queen's, and those of other nobles—played music.

The long day ended with the final service of fruit and wafers. The Knight Marshall provided a napkin, and as the torches were lighted, the queen washed. Grace was said, after which the trumpets signaled the final ceremony. The mayor of London served the Queen her "void"—a cup of hippocras and spices before departure—for which he received the gold cup as his fee. Finally, Queen Elizabeth departed "with God's blessing, and to the rejoicing of many a true English man's heart."[19]

The next morning, Elizabeth, "my lady the king's mother," and 80 gentlewomen attended the king's mass in St. Stephen's Chapel. The queen next sat in state in the Parliament Chamber with "my lady the king's mother" on her right and her aunt, the duchess of Bedford, and sister Cecily on her left. The duchess of Suffolk, the duchess of Norfolk, and scores of ladies and gentlewomen attended her at her side tables. After dinner the ladies danced, as the festivities concluded. The next morning, Elizabeth and her attendants departed for Greenwich, while Parliament resumed its session.

Attendance at Queen Elizabeth's coronation indicates the broad support Henry was building for his reign. All lords were invited to coronations, and the list of attending guests included the archbishops of Canterbury and York, 13 bishops, 17 abbots, 2 dukes, 19 earls, 25 lords, 31 bannerets, and 150 knights, many accompanied by their ladies and attendants. The Tudor dynasty emerged from the year 1487 stronger than when it began. Henry's victory over Lambert Simnel added stature and power to his nascent reign—and provided him the opportunity to assess the competence and loyalty of his nobles. By the end of the year, the king had stabilized his executive advisors and built trust among his followers. Dissident forces still existed, but this first Tudor king had laid a solid foundation that would resist and repel them. Future threats to his title would receive little support from his nobles.

CHAPTER 9

"MY LADY THE KING'S MOTHER"

Queen Elizabeth's relations with her mother-in-law were complex. Margaret Beaufort, countess of Richmond and Derby, undoubtedly meant well—as do most competent, energetic women who take charge of the world they inhabit. Her interactions with both Henry and Elizabeth were motivated by a tenacious love that was both admirable and intimidating. Once Henry VII became king, Margaret's frustrations as a mother deprived of her son for 24 years turned into a fierce resolve to help Henry succeed as England's monarch.

For Queen Elizabeth, "my lady the king's mother" may have substituted, in part, for her own mother ensconced behind the doors of Bermondsey Abbey. But a mother-in-law is not a mother, and the ever-present force of Margaret's powerful personality may have grated against the queen's soul at times. "My lady the king's mother" was ever present during the early years of the queen's marriage to Henry. Heraldic accounts of royal events invariably connect "the queen and my lady the king's mother" as if they were one individual. Even William Paston picked up that phrasing when he wrote on September 10, 1493, that the king, the queen, and "my lady the king's mother...lie at Northampton and will tarry there till Michelmas."[1] The phrase became a commonplace in official records and conferred a status on Margaret above that of countess of Richmond and Derby. But more important from Elizabeth's perspective, "my lady the king's mother" was *always there*—perhaps a comforting presence during the Lambert Simnel rebellion when Henry summoned both women to his side, but likely an irritant when privacy was paramount.

The two women frequently collaborated on projects. Queen Elizabeth and Lady Margaret together were licensed on February 6, 1486, to found a perpetual chantry of one chaplain in the parish church of the Holy Trinity, Guildford, Surrey,[2] an indicator of the many interests they shared. Without doubt, the king's mother contributed significantly to the welfare and good order of the queen's household: Margaret's *Ordinances* assured practical, sensible, and comfortable arrangements when Arthur was born. Behind the *Ordinances*, however, lay an obsessive, compulsive personality that might be disconcerting to others. Margaret's precise instructions bespeak a dominant personality who expects to run the show.

Margaret Beaufort's character had been formed by years of personal misfortune and *realpolitik*. She barely knew her father, John, first duke of Somerset, an aspiring, ambitious man whose life was dogged by bad luck and irresponsible actions. As a boy of 16, Somerset embarked for France to fight in the waning decades of the Hundred Years War. Captured in March 1421, he was held for ransom for 17 years. Finally released in 1438,[3] his huge ransom of £24,000 impoverished him, and his long captivity made it difficult to arrange an advantageous marriage. In 1442, he married a widow of the wealthy gentry, Margaret Beauchamp of Bletsoe, already the mother of five children. Created duke in March 1443, Somerset led another expedition to France, hoping to improve his finances and restore his reputation. That foray was even more disastrous than his first: it cost England £26,000 and alienated allies with extraordinary taxes levied by Somerset.[4] Returning to England in disgrace, Somerset died in 1444 amidst rumors of suicide. His daughter Margaret, born on May 31, 1443, could not have remembered her father, except for the stories of his fall from grace.

Left fatherless at age one, Margaret grew up with five siblings from her mother's first marriage to Oliver St. John. In 1447, her mother married for a third time to Lionel, lord Welles, and gave birth to two more sons. Margaret Beaufort's childhood was spent in the midst of that large and apparently happy family. She retained close ties with her siblings of the half-blood during the rest of her life and actively contributed to their well-being and prosperity.

This happy childhood ended abruptly with her marriage at age 12 to Edmund Tudor, earl of Richmond. Margaret immediately became pregnant and was thrust into the midst of the Lancastrian-York fight for the throne of England. Richmond, a staunch Lancastrian and half-brother of Henry VI, was captured by the Yorkists and imprisoned in Carmarthen Castle, where he died on November 1, 1456. A widow and pregnant at age 13, the countess of Richmond gave birth to Henry Tudor on January 28, 1457, at Pembroke Castle, home of her brother-in-law, Jasper Tudor.

Although her Richmond estates provided wealth and a steady income, the 13-year-old Margaret and her newborn son needed more protection than Jasper, earl of Pembroke, could provide. In March 1457, she and Pembroke began arranging a marriage with Sir Henry Stafford, second son of the duke of Buckingham. Stafford was a Lancastrian who fought with the forces of Henry VI at Towton. After Edward IV's victory, however, Stafford switched to the Yorkist side and secured pardons for himself and his wife. Margaret's inheritance was thus saved, but she lost her son Henry whose wardship and marriage were assigned to William, lord

Photo 5   Pembroke Castle. During the Wars of the Roses, Jasper Tudor moved his widowed sister-in-law, Margaret Beaufort, countess of Richmond, to this fortress in south Wales after her husband's death. Here, the Countess at age thirteen gave birth to Henry Tudor on 28 January 1457. Photo by Geoffrey Wheeler, London.

Herbert, a Yorkist who had captured Pembroke Castle on September 30, 1461.

Margaret Beaufort remained a Yorkist for the next 22 years. Her marriage to Sir Henry Stafford developed into a close and apparently happy companionship. They had no children, perhaps because of complications related to the trauma of Margaret's first pregnancy. Their Yorkist ties were strengthened when Stafford's nephew, the second duke of Buckingham, married Katherine Wydeville, sister of Edward IV's queen. At the same time, Margaret's cousin, Henry Beaufort, third duke of Somerset, remained fiercely loyal to the Lancastrian cause—with the exception of a brief interlude in 1462–63 when he aligned himself with Edward IV. Somerset's Yorkist affiliation ended abruptly in November 1463 when he defected back to the Lancastrians, was captured after the battle of Hexham in May 1464, and immediately executed.

The attainder of Somerset allowed Lady Margaret and Sir Henry Stafford to obtain the Beaufort manor at Woking, which provided an elegant base for their increasing status in the Yorkist reign.[5] Margaret's situation remained tenuous, however, as Jasper Tudor continued to lead skirmishes against Edward IV in northwest Wales. Meanwhile, Margaret tried to remain in touch with her son and to work for his best interests. She negotiated his admission into the Order of the Holy Trinity in 1465, a confraternity of brethren at Knaresborough in Yorkshire devoted to redeeming Christians imprisoned by the Turks.[6] In September 1467, Margaret visited her son, age 10, for a week at the Raglan estate of his custodian, Lord Herbert.

During the rebellion of Warwick and Clarence against Edward IV in 1469, Lord Herbert was captured and killed in July at the battle of Edgecote, throwing Henry Tudor's wardship into limbo. The 12-year-old Henry, who was fighting with Herbert's troops loyal to Edward IV, was safely rescued. Months later when Edward IV fled to exile in Holland, Jasper Tudor took charge of his nephew Henry and brought him to London for the Lancastrian Parliament that opened on November 26, 1470. Mother and son were reunited and arranged a meeting with King Henry VI, the boy's uncle of the half-blood. Vergil writes that Henry VI observed the 13-year-old boy and predicted his destiny: "This truly, this is he unto whom both we and our adversaries must yield and give over the dominion."[7] Even Vergil, that official Tudor historian, reports this divination in the passive voice, however—"the king...is reported to have said"—making clear that the story was based on hearsay. Sir Henry Stafford and Margaret tried to persuade George, duke of Clarence, to return Henry Tudor's paternal inheritance, which Edward IV had granted to Clarence. They should have known better. Clarence never let justice stand in the way of greed. He did, however, agree that Henry would inherit the honor of Richmond at Clarence's death.[8] The Staffords placed themselves in a risky position by meeting with the enemies of Edward IV. Their position became more perilous when Margaret's cousin, Edmund, fourth duke of Somerset, visited them at Woking to ask that they join the Lancastrian forces fighting Edward. Stafford gave his answer when Edward IV returned to England to regain his crown. Margaret Beaufort's husband joined Edward's army as it marched past Coventry on the way to London. The countess of Richmond, once more, found herself a Yorkist on the opposite side from her Beaufort-Lancastrian roots.

At the battle of Barnet on April 14, 1471, Sir Henry Stafford was wounded while fighting with Edward IV's army. At Tewkesbury on May 4, Margaret's Lancastrian cousin the duke of Somerset was captured and executed after the Yorkist victory. It was her husband's loyalty to Edward IV that saved Margaret—and several of her family. Her mother, the dowager duchess of Somerset, received a pardon from Edward IV, as did Margaret's half-brother, John Welles. But Margaret's son, Henry Tudor, was irrevocably linked to the Lancastrian cause and fled to Brittany with his uncle Jasper. Bernard André claims that Margaret cautioned her son not to accept any pardon that might be offered by Edward IV.[9] If so, that was good advice. But it meant that the mother would not see her son for the next 14 years. Another hard blow fell within months. Margaret's husband of 14 years, Sir Henry Stafford, died on October 4, 1471, perhaps of complications from his wounds received at Barnet.

Within the year—probably in June 1472—Margaret married Thomas, lord Stanley, who served as steward of Edward IV's household.[10] Stanley's affiliation with the court brought Margaret into close contact with Queen Elizabeth Wydeville, with whom she shared the experience of having grown up in a Lancastrian household but converted to the Yorkist cause by marriage. The Stanleys were also connected to the Wydevilles by marriage: Lord Stanley's son and heir, George, had married the queen's niece Joan, daughter of Jacquetta Wydeville and Lord Strange of Knockin. The friendship between Queen Elizabeth Wydeville and Margaret grew: the countess attended the queen at the Fotheringhay reburial of Richard, duke of York,[11] and carried Bridget, the last royal child born to Edward IV and Elizabeth, at her baptism in 1480. By June 3, 1482, Margaret had earned the king's trust sufficiently to negotiate inheritance rights of her son Henry to the dower property of her mother, the dowager duchess of Somerset, who died in May.[12] The agreement required that Henry Tudor return from exile "to be in the grace and favor of the king's highness,"[13] a stipulation that events of 1483 rendered moot.

The sudden death of Edward IV, Parliament's declaration of illegitimacy for his children, and the accession of Richard III constituted tricky times for everyone in England, but especially for Margaret Beaufort. At the double coronation of Richard III and Queen Anne, Margaret carried the queen's train. Within months, she was plotting with queen dowager Elizabeth Wydeville to marry her son Henry Tudor to Elizabeth of York—or if that were not possible, to the second-born princess, Cecily. The marriage agreement placed Margaret Beaufort, countess of Richmond, firmly in the camp of those dedicated to overthrowing Richard III. Once Henry Tudor, earl of Richmond, fought his way to the throne and married Elizabeth of York—a young girl whose entire life had been ruled by ambitious men—"my lady the king's mother," pragmatic and experienced, stepped in to take charge of the world she knew so well.

In one of his first acts as king, Henry created his mother a *femme sole*, a legal status that allowed her to own property and transact business in her own right, irrespective of her husband. Among the properties conveyed to her in September 1485 was the London mansion of Coldharbour.[14] During Edward IV's reign, that massive residence on the Thames had been extensively renovated and decorated for the State visit in 1480 of his sister Margaret, dowager duchess of Burgundy. Richard III transferred ownership of Coldharbour to the College of Heralds, but Henry VII cancelled that grant in favor of his mother.

Coldharbour became central to Tudor hospitality. Margaret welcomed Elizabeth of York there during the months before her marriage to Henry.[15] Edward Stafford, the young duke of Buckingham, also lived at Coldharbour, his wardship granted to Margaret on August 3, 1486.[16] So, too, Edward, earl of Warwick and son of Clarence, lived at Coldharbour until Henry VII sent that Yorkist heir to the more secure Tower. During the Cornish insurrection in June 1497, Queen Elizabeth and her young son Henry, duke of York, spent a week at Coldharbour before seeking refuge in the Tower. And in 1501, "my lady the king's mother" invited the mayor and City fathers of London to Coldharbour to celebrate the wedding of Prince Arthur.

Margaret wielded both personal and political power. She astutely arranged marriages that aligned her relatives with prominent families. The marriage of George Stanley, Margaret's stepson, to Joan, daughter of Lord Strange and Jacquetta Wydeville, had already connected her family with the Wydevilles, whom she apparently liked. Anthony Wydeville, second Earl Rivers, had taken as his second wife Mary FitzLewis, granddaughter of Edmund, second duke of Somerset, and first-cousin-once-removed of Margaret. In later years, Margaret reserved a room in her household for Lady Rivers.[17] Whether Margaret had anything to do with the marriage of Katherine Wydeville, dowager duchess of Buckingham, to Jasper Tudor is unclear, but she was surely a player in the marriage of Thomas Grey, son of the marquess of Dorset and nephew to Elizabeth of York, to Eleanor, daughter of Margaret's half-brother, Oliver St. John.[18]

The marriage of Cecily, second daughter of Edward IV, to Margaret's half-brother John, viscount Welles, best shows the shrewd hand of "my lady the king's mother" at work. The Welles family had not fared well during the reigns of Edward IV and Richard III, thanks to their Lancastrian ties. Margaret always retained great affection for them, partly because Lionel, lord Welles and third husband of her mother, was the only father figure she had ever known. Margaret's half-brother John Welles, penniless due to Edward IV's attainders, lived with their mother, the dowager duchess of Somerset. Under Henry VII, his attainders were reversed and his barony of Welles restored in 1485.[19] Cecily, the queen's sister, had lived with Margaret since September 1485. Next heir to the throne after Elizabeth, this most beautiful of Edward IV's daughters needed protection from men who might use her to challenge Henry's throne. Margaret forestalled that threat by marrying Cecily to her half-brother, John, viscount Welles, a man 20 years older than his lovely wife.

Margaret seems to have been genuinely fond of Cecily. When Welles died in 1499, Margaret helped Cecily retain property rights to some of her husband's estates, which should have reverted to children from the first marriage of Lionel, lord Welles. Cecily had given birth to two daughters, but both died before their father, who left no heirs. His Will gave Cecily a life interest in his estates, a provision that was challenged by the precedent Welles heirs. Margaret interceded to protect the interests of Cecily, whose claim prevailed (perhaps assisted by Margaret's son and Cecily's brother-in-law, Henry VII). Margaret also issued a special dispensation permitting Cecily to worship regularly in Margaret's household.[20]

Three years later in 1502 when Cecily remarried without the king's permission, Margaret provided a home for the disgraced couple, who were banished from the Court. This second marriage of Cecily to Thomas Kyme, a mere esquire, infuriated Henry who could have profited financially and politically by a more advantageous union for the sister of his queen. Thomas and Cecily Kyme sought refuge at Margaret's Collyweston manor near Stamford.[21] When Henry expropriated the Welles inheritance of Cecily, Margaret again helped negotiate a settlement that allowed Cecily to keep a life interest in part of it. Cecily and her new husband ultimately moved to the Isle of Wight, where the former princess gave birth to two children who were never recognized by their royal relatives. In 1506, Margaret reserved a room for Cecily's use at her Croydon manor and paid part of her funeral expenses when she died on August 24, 1507.[22]

Family was paramount to "my lady the king's mother," who fought fiercely for those she loved—even if it sometimes meant opposing her son, the king. Those subjected to well-intentioned interventions, however, may not always appreciate a matriarch *sans pareil*. In July 1498, the Spanish sub-prior of Santa Cruz wrote to Ferdinand and Isabella about the relationship of Margaret and Elizabeth of York:

> The Queen is a "very noble woman" and much beloved. She is kept in subjection by the mother of the King. It would be a good thing to write often to her, and to show her a little love.[23]

A week later, Pedro De Ayala confirmed that assessment:

> The King is much influenced by his mother and his followers in affairs of personal interest and in others. The Queen, as is generally the case, does not like it.[24]

That the Spanish were correct in assessing the mother-in-law's control over the queen may be confirmed by a deposition in Nottingham regarding the "treasonable language" of John Hewyk, a yeoman of the crown. Alice, wife of William Jefferson, testified that Hewyk told the townsfolk of Howes after "coming home from the King and the Queen" that "he had spoken with the Queen's Grace and should have spoken more with her said Grace, had not been for that strong whore the King's mother."[25] Margaret, ever vigilant, may have stepped in to protect the gracious queen from a foul-mouthed, opportunistic servant—or she may have been intruding inappropriately in the queen's business. By 1500 Elizabeth of York, consort to Henry for 14 years, should have been able to fend for herself.

If Margaret's love for the queen and royal children was overly possessive, it was also genuine. She kept a suite of rooms reserved for Queen Elizabeth at her Collyweston estate,[26] and in a 1497 letter to Thomas Butler, the queen's chamberlain, she wrote:

> ...blessed be God, the King, the Queen, and all our sweet children be in good health. The Queen hath been a little crased, but now she is well, God be thanked.[27]

Concern for the welfare of Elizabeth and her children continued years after Margaret first wrote her *Ordinances*. Thus when Elizabeth of York gave birth to the second Tudor heir, it was only appropriate that the new baby was named Margaret after "my lady the king's mother."

CHAPTER 10

LIFE WITH HENRY

Queen Elizabeth's first two years of marriage—dominated by the birth of Arthur, the Lambert Simnel rebellion, and her coronation—repeated the pattern that had come to define her life: moments of glory interspersed with periods of peril. Now her wheel of fortune was about to embark on a long upward swing of gracious living and pleasurable pastimes before it once more plunged this queen into the depths of despair. While Queen Elizabeth and her family suffered the traumas commonplace to the era—the early deaths of three children, bouts with disease—her life with Henry was, on the whole, quite gratifying. Although another rebellion would add considerable uncertainty to Henry's reign, Elizabeth of York looked forward to 14 years of happy marriage and a thriving family.

The court of Henry VII and his "Gracious Queen" replicated the customs and traditions of the court of Edward IV and Elizabeth Wydeville, the royal world in which Elizabeth of York had grown up. It was in this private sphere that Queen Elizabeth made her contributions to the Tudor dynasty. The queen surrounded herself with her Wydeville relatives for both emotional support and physical comfort. King Henry, too, relied on men with Wydeville connections for his initial nucleus of loyal nobles— Edward Stafford, third duke of Buckingham; Henry Bourchier, second earl of Essex; Thomas Grey, marquess of Dorset; and Sir Edward Wydeville. The marriage of his uncle Jasper to Katherine Wydeville, dowager duchess of Buckingham and aunt to the Queen, solidified those relationships.

The royal households moved frequently. Their enormous retinue consumed food and created waste in almost stupefying amounts, while stretching the resident household staff to its limits. After residence of a month or two in one palace, general cleanliness and good health required the Court to move on to permit both property and staff a chance to recuperate. Although the king and the queen each kept separate households, Henry and Elizabeth spent much time together.

At the conclusion of his second Parliament, Henry joined Elizabeth and his mother at Greenwich for the 1487 Christmas season. Greenwich Palace offered a comfortable residence with buildings close to the Thames and convenient access from barges. Originally a country house built by Humphrey, duke of Gloucester, Queen Margaret of Anjou made extensive renovations before Edward IV gave Greenwich to his consort Elizabeth Wydeville as part of her dower property. Gardens surrounded the buildings with their two courts—one for the king and another for the queen.[1] The queen's residence included a great chamber, a parlor, and a gallery overlooking a garden with private arbor.

Celebrating Christmas Eve 1487 at Greenwich, the king, wearing a gown of purple velvet furred with sables, attended the Mass of the Vigil with his nobles before going to Evensong with his Officers of Arms. On Christmas Day, the king and the queen dined separately—Henry with his attendant nobles in the Great Chamber, Elizabeth and the king's mother with their attendants in the queen's chamber. Members of Queen Elizabeth's family included her sister Cecily and at least two aunts, the duchess of Bedford and the countess of Rivers.

New Year's was traditionally a day of gift giving, when the nobility distributed gifts to each other and to their Officers at Arms. At the loud, colorful, and joyful New Year's celebration, official *largesse* was "cried" throughout the hall. The Officers of Arms received £6 from King Henry and 40s from Queen Elizabeth, for which each in turn was acknowledged by special cries. The king's mother gave 20s and was cried three times:

> *De hault, puissaunt, et excellent Princesse, la mer du Roy notre Souveraigne, Countesse de Richemonde et de Derbye, Largesse.*

> [From the high, mighty, and excellent Princess, the mother of the King, our Sovereign, Countess of Richmond and Derby, *Largesse!*][2]

Jasper Tudor was similarly cried for his gift of 40s, as was his wife, Katherine Wydeville, for her gift of 13s 4d (a mark):

> *Largesse de hault et puissaunt Princesse, Duchesse de Bedford et de Buckingham, Countesse de Pembroke, Stafford, Harford, et de Northampton, et Dame de Brecknok, Largesse.*

[*Largesse* from the high and mighty Princess, Duchess of Bedford and of Buckingham, Countess of Pembroke, Stafford, Harford, and of Northampton, and Lady of Brecknock, *Largesse*.][3]

On New Year's Day in the third year of Henry VII's reign, Katherine Wydeville was among the highest ranking women in the Court. Since her youth she had enjoyed high status as wife of the duke of Buckingham, but her marriage to Jasper Tudor conferred even higher ranking because the king's uncle took precedence over other dukes. Katherine Wydeville now enjoyed the same honorific that distinguished her mother, Jacquetta of Luxembourg, duchess of Bedford for 39 years.

Cries echoed throughout the Great Hall, announcing each donor of gifts to the Officers of Arms. John Fox, bishop of Exeter and Keeper of the Privy Seal, gave 20*s*; the earl of Arundel 10*s*; the earl of Oxford 20*s*; his lady, the countess of Oxford, 20*s*; the earl of Derby 20*s*; the earl of Devonshire 13*s* 4*d*; Lord Welles and Lady Cecily 20*s*; Sir William Stanley, the king's chamberlain, 10*s*; the earl of Ormond 20*s*; Lord Strange 10*s*; the Treasurer 6*s* 8*d*; and the Controller, a crown. The Secretary who gave 6*s* 8*d* was not cried, since custom prohibited recognition for clergymen or for those who ranked lower than viscount. Barons, bannerets, knights, esquires, and their wives were cried in general. The herald who carefully recorded each gift pointedly noted that there were "many lords more in the Court, some coming and some going, which gave no rewards to the Officers of Arms."[4] Nevertheless, the evening ended happily with "a goodly Disguising."

The herald's comment about the lords who gave no gifts implies a political, as well as pleasurable, aspect of these year-end revels. The *largesse* of the king and nobility constituted bonuses to their officers and personal recognition of loyal service. During this festival, the Court became one harmonious body. Although strict hierarchy was maintained (especially in seating assignments), the nobility and their retainers together enjoyed the same disguisings, laughed at the same jesters, and feasted at communal banquets. The celebrations enhanced camaraderie and smoothed over frayed feelings and dissonances from the working year. As the New Year began, harmony and good will prevailed.

Disguisings traditionally entertained the Tudor Court during the holiday. Queen Elizabeth loved the dancers and singers who suddenly appeared dressed in elaborate, sometimes fantastic, costumes. Their stately manners and deliberate movements culti-vated a sense of mystery enhanced by their isolation from the rest of the revelers. Disguisers spoke to no one and remained aloof from the guests, dancing and interacting only within their group, some of whom were well-known members of the court. Silent and aloof, the disguisers performed, then left as mysteriously as they arrived.

Political symbolism blended with religious ceremony. On the eve of Twelfth Night, the king attended Evensong in his surcoat with tabard sleeves and hood, wearing his cap of Estate. John Morton, archbishop of Canterbury, presided at the service. The next morning at Matins, the Court displayed their robes of Estate in full royal procession. The king and queen wore their crowns and the king's mother a "rich Coronal."⁵ Jasper Tudor, duke of Bedford, carried the cap of Estate before the king, while the earl of Oxford, Great Chamberlain of England, carried the king's train. Queen Elizabeth, the king's mother, and their attendants followed the king's party. Margaret Beaufort was dressed "in like Mantel and Surcoat as the Queen," a significant sartorial symbol that she possessed rank and status commensurate with the queen, although she walked slightly behind "aside the queen's half train" with Master Fowler carrying her train over his right arm. The countesses of Oxford and of Rivers followed, wearing circlets on their heads. Attendants, ladies, and gentlewomen completed the procession.

After High Mass, the king and queen kept Estate in the hall where they dined. The king, wearing a crown of gold set with pre-cious stones, sat under a cloth of Estate with the archbishop of Canterbury on his right and the queen, also crowned, on his left. The queen sat beneath a cloth of Estate hanging somewhat lower than the king's. The earl of Oxford tended to the king's crown, and the earl of Ormond, the queen's chamberlain, knelt between the queen and the king's mother to tend to Elizabeth's crown while she ate. At the formal dinner served by attendants in robes of velvet and damask, Jasper Tudor headed the table on the right side of the hall, sitting next to the French ambassador. Following in order were the duke of Suffolk, another French ambassador, and other nobility. On the left side of the hall, the queen's sister Cecily presided over the table with the countess of Oxford, the countess of Rivers, Lady Strange, and other noble ladies and gentlewomen.

After the first course, the dean and canons of the King's Chapel, who sat at the middle table, sang a carol. At conclusion of the second course, the minstrels played. The Officers of Arms then descended from their stage, and the Garter King of Arms thanked the king for his *Largesse* and requested permission to thank the queen. That granted, he cried the *Largesse* of both king and queen. The banquet concluded with the king's Marshal drawing the surnap (large napkin) and making Estate to the king and queen and "half Estate" to the king's mother and the archbishop of Canterbury.

By Easter 1488, the Court, including Queen Elizabeth and the king's mother, had moved to Windsor Castle, where the bishop of Exeter conducted the Divine Service. Edward IV had modernized Windsor Castle by adding a bay window to the queen's chamber, constructing a new gallery and roof near the jewel house, and improving the gardens.[6] The splendid new Chapel of St. George was still under construction with the carved stalls and canopies of the Chapel in place, but the walls and vaulting of the nave unfinished.[7] The royals remained at Windsor for the annual Knights of the Garter celebrations on St. George's Day, April 23, rituals in which Elizabeth of York had participated since age 10.

The Order of the Garter, established by Edward III, celebrated the ideals of English knighthood and constituted the highest honor an individual could receive. Membership was restricted to the king and 25 knights chosen for distinction in serving the realm. Deeds in arms, noble lineage, and court connections determined those nominated to join the Order. Garter Knights served until death, unless "degraded" for some heinous offense such as treason—a rare occurrence. The Chapter met annually to affirm fraternal ties, with each knight proudly occupying his assigned stall in the chapel of St. George during religious vigils and masses.

The selection of men to become Garter knights and the rituals of the ceremony strengthened personal loyalties and reinforced political hierarchy. For Henry Tudor, who was still building affinities with England's nobility, the ceremony of the Garter was particularly important. The Garter procession visibly displayed the magnificence that made the king preeminent among nobles, and the rituals emphatically emphasized hierarchy. On entering and exiting the chapel, each knight first bowed to the altar, then turned to recognize his sovereign king, God's anointed representative on earth. During the three-day retreat, the king and his

knights worshiped together in the chapel, discussed issues per-
taining to the brotherhood in the chapter house, and feasted
together at sumptuous evening banquets. Companionship, camaraderie, and fealty intensified during the Garter's annual
ceremonies.

On the morning of St. George's Day 1488, the king, the queen,
and "my lady the king's mother" attended Matins dressed in similar Garter robes. During *Te Deum* and *Benedictus*, the queen and
the king's mother were sensed after the king, but only the king
and queen kissed the Pax. Following Matins, the king, the queen,
and the king's mother went in procession around the cloister.
Anyone who harbored doubts about Henry Tudor's place in the
ranks of English kings was reassured by the presence of Elizabeth
of York, who had ridden in Garter parades for years. Continuity of
the monarchy prevailed.

The Garter feast, held the following Sunday, included an illustrious assembly of clergy, nobility, and ambassadors. In addition
to the king's Council, the archbishops of Canterbury and York,
the bishops of Lincoln and Exeter, and the Chief Justice of the
King's Bench were present. Ambassadors from France, Spain,
Flanders, Brittany, and Scotland indicated Henry's increasing
interest in foreign policy. That afternoon, Henry held a long meeting with his guests in the chapter house of the College, after which
all went to Evensong.

During the first procession, Queen Elizabeth and "my lady the
king's mother" wore Garter gowns of the preceding year and rode
in a chair covered with cloth-of-gold and carried by six horses harnessed in the same cloth-of-gold. Twenty-one ladies and gentlewomen rode behind the queen's chair, all wearing crimson velvet
gowns that contrasted vividly against their white horses saddled
and harnessed with cloth-of-gold. White roses, the badge of York,
decorated the horses' half-trappings. Sir Roger Cotton, Master of
the Queen's Horse, led the queen's horse of Estate with a saddle of
cloth-of-gold on which were three crowns of silver gilt. At
Evensong, the king and knights of the Garter were sensed, but not
the queen or the king's mother.

The next morning, the knights of the Garter reassembled on
horseback wearing livery of the new Garter year—mantles of
white cloth with garters. The king's horse was trapped with the
image of St. George on white cloth-of-gold. Processing in the
order of their chapel stalls, the Garter knights rode to the chapel

for Matins, where the queen and the king's mother joined them and stayed for the Mass. The queen and the king's mother also attended Evensong that day, but at the Garter feast the king dined alone with his nobles and the ambassadors. The queen and "my lady the king's mother" joined them only for the procession to the chapel.

A song composed especially for this Garter feast celebrated the king with its refrain:

England now rejoice, for joyous may thou be,
To see thy King so flowering in dignity.[8]

The song recognized the presence of ambassadors from France, Spain, Scotland, Brittany, and Flanders before paying special tribute to the queen and the king's mother:

O knightly Order, clothed in robes with Garter:
The Queen's Grace, thy Mother, in the same.

Included among the queen's attendants were her 12-year-old sister Anne, her aunt the countess of Rivers, and her cousin lady Margaret of Clarence. At the king's special request, the queen's uncle "Lord Wydeville" also attended services in the chapel.[9]

Queen Elizabeth's life seems dominated by ceremony partly because the heralds recorded public events in great detail, while her daily routines did not merit entry into official documents. Yet, a substantial portion of the queen's life was devoted to public ceremony, especially during the year following her coronation and before her increasing family consumed her time and energies. The raison d'être for a queen consort resided in the majesty, affinities, and heirs she contributed to the king. In the case of Elizabeth of York, her presence visibly symbolized the union of the factions that just three years earlier had embroiled England in civil bloodshed. Elizabeth's public appearances added stability to Henry's throne, especially as the Tudor king settled into the hard, long-term job of governing the nation conquered by his sword.

Henry and Elizabeth spent much time together—perhaps in part because the queen's dower income did not sufficiently support her household and the magnificence demanded by public appearances.[10] In May 1488, Henry supplemented Elizabeth's dower by ordering the town of Bristol to pay the queen £102 15s 6d from its farm and the sheriff of Bedford to provide another £20 for life. But even after Elizabeth received reversion rights to Yorkist estates in 1492, the couple frequently shared residences. Apparently, they genuinely liked each other.

In spring 1488, Elizabeth clearly influenced the king, who chose Dame Elizabeth Darcy as governess for Prince Arthur.[11] The "Lady Mistress to our dearest son, the Prince" had supervised the nursery of Edward V, the queen's brother.[12] Lady Darcy received 20 marks sterling per half-year and was assisted by Agnes Butler and Evelyn Hobbes, who each received 33s 4d, and by Alice Bywymble, who earned 26s 8d for the half-year.[13]

Whitsuntide 1488 found the royal couple at Windsor Castle. During the summer the king hunted in his park at Woodstock and in the forest of "Whichwood," but by All Hallows Day the family gathered once more at Windsor.[14] The summer was an eventful one with the death of James III of Scotland on June 11, 1488 rendering irrelevant the proposed marriage with queen dowager Elizabeth. A greater personal loss for both the queen dowager and Queen Elizabeth was the death of Sir Edward Wydeville, that adventurous spirit who died fighting for the lost cause of Breton independence from France. Sir Edward's death at the battle of St. Aubin du Cormier on July 28, 1488, left the queen with only one Wydeville uncle: Richard, third earl Rivers. This uncle never married and stayed close to his Grafton estates in Northamptonshire. In the tradition of Wydeville ancestors who had resided in the Grafton area since the twelfth century, lord Rivers served as Justice of the Peace in Bedfordshire, but unlike his father and his brothers, he made no significant contributions to the reigns of Edward IV and Henry VII.

By autumn, the king, the queen, and their households moved to Westminster for meetings with the Great Council. The central event of this season featured an ambassador from the Pope who brought special gifts of a sword and a cap for England's king. The arrival of the Pope's Cubiculer (chamberlain) in London caused the king, the queen, and the king's mother to move from Westminster to Bishop's Palace next to St. Paul's Cathedral. The journey was made in "so great a mist upon Thames, that there was no man could tell of a great season in what place in Thames the King was."[15] In a grand ceremony at St. Paul's attended by ambassadors from France, the Holy Roman Empire, Spain, Brittany, Flanders, as well as "divers other strangers, as Scots, Easterlings

[Baltic merchants of the Hanseatic League] and others," archbishop Morton girded the sword around the king and placed the
cap on his head, a highly honorific ritual in which the Pope sym-
bolically armed and crowned the king of England. Henry celebrated with a great feast, opened his household to his guests, and
sent ambassadors throughout Europe to proclaim his enhanced
stature.

It is difficult to gauge the personal interactions of Henry and
Elizabeth from behind the recorded formalities of public appearances. Only tantalizing wisps of clues indicate their close personal
affection. In Michaelmas Term 1488, a Writ under the Privy Seal
granted to "Elizabeth, the queen, by way of reward—c marks."[16]
We have no way of knowing why the king gave Elizabeth 100
marks.

Christmas 1488 was celebrated at the royal residence at Sheen
(Richmond), where Queen Elizabeth was accompanied by the
king's mother, her sister Anne, her cousin Elizabeth Stafford, her
cousin Margaret of Clarence, her aunt Lady Rivers, and many others. Sheen had been a favorite residence of Elizabeth's mother
because of its proximity to the Carthusian charterhouse and to
the Bridgettine Abbey of Sion, both of which Elizabeth Wydeville
patronized. Sheen, unlike other palaces, offered the royal couple
privacy created by a moat that divided the royal lodgings from the
Court.[17] Life was beginning to settle into a routine punctuated by
the festivals that dominated the medieval calendar.

Easter 1489 found the king, the queen, and "my lady the king's
mother" at Hertford, an ancient moated castle where Edward IV
had added a brick gatehouse during the early 1460s.[18] Henry
departed northward in May to investigate the murder of the earl
of Northumberland and spent Whitsuntide at Nottingham before
returning to Windsor for summer hunting and sport. This year,
the Feast of St. George was delayed until July 19, during which
celebration viscount Welles, half-brother of the king's mother and
husband of the queen's sister Cecily, was installed as Garter
Knight. At the Requiem Mass on the morning after the Garter
Feast, the swords, helms, and crests of the deceased earl of
Northumberland and of Sir Edward Wydeville were offered.

For the Feast of St. George in 1489, Henry sent gifts from the
Great Wardrobe to Elizabeth and his mother that included robes
of sanguine cloth furred with "miniver pure" (white belly skins of
squirrel) and a "garter with letters of gold."[19] Elizabeth also

received "cloth of black velvet, russet cloth, Flanders web, backs of grey (winter squirrel fur), and single shoes."[20] For the office of her robes, Henry sent sheets of Holland cloth, long buckram, canaber cloth, beds of feathers, counterpoints of verdour, brushes, fringe, and thread. For the office of her beds, she was given "cloth of white blanket, singly set velvet, canaber cloth, cords, counterpoints, beds of down, beds of feather, carpet, worsted of the middle assise, London thread, mantelle, standards, trussiny coffers, crochettes of the middle and lesser assise, tapet hooks, hammer of iron, bags of canaber cloth, sheets of Holland cloth."[21] Thus, Henry continued to supply the queen's basic requirements. When expenditures exceeded her budget, the king's treasury covered expenses.

In Fall 1489, the queen prepared to enter confinement for the birth of her second child. Meanwhile, Prince Arthur was almost three years old and not yet dubbed knight or created Prince of Wales. That deficiency was remedied on St. Andrew's Eve 1489, when Arthur shared the spotlight with his newly arrived sister.

CHAPTER 11

THE ROYAL FAMILY

Queen Elizabeth's confinement for the birth of her second child began with ceremonies mandated by Margaret's *Ordinances*. Since each heir added to the continuity and stability of the monarchy, entering the birthing chamber was almost a State occasion:

> Upon All Hallow's Eve [1489], the Queen took her chamber at Westminster, greatly accompanied with ladies and gentlewomen; that is to say, the Lady the King's mother, the Duchess of Norfolk, and many other, having before her the great part of the nobles of this realm present at this Parliament. She was led by the Earl of Oxford and the Earl of Derby. The Reverent Father in God, the Bishop of Exeter, sang the Mass in pontifical robes, and after *Agnus Dei*. Then the Queen was led as before.
>
> The Earls of Shrewsbury and of Kent held the towel when the Queen took her rites, and the torches were held by knights. And after Mass, accompanied as before, when she was come into her great chamber, she stood under her Cloth of Estate. Then there was ordained a void of spices and sweet wine. That done, my Lord the Queen's Chamberlain in very good words desired in the Queen's name, the people there present to pray God to send her the good hour.
>
> And so she departed to her inner chamber, which was hanged and sealed with rich cloth of blue arras with fleur-de-lis of gold without any other cloth of arras of imagery, which is not convenient about women in such [a] case. [The images of traditional tapestries were thought to excite the mother and jeopardize the birth.] In that chamber was a rich bed and a pallet, the which pallet had a marvelous rich canopy of gold with velvet, paly [cover] of divers colors, garnished with red roses, embroidered with two rich panes of ermine, covered with Rennes of lawn [fine linen]. Also there was a rich altar well furnished with relics, and a rich cupboard well and richly garnished. Then she recommended her to the good prayers

of the Lords, and my Lord her Chamberlain drew the traverse. From then forth no manner of officer came within the chamber, but ladies and gentlewomen, after the old custom.[1]

An exception was granted, however, for a group of French ambassadors who desired to visit the queen. François de Luxembourg, Viscount of Geneva[2] and cousin to queen dowager Elizabeth, was admitted to the queen's chamber in a rare relaxation of protocol, along with three others of his company, the queen's chamberlain, and the Garter King of Arms. Queen dowager Elizabeth and "my lady the king's mother" attended the queen during her second confinement, the only known appearance of Elizabeth Wydeville outside of Bermondsey Abbey between her entrance in February 1487 and her death in June 1492.

During the month that Queen Elizabeth spent within her birthing chamber, her 3-year-old son, Arthur, was created Prince of Wales. On November 21, he arrived at Sheen, where he stayed until November 26 when he boarded the king's barge for the trip to Westminster. Before Chelsea, he was joined on his barge by lords spiritual and temporal, including the bishops of Winchester, Ely, Salisbury, and Durham, seven earls, and "divers other lords, knights, and esquires, kings of arms, heralds, pursuivants, trumpets, and minstrels."[3] At Chelsea, the mayor of London and representatives of the guilds joined the procession with barges decorated with banners and pennons. At Lambeth, ambassadors and merchants of Spain greeted the flotilla by casting apples into the Thames "all in rejoicing of the Prince's coming." From the landing at King's Bridge (a pier) in Westminster, Arthur's way to the King's Bench in Westminster Hall was lined on both sides with members of the crafts standing in order. At Westminster Hall, the mayor, aldermen, and others received the prince before proceeding to the king's presence in the Great Chamber of the Brick Tower.

All this visual display reveals Henry's astute use of political symbolism. The Prince of Wales ceremony officially designated the heir apparent of England, and the public exhibition of Arthur proved to participants and spectators that the Tudor monarchy was thriving and secure. As England's future monarch sailed down the Thames surrounded by prelates, nobles, and citizens, both foreign visitors and English subjects witnessed the future—and popularity—of the Tudor dynasty. The Spanish, in particular, responded exuberantly to the prince, already betrothed to their *infanta* Katherine of Aragon. Henry exploited the *carpe diem* moment to show the most powerful country in Europe that his small island nation was worthy of that liaison.

On November 29, when the king went to dinner, Prince Arthur held the towel—the child standing alongside the earls and lords who bore the water, made the assay, and carried the basin. The prince was learning his lessons in royal ritual and responsibility. That night as Arthur and 19 adult men were initiated as knights of the Bath, his mother was laboring to deliver her second child, a princess who arrived at 9:00 p.m. Never had the promise and prospects of this young Tudor dynasty been brighter!

The next morning after Mass, Prince Arthur was conveyed through St. Stephen's Chapel to the lower end of the stairs near the vicar's lodging, where he mounted his horse. The earl of Essex bore the prince's sword and spurs as they rode into Westminster Hall, dismounting before the King's Bench. The prince led the other initiates of the knights of the Bath into the White Hall to await the king. The marquess of Berkeley and the earl of Arundel led the prince to the king's presence, where the earl of Oxford, Great Chamberlain of England, took the sword and spurs and presented the right spur to the king. The king commanded the marquess of Berkeley to set the right spur on the prince's heel, as the earl of Arundel placed the other on his left heel. The king belted on Arthur's sword and dubbed his three-year-old son knight of the Bath. After the other 19 knights were dubbed, the king created a pursuivant for Prince Arthur.

The all-night vigil and morning ceremony concluded, Arthur went to the king's closet to put on his robes of Estate. The marquess of Berkeley led the prince to the Parliament Chamber with the earl of Arundel and earl of Derby bearing his cape and coronal, the golden rod, and the ring of gold. The earl of Shrewsbury carried the prince's sword with its pommel upward. The king then created his son Prince of Wales and earl of Chester. That day Prince Arthur sat under the cloth of Estate in the Parliament Chamber for a celebratory banquet. After the minstrels played, the Garter King cried the prince for his *Largesse*, distributed by Sir Thomas Lovell, treasurer of the king's chamber, and thanked the king in the name of all Officers of Arms.

Even as this ceremony proceeded, the queen was giving birth to a second heir. Arthur's newborn sister entered the royal spotlight the following day and was christened on the morning of

St. Andrews Day, November 30, 1489. The font from Canterbury, traditionally used for christening royal children, had been moved to Westminster Abbey where it was placed under a round canopy with a large gilt boll. The marchioness of Berkeley carried the baby from the queen's chamber to Whitehall, assisted by the earls of Arundel and Shrewsbury. At the front of the procession to Westminster Abbey were knights, esquires, yeomen, and other gentlemen of the Crown carrying 120 torches. Officers of Arms, the Garter King of Arms, and the constable and marshal of England followed with their staves of office. The earl of Kent carried a pair of gilt basins, the earl of Essex the taper, and viscount Welles a Salt of gold decorated with precious stones. Lady Anne, the queen's sister, immediately preceded the marchioness and baby, carrying the christening robe with its "marvelous rich cross lace."[4] At the porch of the church, which had been decorated with a ceiling of embroidery work, the baby was received by John Alcock, bishop of Ely, who christened and named her Margaret, after "my lady the king's mother." The baby's godfather was John Morton, archbishop of Canterbury and Chancellor of England; her godmothers were "the high and excellent Princess my lady the king's mother, and the duchess of Norfolk, daughter of the good Talbot, earl of Shrewsbury."[5]

As soon as the baby was lowered into the font, torches and taper were lighted, and the Officers of Arms put on their coats of arms. Thomas Rotherham, archbishop of York, then carried the newly christened Princess Margaret to the high altar for confirmation where the marchioness of Berkeley stood as confirmation godmother. After spices and wine, the joyous procession returned to the palace to the sounding of trumpets. Lady Buckingham, assisted by Lord Strange, carried the train of Princess Margaret's christening robe. Four knights bannerets carried the canopy over the baby, whose presents included a silver-and-gilt chest filled with gold from "my lady the king's mother."[6]

With the Christmas season imminent, the royal family stayed at Westminster. But an outbreak of measles among the ladies of the Court cut short the holiday. Several deaths resulted from the measles, including that of Lady Neville, daughter of William Paston. The epidemic forced the queen's churching to be held privately on St. John's Day, December 27. The next day, the king, the queen, and the Court boarded barges and moved to Greenwich.

New Year's Day was celebrated with traditional gifts to the king's Officers of Arms: the queen gave the officers 40*s* and "my lady the king's mother" 20*s*, receiving the customary cries of *Largesse*. On Twelfth day, ambassadors from Spain dined with the king, but the measles epidemic curtailed the usual revelries. No disguisings and very few plays were presented during this holiday, but an "Abbot of Misrule" provided good sport. The king then went hunting in Waltham forest before he returned with his Court to Westminster.

By Candlemas Day, the measles epidemic had subsided sufficiently for the king, the queen, and "my lady the king's mother" to go in procession with the lords of Parliament into a richly decorated Westminster Hall to celebrate the infant Christ's presentation at the Temple of Jerusalem. The king wore a rich purple robe decorated with gold cord and furred with sables, as he led his nobles and the French and Spanish ambassadors to services conducted by the bishop of Exeter. Negotiations for the marriage of Prince Arthur to Princess Katherine of Aragon assured that ambassadors from Spain were continuously present in England from this time onward. This evening the queen and "my lady the king's mother" joined the king in the White Hall for a play. Also attending were selected courtiers, "but no strangers [foreigners]."[7] The king remained at Westminster for the Lenten season, then joined his household at Sheen during Passion Week.

King Henry VII spent freely and generously on his family's needs and pleasures. Not at all the penurious penny-pincher for which he became infamous after Elizabeth of York's death, the king paid his staff generously. Among the attendants of Prince Arthur, Thomas Poyntz received 40 marks on March 11, 1488, for his service to the king and Arthur.[8] Arthur's physician Stephen Bereworth was granted a life annuity of £40 on May 30, 1488, for "his medical attendance upon Arthur, the King's firstborn son."[9] John Whiting, sewer to Arthur, received a grant-for-life and was paid 20 marks on February 3,. 1489, 20 marks on November 20, 1489, 20 marks on January 23, 1490.[10] Thomas Fissher, yeoman of the prince's cellar, received 40s on March 29, 1490,[11] and Richard Howell, marshal of Arthur's household, 10 marks on January 9, 1490.[12] John Almor, sergeant-at-arms for the prince was paid wages and fees of 12d a day.[13]

Dame Elizabeth Darcy, Lady Mistress of the Prince, continued to govern Arthur's nursery, assisted by Agnes Butler, Evelyn

Hobbes, and Alice Bywymble. In June 1487 a general order paid the wages of the Lady Mistress, nurses and other gentlewomen a sum of £46.[14] During Easter term 1488, Dame Darcy was paid her annual salary of 40 marks, plus expenses.[15] At Michaelmas 1488, she received another 20 marks sterling for the half-year, while Agnes Butler and Evelyn Hobbes each received 33s 4d and Alice Bywymble 26s 8d.[16] In July 1489, their salary for three quarters of the year to Midsummer amounted to £20 sterling for Dame Darcy, and 50s each for Agnes Butler and Evelyn Hobbes.[17] Katherine Gibbes, Arthur's nurse, received a grant-for-life of £20 on April 28, 1490, from the king's Exchequer.[18]

Arthur's early education began under the tutelage of John Rede, former headmaster of Winchester College,[19] who was soon joined by Bernard André, the poet and historian who served as Arthur's tutor from 1496 to 1500. After reading and grammar, Arthur progressed to oratory, history, and biblical studies. He read authors in French, Latin, and Greek. In late 1499, Thomas Linacre, recently returned from a decade of studies in Italy, became Arthur's principal tutor.[20] Linacre's degree in medicine from the university at Padua, his years of studying Greek at Florence, and his translations in Latin placed him among the leading humanists in England. By age 15 Arthur had read 33 works in Latin, including Cicero, Homer, Livy, Ovid, Thucydides, and Virgil.[21] His further training in arms and archery (especially the long bow) produced a well-rounded prince not only versed in the humanist learning then current on the Continent, but also proficient in the arms that distinguished Burgundian nobility.[22]

King Henry was intent on securing a consort for Arthur who would be worthy of such a man, and negotiations for Arthur's marriage to Katherine of Aragon proceeded as rapidly as political reality permitted. In late 1487 or early 1488, Ferdinand and Isabella of Spain sent Roderigo Gondesalvi de Puebla to England, followed by a letter dated April 30, 1488, that authorized him to conclude a treaty of marriage between the Princess Katherine and Arthur.[23] By July, De Puebla was discussing with Henry's commissioners Richard, bishop of Exeter, and Giles Daubeney, chamberlain of the Exchequer, the amount of the marriage portion, the conditions of its payment, and the jointure to be given by Henry to Princess Katherine.[24] On December 11, 1488, Henry appointed additional commissioners: Thomas Savage, Doctor of Civil Laws and chancellor of the earldom of March, and Richard Nanfan, knight for the king's body.[25]

To assure that the prince was properly appareled for his increasingly important royal role, he received regular deliveries from the Great Wardrobe. In 1489, the grant included

> divers robes, tunics, and other ornaments, things, and stuffs for the said lord prince, and also the mistress-nurse and other servants of the same prince, made of cloth of fine white doubly set velvet, damask, satin, sarcenet, fustian, furs of ermines, black bogy [imported skins of lamb's leg]; with sheets of Holland cloth, brushes, crochettes, tapettes, iron hammers, and other things necessary for him.[26]

King Henry also began to establish Prince Arthur's authority in the realm. On May 20, 1490, Thomas, earl of Surrey, was appointed Arthur's underwarden of the Marches with power to array the men of Northumberland to defend Berwick and to keep the peace along the marches with Scotland.[27] To support his expenses, Arthur received a grant of the principality of Wales on December 1, 1490, including castles, towns, and rents sufficient "for the maintenance of his state in accordance with the nobility of his race and the excellence of his name."[28] A grant of livery enabled him to "sustain the honor of the dukedom." On October 2, 1492, Arthur was delegated power to grant licenses to elect minor prelates and to present benefices of less than 40 marks. He was also appointed "keeper of England and the King's lieutenant there, while the king is in remote parts."[29] Before the prince turned six, he was granted the power to appoint justices of *oyer* and *terminer* in the counties of Salop, Hereford, Gloucester and Worcester, and the marches of Wales; to array men of arms; to have retainers with his own livery of cloths and badges; and to execute justice in the marches of Wales.[30] Although his Council carried out these provisions, actions were taken in the prince's name. Just after Arthur's seventh birthday, Henry granted estates and rents to fund the prince's own household, including 12 castles, 6 manors, several towns, and 20 lordships, the rents amounting to more than £465.[31]

Ferdinand and Isabella ratified the marriage treaty of Arthur and the *infanta* Katherine at Medina del Campo on March 28, 1489.[32] Later, Henry VII stipulated that Princess Katherine would be

> ...sent to England as soon as she has completed the twelfth year of her age, and the Prince of Wales the fourteenth year of his age.[33]

The marriage portion of the princess was 200,000 scudos (4s 2d each scudo) with 100,000 scudos to be paid within four days of marriage, 50,000 within the next year and the remaining 50,000 within the second year. The payment would be made in England in coin or vessels of gold and silver appraised in England at the time of payment.[34]

The marriage was jeopardized, however, by another pretender to Henry's throne. In October 1491, a young man appeared in Ireland claiming to be Prince Richard, Queen Elizabeth's younger brother who had disappeared from the Tower in late 1483. "Richard, duke of York" claimed his rights as king of England. This new threat to Henry's crown caused Ferdinand and Isabella to procrastinate in negotiating their daughter's marriage to Arthur Tudor.

While King Henry began pursuing this newest claimant to England's throne, Queen Elizabeth gave birth to a second son on June 28, 1491, at Greenwich Palace. Named after his father, Prince Henry would become one of the most famous monarchs in English history. At this moment, however, the future Henry VIII, although welcomed and feted, lived in the shadow of his older brother, Arthur, the Tudor heir educated and cultivated to become England's next monarch.

The year 1492 brought sadness and sorrow to Queen Elizabeth. Her mother died at Bermondsey Abbey during the night of June 7/8, 1492. Elizabeth Wydeville's body was transported by barge to Windsor Castle, where she was buried next to her beloved husband, Edward IV, with rites so truncated that the contemporary scribe commented on the low hearse—"such as they use for the common people"—the inferior tapers, and the scanty attendance at her funeral.[35] The queen dowager's daughters Anne, Katherine, and Bridget attended the funeral, along with her son Thomas, marquess of Dorset. Neither Queen Elizabeth nor her sister Cecily were present. The queen was already in confinement awaiting the birth of her fourth child, and Cecily, whose husband Viscount Welles represented her, may have been ill or in confinement herself. The contemporary scribe merely commented that Queen Elizabeth had taken to her chambers and "I suppose she went in blue [the royal color of mourning] in likewise as Queen Margaret, the wife of King Henry the VI, went in when her mother the Queen of Sicily died."[36]

Elizabeth of York gave birth to a royal princess on July 2, 1492—barely a year after the birth of Henry—and named her Elizabeth.

Perhaps sickly from birth, this child lived just three years and died of "atrophy" in October 1495. At her death, the princess received a royal burial that cost £318 9s 7d paid to John Shaa.[37]

Queen Elizabeth's growing family may have distracted her from the rumors that her brother Prince Richard, reputedly murdered in the Tower of London at age 10, had appeared in France, Burgundy, and Ireland. Stories from the Continent described a charming young man whom King Charles VIII of France and duchess dowager Margaret of Burgundy officially received as "Richard, duke of York." Reports that her younger brother was alive surely reached Elizabeth. Yet no contemporary document— not one—mentions Elizabeth's reaction to the possible survival of her brother. The absence of information regarding any interaction between Queen Elizabeth and the man who became known as "Perkin Warbeck" is stunning, given this individual's dominance of her husband's domestic and foreign policies for the next eight years and Perkin's own residence in Henry's Court after his capture.

Those who remembered Lambert Simnel (just about everyone) immediately suspected that "Richard, duke of York" was yet another imposter, but the possibility that Prince Richard may have escaped from the Tower could not be absolutely eliminated. Did Elizabeth's heart leap with joy at the possibility that she might see her little brother again? Or did she perceive him as a threat to her own royal family? The historical record, as usual when dealing with the personal aspects of royal lives, gives no clue about Elizabeth's reactions to and interactions with Perkin Warbeck.

During their childhood years, Elizabeth's younger brother Richard had lived with his mother and sisters (the heir to the throne, Edward, Prince of Wales, resided in his own household at Ludlow castle). On May 1, 1483, when Richard, duke of Gloucester, took custody of Edward V, queen dowager Elizabeth, her five daughters, and son Richard fled to Westminster Sanctuary. During the next 6 weeks, the 17-year-old princess Elizabeth and 9-year-old Richard shared miseries and trauma, facing a future fraught with dangers. Eight years had passed since that dreadful day when the archbishop of Canterbury removed Prince Richard from Sanctuary. Elizabeth had become queen consort and mother of two sons, whose achievements replicated those of her brothers. Did she recall memories of her brothers with each celebration of her own sons? How did she respond to news that the youngest of her brothers was alive and well and living in France? The records provide no answers.

To fight this threat to his throne, Henry planned a foray into France—partly to promote the interests of Brittany and partly to undercut French support for "Richard, duke of York." Before departing, Henry determined that Elizabeth's dower was "insufficient to maintain the Queen's dignity" and took steps to augment it. He granted Elizabeth reversion rights to the property of her grandmother, Cecily, duchess of York. An initial grant-for-life included 44 lordships and manors, 4 hundreds, 4 forests, 3 boroughs, 2 fee farms, and the castle of Brugewater. A second grant-for-life on February 1 gave the queen reversion rights upon the death of the king and of Cecily, duchess of York, to another 37 lordships and manors, 3 boroughs, 1 fee farm, 3 offices of feodary or bailiff, and the receivership of the castle-guard monies of Rochester.[38]

During this critical year of 1492, the world was rapidly changing. Europe was altered forever. Lingering vestiges of the Crusades ended when the army of Ferdinand and Isabella conquered Granada, the last foothold of the Moors in Spain. The conquest of Granada was celebrated in England on April 6, with a gathering of the Mayor and "a great multitude of the Citizens in their liveries" at the door of St. Paul's. Archbishop and Chancellor John Morton praised the Spanish victory over the Moors.[39] That same year Columbus discovered the "new world," infusing England and the Continent with an exciting, adventurous spirit and introducing new political challenges. Within a few years, Henry, too, would license English ships to explore the "islands" to the west.

When Henry VII sailed for Calais on October 6, 1492, Queen Elizabeth's financial situation was reasonably secure, but she was left alone in London with four small children: Arthur age six, Margaret three, Henry one, and Elizabeth, an infant of three months. Elizabeth of York was nine years old when her own mother had found herself in exactly the same position—presiding over the royal family in England while her husband sailed off to war with France.

Did this Queen Elizabeth—in addition to her fears about the king's safety—wonder whether her husband would meet the individual who claimed to be her brother, Prince Richard, duke of York?

CHAPTER 12

FESTIVALS AND CHALLENGES

Perhaps Queen Elizabeth was privy to Henry's war plans and knew that he hoped to emulate her father's invasion of France 17 years earlier. Shrewd enough to comprehend that armed battle would ravage England's resources, Henry VII followed the example of Edward IV in negotiating peace at great cost to the French treasury and at great profit to his personal coffers. By November 9, 1492, Henry had concluded the Treaty at Étaples with Charles VIII, who agreed to pay the King of England 50,000 crowns a year for the rest of his life.[1] The Treaty also required Charles VIII to cease and desist from offering aid to rebels who challenged Henry. Perkin Warbeck was forced, thereby, to leave France and move on to Burgundy where he received a warm and financially rewarding welcome from dowager duchess Margaret.

Henry VII was back home in time to celebrate a royal Christmas at Westminster. Once more the records provide no information— not a word—regarding what Henry told Elizabeth about the man in France who claimed to be her brother. Frustratingly devoid of personal particulars—the interactions and ambiguities that constitute the richness of human experience—the historical documents record only the facts of politics and power plays. At home, Henry set to strengthening his political ties with his people.

The king had taxed the merchants of London with "benevolences" to fund his foray into France, forced assessments that were renamed "malevolences" by the contributors.[2] During the year following his return to England, Henry worked to assuage the financial anguish of his London supporters and to win back their good will. In a grand gesture of conciliation and appreciation, the king invited the mayor and his brethren to a "royal feast" on Twelfth Night 1494.[3] The contemporary report of the evening provides a rare and fascinating glimpse into the elaborate festivities of the

royal holidays, particularly the music and disguisings so loved by
Queen Elizabeth.

Representing the king at the "great dinner in the White
Hall"—a singular honor—was Sir William Stanley, chamberlain
of the king's household. Sir William presided at the high table
during the dinner honoring London's mayor, aldermen, and distinguished citizens. The ensemble then moved to Westminster
Hall, which was festively decorated with arrases and furnished
with stages for the evening's entertainment. Around 11 o'clock,
the king arrived with ambassadors from France and Spain, followed by the queen with her ladies and gentlewomen. The king's
players presented an "interlude," a brief play that entertained the
guests:

> But ere they had finished their play, came in riding one of the King's
> Chapel named "Cornish" [William Cornish, gentleman of the
> Chapel Royal], appareled after the figure of Saint George, and after
> followed a fair virgin attired like unto a King's daughter and leading
> by a silken lace a terrible and huge red dragon, the which in sundry
> places of the hall as he passed, spit fire at his mouth. And when the
> said Cornish was come before the King, he uttered a certain speech
> made in Ballad Royal, after finishing whereof he began this anthem
> of Saint George, "O Georgi deo Care" [O George, beloved of God],
> whereunto the King's Chapel which stood fast by answered,
> "Salvatorem Deprecare, ut Gubernet Angliam" [Intercede with the
> Savior, that he may govern England]. And so sang out all the whole
> anthem with lusty courage. In pastime whereof the said Cornish
> avoided [left] with the dragon, and the virgin was led unto the
> Queen's standing.[4]

This early appearance of William Cornish as an actor revealed little of the later importance he would wield in the developing music
and drama of the Tudor court. The enactment of St. George and
the anthem of tribute to the king represented typically traditional
entertainment in the English court. So, too, the music and dancing that followed:

> Then came in from the same place where Cornish before came
> from, as from the lower part of the hall, 12 gentlemen leading by
> kerchiefs of pleasance 12 ladies being all costiously and goodly dis-
> guised, as well the men as women, having before them a small
> Tabret [drum] & a subtle fiddle, the which gentlemen leaped and
> danced all the length of the hall as they came, and the ladies slode

[slid] after them as [if] they had stood upon a frame running, with wheels. They kept their traces so demure and close that their limbs moved all at once.

When they were come before the King, they dissevered [divided] them by 2 & 2, and so danced a certain of dances, and then by 3 & 3, and lastly by 4 & 4, and thus continued by a large hour, all which season it was wonderful to behold the exceeding leaps....[5]

The men leapt so vigorously that spangles of gold fell from their costumes, although the ladies never varied from their demure movements.

Thoroughly pleased, the mayor and his brethren next proceeded to a banquet sufficiently sumptuous to mollify any residual irritation from the king's "malevolences":

A table of stone...was garnished with napery, lights, and other necessaries, whereat the King, the Queen, and other Estates as it pleased his Grace to command being set. Anon from the kitchen...came the foresaid 12 gentlemen being still in their disguised apparel, bearing every each of them a dish, and after them as many knights and Esquires as made the full number of 60, the which 60 dishes were all served unto the King's mess and forthwith were as many served unto the Queen. Of the which six score dishes was not one of flesh or of fish, but all confections of sundry fruits and conserves, and so soon as the King and the Queen and the other Estates were served, was then brought unto the Mayor's stage 24 dishes of the same manner service, with sundry wines and ale in most plenteous wise.

And finally as all worldly pleasure hath an end, the board was reverently withdrawn, and the King & Queen with the other Estates with a great sort of lights conveyed into the Palace, and the Mayor with his company yood [went] to the Bridge where two barges tarried for them and so came home by breaking of the day.[6]

An evening spent with the king reinforced political loyalties at a time when Henry was increasingly harassed by the peregrinations of "Richard, duke of York" through the courts of Europe. Everywhere "Richard" claimed his right to the throne of England. After the Treaty at Étaples ended his five months residence in France (where Charles VIII had received him as "the son of King Edward"),[7] "Richard" moved on to Brabant, where dowager duchess Margaret welcomed him to her court at Malines as her nephew.[8] Since she had also sponsored Lambert Simnel, Margaret's support of this latest challenger to Henry VII surprised no one. Margaret's enmity toward Henry VII—the man who killed her brother Richard III—was vengeful and unrelenting.

There is something odd, however, in Margaret's unwavering endorsement of the young men she adopted as her nephews and her apparent disregard for her beautiful niece, England's reigning queen consort. Of the many perplexities in the eight-year odyssey of "Richard, duke of York," Margaret's financial support and personal endorsement of her "nephew" in ways that endangered her niece Elizabeth remain unexplained. Margaret would have met her niece during her visit to England in 1480 when Elizabeth was 14 years old. Then, the young, beautiful "my lady the Dauphine" was the preeminent daughter of York, a role dowager duchess Margaret had enjoyed in her youth. Her displacement as the reigning Yorkist daughter, the long-standing rivalries between Burgundy and France, and the expectation that Elizabeth as queen of France would outrank the dowager duchess of Burgundy may have provoked an invidious enmity in the older woman. Envy, added to Margaret's hatred of Henry for killing her brother Richard III, may explain her actions. Whatever the causes, Elizabeth of York once more became a sacrificial lamb on the altar of political ambition, an offering tendered this time by her aunt.

The dowager duchess's support of "Richard, duke of York" also threatened the nation of her birth. When Margaret persuaded her step-son-in-law Maximilian, archduke of Austria and regent of the Burgundian Netherlands, to adopt the cause of "Richard," she aided and incited the expansionistic dreams of European rulers. France and Burgundy had always pursued every opportunity to destabilize that small island across *La Manche*. Now Austria hoped to seize it—with help from the Yorkist-born sister of Edward IV, Richard III, and Clarence. In exchange for Margaret's funding of the fleet that invaded England, "Richard" signed a deed in December 1494 acknowledging his debt to the dowager duchess of Burgundy for "8,000 gold écus of the coin and mint of the King of France." In January 1495, he signed a second document granting England to Maximilian in case of his death.[9]

As early as the summer of 1493, Henry VII had proclaimed "Richard" an imposter foisted on England by the "malice" of

Margaret of Burgundy. In a letter to Gilbert Talbot, dated July 20, 1493, Henry identified the young man as

> another feigned lad called Perkin Warbeck, born at Tournay, in Picardy, which at first into Ireland called himself the bastard son of King Richard; after that the son of the said Duke of Clarence; and now the second son of our father, King Edward the IVth.[10]

The multiple identities explicitly recall Lambert Simnel and undercut the credibility of this latest imposter—whom England forever after would know as "Perkin Warbeck."

Unfortunately, Henry's identification of the impostor did not diminish the enthusiasm of rival monarchs for promoting Perkin's cause. Pleas to the rulers of Europe solicited support for Perkin: in a letter to Isabella of Castile in August 1493, "Richard, duke of York" describes how "at about age nine" he was destined for death, but saved by the "divine clemency" of the lord commissioned to kill him.[11] A letter from Margaret of Burgundy to Isabella identifies Richard as her nephew.[12] Although Isabella and Ferdinand remained loyal to Henry VII, the uncertainty of his right to England's throne most certainly delayed negotiations for the marriage of Arthur and Katherine. Then, as if to poke a finger directly into Henry's eye, Maximilian received "Richard" in his court as "the son of King Edward of England" and seated him at the high table during his wedding banquet on March 16, 1494.[13]

Henry responded by creating an English "Duke of York," conferring that title on his son Henry with elaborate celebrations beginning on All-Hallows Day 1494. In addition to voiding "Richard's" claim to the title, the ceremonies distracted the English nation from the stories arriving from the Continent. Once more, the Tudor dynasty displayed its magnificence with all the splendor of medieval romance, beginning with solicitations from the ladies of the Court for tournaments following Prince Henry's investiture:

> ...for the pleasure of our sovereign lord, the Queen's grace and the ladies, remembering themselves that ancient custom of this his noble realm of England at such royal feasts to be great and notable acts of arms, for the continuance of the which, and for the exercise of the same, and lest any other should take that enterprise before them, they besought the King's grace to license and to permit them at the said feast to hold and to keep a "justes royall"...[14]

In preparation for the celebrations, the king, the queen, and "my lady the king's mother" moved from Sheen to Westminster on October 27. Two days later, Prince Henry left Eltham, his palace home, to ride through the streets of London:

> At afternoon, about three of the clock came through the City the Duke of York, called Lord Henry, the King's second son, a child of four year of age or thereabouts, which sat upon a courser and so rode to Westminster to the King with a goodly fellowship [Henry was 3 years, 4 months old].[15]

The mayor, the aldermen, and "all the crafts in their liveries" escorted the prince through the city.[16]

Preceding his creation as duke of York, Prince Henry and 22 others, including Lord Harington (son of Thomas Grey, marquess of Dorset), performed the rituals that made them knights of the Bath. On October 31, Henry was created duke of York "with the gift of a thousand pound by year."[17] Queen Elizabeth did not attend the ceremony, but joined the grand, celebratory procession that featured "Lord Harry, Duke of York, in his harness [armor]."[18] The king and queen wore their crowns and 10 bishops their miters.

The tournaments began at Westminster on November 9, with the king and queen attending in their special "house":

> It was the most triumphant place that ever I saw. First, to see the King's grace and the Queen's so richly emparelled, his house and stage covered with cloth of Arras blue, enramplished with fleur-de-lis of gold, and within...hanged with rich cloth of Arras of other stories and two cloths of Estate, one for the King, another for the Queen, and rich cushions of cloth of gold, accompanied with the substance of the great Estates of this realm, as the Duke of York, the Duke of Bedford, the Duke of Buckingham, and many other, earls, barons, bannerettes, and knights....[19]

During the first day of the tournament, the four challengers wore the king's livery of green and white with the queen's heraldic crest of blue and murrey on their helmets. On the second day, they wore the blue and white livery of "my lady the king's mother."[20] That evening after supper and dancing, the prize was awarded to the earl of Suffolk by the five-year-old "high and excellent princess the Lady Margaret, the King's eldest daughter."[21] Queen Elizabeth

Photo 6   Henry VIII as a child (1491–1547, reigned 1509–47).
Erasmus described Henry at age nine as "having already
something of royalty in his demeanor, in which there
was a certain dignity combined with singular courtesy."
Fonds bibliothèque Méjanes (Aix-en-Provence, France).

was following the example of her own mother in introducing her children to royal ceremony at an early age.

The third day of the tournament featured the running of the course with spears, followed by sword fighting. "Four fair ladies" led the knights on horseback into the lists with laces woven of white and blue silk. The ladies rode white horses and wore white satin gowns with crimson satin sleeves.[22] The knights displayed ostrich feathers on their helmets and rode horses trapped with black velvet purled with gold.[23] Again, the king and queen watched from their luxurious house. Again, Princess Margaret awarded the prizes for the day. The tournaments were elaborately and traditionally English in their rituals and ceremonies. Within six years, this martial test of arms would forever change when pageantry and drama introduced allegory and romance into the lists.

Although England had created Prince Henry as duke of York, "Richard's" advocates in Europe were not deterred. Even while the tournaments at Westminster were proceeding, Margaret of Burgundy and Maximilian of Austria were planning to invade England with an army led by "Richard, duke of York." Indeed, supporters for the imposter were apparently embedded deep within the English Court. In January 1495, King Henry's own chamberlain of the household, Sir William Stanley, was convicted of treason and beheaded on February 16 for his alleged support of Perkin. The idea that his chamberlain—the man who controlled access to the king's most private chambers, the man who had represented the king at his Twelfth Night dinner a year earlier—favored "Richard, duke of York" stunned the Court and scared those intimate to Henry. If the charges were true, even trusted servants were rallying to the cause of this alleged son of Edward IV.

Henry took immediate steps to thwart competition from other Yorkists. The unmarried sisters of his queen constituted targets of opportunity for powerful men bent on challenging the king, and Henry rapidly counteracted that threat. The youngest sister, Bridget, was no problem since she had entered the Dominican convent at Dartford in 1490 and was safely secluded as a nun of that order. Cecily, the second of Edward IV's daughters, remained safely wed to Viscount Welles, half-brother of the king's mother. The queen's sisters Anne and Katherine, however, loomed as tempting wives for contenders to the throne. The marriages of both princesses in 1495 reveal how Henry's marital policy attempted to secure internal support for his reign.

On February 4, 1495, Princess Anne was married to Thomas Howard, eldest son of the duke of Norfolk. Both the father and grandfather of Thomas Howard had been strong Yorkists who fought with Richard III at Bosworth. Ten years later, the family was attempting to redeem itself, and the Tudor king was determined to cement an affinity by embracing Norfolk's son within the royal family. After his marriage, Thomas Howard gained favor by fighting against the Cornish rebels in 1497. Later that year he joined his father in opposing the Scots and earned a knighthood. Henry VII succeeded in converting the Howards from Yorkist to enduring Tudor supporters. Anne died in 1511, but Thomas Howard lived to become the third duke of Norfolk—that powerful and infamous uncle of Anne Boleyn and Katherine Howard, two of Henry VIII's six wives.

The marriage of Princess Katherine to William Courtenay, son of Edward Courtenay, took a bizarre and unexpected turn, however. Edward Courtenay, a long and devoted follower, had lived in exile with Henry in Brittany and fought with him at Bosworth. He became earl of Devon in October 1485, participated in Henry's coronation, fought at Stoke in 1487, and was elected knight of the Garter in April 1494. His son William married Princess Katherine in 1495, another reward for proven loyalty. William himself had been made knight of the Bath at Queen Elizabeth's coronation in 1487 and accompanied the king to France in 1492. In 1502, however, Sir William Courtenay was charged with treason for his alleged support of Edmund de la Pole, earl of Suffolk (nephew of Edward IV and another contender for the throne). Thrown into prison, William Courtenay depended on Queen Elizabeth to support her sister Katherine and the three small Courtney children.

Henry's marital policy was part of ordinary crown business, which frequently intermingled with the personal. Other family matters that needed attention included the disposal of the property of Cecily Neville, duchess of York and the queen's paternal grandmother, who was nearing death: her castle, manor, lordship, and town of Fotheringhay were granted to Queen Elizabeth on March 27, 1495.[24] Death also claimed the youngest royal daughter, Elizabeth, at age three in autumn 1495. The child's body was transported from Eltham to Westminster, where she was buried on the left side of St. Edward's altar.[25] Queen Elizabeth was already pregnant with a fifth child, who was born around March 18, 1496.

Christened "Mary," this princess would become the grandmother of Lady Jane Grey, queen of England for those nine turbulent days in 1553. Elizabeth of York was back to her royal duties by November 1496, when she accompanied the king to the Sergeant's feast at the bishop of Ely's palace in Holborn.

All these personal events took place under the increasingly dark shadow cast by Perkin Warbeck's pending invasion of England. On July 3, 1495, a small troop of about 150 men led by "Richard, duke of York," arrived in Kent. "Richard" watched from his ship as his men were captured and slaughtered.[26] He then sailed for Ireland, where his ships laid siege to Waterford for 11 days before sailing on to Scotland, where James IV—pleased with the opportunity to tweak his neighbor south of the Tweed—received "Richard" warmly.

Almost immediately, James IV married his handsome guest to a royal wife, Katherine Gordon, daughter of George Gordon, second earl of Huntly and relative of King James. A year later, James IV placed "Richard" at the head of a raiding party that invaded England on September 17, 1496. Burning houses and ravaging villages, the Scots advanced little more than four miles across the border before retreating when they heard that Lord Neville was approaching with 4,000 men.[27] King James's disgust at "Richard's" failure to fight because of concern for "his own natural subjects and vassals" caused the Scottish king to temper his enthusiasm for the young lad.[28] The welcome mat for "Richard, duke of York" was wearing thin, and in July 1497 he left Scotland with his wife and son, sailing once more for Ireland. From there he launched an invasion of England that would lead to his inevitable demise.

Other threats harassed Henry. In May 1497, the commons of Cornwall, angered by taxes, marched toward London with a company reported to number around 15,000 men.[29] Henry diverted 8,000 soldiers who had been headed north to the Scottish borders toward Exeter to fight the Cornishmen. Henry himself left Sheen to lead the defense. The next day, Queen Elizabeth and prince Henry (about to celebrate his sixth birthday) moved to Coldharbour, the large house on the Thames belonging to "my lady the king's mother," for six days before seeking protection in the Tower of London. The City instituted a general watch and the mayor sent wine and food to troops in the field.[30] The Cornishmen, when confronted by the king's mounted troops, soon discovered that their best interest lay in securing a pardon, and after a skirmish at Blackheath and the capture and execution of their two leaders, Henry quelled this rebellion by the end of June.

After such trauma, the Court welcomed the good news brought by John Cabot upon his return in mid-August 1497 from exploring the new world. Sailing out of Bristol at the beginning of summer on an expedition commissioned by King Henry, Cabot reported that he had planted the flag of England on the new found land, and he exhibited snares for catching game and a needle for making nets gathered from native sites. Henry paid £10 to "him that found the new isle" and promised further support.[31] Five years would go by before three natives of this new world would appear in London, but the excitement of Henry and his subjects was palpable at the news of an unknown civilization.[32] England would not defer to Spain in exploring the new world!

The euphoria inspired by this discovery ended on September 7, 1497 when three small ships carrying 100–120 men, including "Richard, duke of York," his wife, and son, landed in Cornwall near Land's End. Proclaiming himself "King Richard IV," he led his men in an assault on Exeter on September 27.[33] His timing was dreadful, since the Cornishmen had just learned their painful lesson at Blackheath. No nobles and few gentlemen took up his cause, and when the town of Exeter refused to admit "Richard IV," he sent his wife and son to St. Michael's Mount, mounted his horse in the middle of the night, and fled to Sanctuary at Beaulieu Abbey. Whatever the truth about this young man's heritage, he clearly lacked the Plantagenet penchant for fighting. Deserting his troops not only demoralized his men, but also destroyed any credibility "Richard" might claim as a leader. From this point on, the imposter became little more than a figure of ridicule, a joke that resonated in the very name assigned him by Henry VII: Perkin Warbeck.

Aware that his charade was over, Perkin left Sanctuary and threw himself on the mercy of the king, who was at Taunton with his son Arthur, age 11, and many members of the nobility.[34] Included in the king's party were several who should have been able to identify the true prince Richard, son of Edward IV. In particular, Thomas, marquess of Dorset, the prince's half-brother, had spent weeks with him in Westminster Sanctuary just 14 years earlier. Surely some vestige of the child would have been visible in the face of the 23-year-old adult, especially since Perkin consistently cited 3 birthmarks, including one under his eye, to verify his identity as Richard. Frustratingly, the records include no evidence of any effort to examine the person who called himself "Richard IV" by those who knew the prince as a child.

Henry's subsequent treatment of his captive only confounds the perplexities that still enshroud Perkin. The king sent for Perkin's wife, Lady Katherine Gordon, who had moved to Sanctuary at St. Buryan, a small village between Land's End and Penzance.[35] In recognition of her royal Scottish rank, Henry ordered a satin dress with velvet ribbons, a riding cloak and hat, gloves, a kirtle, hose and shoes for her journey.[36] Upon meeting this "woman of goodly personage and beauty,"[37] Henry seemed rather pleased with his war booty and paid £20 sterling for the diet of Lady Katherine while his servant Thomas English delivered her "unto our dearest wife the Queen wheresoever she be."[38]

Queen Elizabeth had just returned from Walsingham Priory, the pilgrimage site in Norfolk associated with the Virgin Mary. She stopped in London for two days, where she lodged at the Great Wardrobe before traveling on to Sheen.[39] On Saturday, October 21, 1497, Queen Elizabeth met Lady Katherine Gordon, the woman who claimed to be her sister-in-law.[40] What could Elizabeth of York possibly have thought when she met this wife of the man impersonating prince Richard, the brother Elizabeth had loved as a child? The historical records are silent—they say nothing!—about the response, the reaction, or the emotions of Queen Elizabeth in this curious encounter. Did Elizabeth ask Lady Katherine to describe "Richard, duke of York"? Did she willingly welcome this woman into her most intimate circle of attendants? Did Elizabeth ask to meet Perkin? The records provide no clues. All we know is that Lady Katherine Gordon became one of Elizabeth's highest-ranking Ladies-in-Waiting and spent the rest of her life in the English court.

The story becomes curiouser and curiouser with Henry's treatment of his captive. This imposter who had consumed the king's energies and England's resources for eight long years was admitted into the king's Court. Although effectively under house arrest, Perkin was treated as a courtier, not as a prisoner. True, Henry Tudor himself had lived in the court of Brittany as a closely watched exile, but he had never attacked Brittany in armed combat, as Perkin had attacked England. Further, Henry Tudor, earl of Richmond, was grandson of a queen and great-grandson of the

king of France. In contrast, Perkin's confession identified himself
as the son of a "controller of the Town of Tournai," although the
records in Tournai identify his father as a boatman of the lower
ranking trades.[41] Perkin's heritage—and actions—hardly merited
residence in the Court of England.

During Perkin's months at Court, he mingled freely among the
courtiers. A dispatch from the Venetian ambassador states that he
had seen Perkin

> who was in a chamber of the King's palace and habitation. He is a
> well favored young man, 23 years old, and his wife a very handsome
> woman; the King treats them well, but did not allow them to sleep
> together.[42]

Perkin was present at Sheen during the Christmas season of 1497
when that favorite residence caught fire on December 30, a tragedy that greatly endangered the royal family:[43]

> This year the King kept his Christmas at his manor of Sheen,
> where, upon St. Thomas day at night in the Christmas week about
> nine of the clock began a great fire within the King's lodging, and
> so continued unto twelve of the night and more, by violence
> whereof much and great part of the old building was burnt, and
> much harm done in hangings, as rich beds, costrings [curtains] and
> other, appertaining to such a noble court. How be it, owing to
> God, no man was, nor Christian creature, thereby perished, which
> was to the King's singular comfort, considering the great and nota-
> ble Court that there was holden, as first the King, the Queen, my
> Lady the King's mother, with my Lord of York, My Lady Margaret,
> and divers other Estates.[44]

Where was Perkin during the fire? Ann Wroe, Perkin's biogra-
pher, suggests that the fire might have been suspicious and that it
began in the king's wardrobe where Perkin usually slept.[45] The contemporary reports do not substantiate that claim. The ambassador
from Venice writes that the fire broke out in the Queen's chamber,[46]
and letters to Milan state that the fire began "by accident and not
by malice, catching a beam about the ninth hour of the night.…
The King does not attach much importance to the fire, seeing that
it was not due to malice."[47] If Henry had suspected Perkin, surely he
would have taken immediate action. The fire offered an excellent

opportunity to punish Perkin on the spot. Instead, Henry remained insouciant and Perkin remained at Court.

Whatever his status within the Court, life was becoming intolerable for "the well favored young man," who attempted escape on June 9, 1498. Fleeing Westminster, Perkin once more sought shelter at a religious site—the Charterhouse at Sheen. Recaptured in just four days, he was sent to the Tower where traitors normally were executed almost instantly. Again, Henry delayed. A year went by before Perkin was accused of collaborating with the unfortunate earl of Warwick in planning an escape from the Tower. That plot discovered, Perkin and Warwick were tried, convicted, and executed within five days of each other. Perkin was hanged on November 23, 1499 and Warwick beheaded (in concession to his nobility) on November 28, 1499. Vergil expresses considerable sympathy for Warwick:

> ...a few days afterwards, Edward earl of Warwick was himself beheaded. The entire population mourned the death of the handsome youth. Why indeed the unhappy boy should have been committed to prison not for any fault of his own but only because of his family's offences, why he was retained so long in prison, and what, lastly, the worthy youth could have done in prison which could merit his death—all these things could obviously not be comprehended by many.[48]

A letter from De Puebla to Ferdinand and Isabella on January 11, 1500, explains that the executions were essential to stabilize the kingdom:

> ...this kingdom is at present so situated as has not been seen for the last five hundred years till now, as those say who know best, and as appears by the chronicles; because there are always brambles and thorns of such a kind that the English had occasion not to remain peacefully in obedience to their King, there being divers heirs of the kingdom and of such a quality that the matter could be disputed between the two sides. Now it has pleased God that all should be thoroughly and daily purged and cleansed, so that not a doubtful drop of royal blood remains in this kingdom, except the true blood of the King and Queen and above all, that of the Lord Prince Arthur. And since of this fact and of the execution which was done on Perkin and on the son of the Duke of Clarence, I have written to your highnesses by various ways, I do not wish to trouble you with lengthy writing.[49]

During the 14 years Henry had been king of England, imposters and rebels had plagued his reign almost without remission. His queen consort, Elizabeth of York, remained loyally and lovingly by his side—inured to personal insecurity and daily uncertainty almost from the moment of her birth. She served her husband and nation graciously, and her subjects grew to love her quiet dignity. During the last months of the Perkin Warbeck episode, she gave birth to another son, Edmund, duke of Somerset, born on February 21, 1499, at Greenwich Palace, news delivered to Ferdinand and Isabella by Don Pedro de Ayala:

> The Queen of England was delivered on Friday of a son, whose christening took place on the following Sunday. There had been much fear that the life of the Queen would be in danger, but the delivery, contrary to expectation, has been easy. The christening was very splendid, and the festivities such as though an heir to the Crown had been born.[50]

What provoked "fear" at the impending birth is unknown, but those fears foreshadowed the tragedy to befall the newborn child just sixteen months later—and his mother four years hence.

Queen Elizabeth recovered from this birth quickly and soon immersed herself in the busy life of a working queen consort. After the execution of Perkin Warbeck, Henry was free of challenges and turned his attention to foreign policy. The king of England planned a trip to Calais to meet with Philip, archduke of Burgundy. When Henry sailed, Queen Elizabeth was at his side.

CHAPTER 13

THE PERSON BEHIND THE PERSONA

Getting to know the person behind the public persona of Elizabeth of York is difficult. Public documents describe her appearance and interpret her actions and emotions through the eyes of observers—many of whom see what they want to see, tell others what they want them to hear, and project onto the queen their own experiences and feelings. The Spanish ambassador De Puebla, for instance, observed Elizabeth closely during the decade he was negotiating the marriage of Arthur and Katherine of Aragon. As an advocate for the marriage, De Puebla's letters to Spain impressed upon his monarchs the splendor of Elizabeth's court, especially the ladies who attended her. When he visited the queen at "an unexpected hour" in July 1488, he found Elizabeth

> with two and twenty companions of angelical appearance, and all we saw there seemed very magnificent, and in splendid style, as was suitable for the occasion.[1]

Ten years later on a Sunday morning in July 1498, he described court ritual:

> The King and Queen heard mass in the chapel and walked in the procession. The ladies of the Queen went in good order and were much adorned.[2]

The Venetian ambassador, Andrea Trevisano, adds another portrait in his September 1497 letter to the Doge when visiting the king at his palace of Woodstock. After being received by King

Henry and Prince Arthur, age 12, the ambassador found the queen at the end of a hall:

> ... dressed in cloth of gold; on one side of her was the King's mother, on the other her son the Prince. The Queen is a handsome woman. [The ambassador] presented his credentials and said a few words in Italian; the Queen answered him through the Bishop of London.[3]

The interactions between Elizabeth and Henry bespeak a mutual affection and respect, with the king deferring to Elizabeth's wishes at times. A letter from Pope Alexander to the king's mother, for instance, states that Henry had promised the queen to appoint her candidate as the next bishop of Worcester (a deference to the queen's wishes that Malcolm Underwood, a modern historian, finds "something of a surprise").[4] Further evidence of Henry's affection for Elizabeth can be teased out of extracts recorded from his Privy Purse expenditures between 1491 and 1505.[5] Contrary to Francis Bacon's claim that Henry "showed himself no very indulgent husband towards [Elizabeth] though she was beautiful, gentle, and fruitful,"[6] the king's Privy Purse accounts reveal a generous, thoughtful, and fun-loving husband and father. If Elizabeth's own dower never sufficiently covered her expenses and never ensured financial independence, Henry and she shared a somewhat muddled system where Henry paid some of her bills and they lent each other money, an arrangement that may not have pleased more independently minded queens, but one that worked for them. Certainly, Henry VII spent freely—lavishly, even—on pleasures that he, the queen, and the royal children loved.

Prince Arthur grew up separately in his own household, while the other royal children lived together at Eltham Palace, near Greenwich. Eltham had been a favored palace of Edward IV and Elizabeth Wydeville—large and luxurious with its Great Hall facing a spacious courtyard. Private royal lodgings separated from the public areas incorporated Burgundian architectural features: brick facades, five-sided bay windows, and a pleasure gallery with spectacular views of the Thames valley.[7] Erasmus described Eltham during his first visit to England in 1499. On a country stroll with Thomas More, the two men encountered the royal children, who were in the Hall surrounded by their attendants:

> In the midst stood prince Henry, then nine years old, and having already something of royalty in his demeanor, in which there was a certain dignity combined with singular courtesy. On his right was Margaret, about eleven years of age, afterwards married to James, king of Scots; and on his left played Mary, a child of four. Edmund was an infant in arms.[8]

Thomas More presented a piece of writing to Prince Henry, embarrassing Erasmus who was unprepared to do the same. During dinner, the prince sent Erasmus a note requesting "something from [the] pen" of Erasmus, who spent the next three days composing a poem for the precocious nine year old.

The children's education included music, which surrounded the king and queen wherever they went. Their minstrels included players of bagpipes, organs, pipes, tabors, trumpets, sackbuts, fiddles, harps, recorders, and horns. So, too, tumblers, jugglers, leapers, wrestlers, dancers, players, and disguisers entertained frequently. In one instance, the king paid an extravagant £12 "to a little maiden that daunceth" and another astonishing £30 to "the young damsel that daunceth."[9] Such amounts are extraordinary for the era, especially when compared to the £2 12*s* his barber earned for three entire months of work from March 25 to June 25, the £10 given to John Cabot for discovering the new world, or the £100 to Robert Vertue for building one of the towers at the Tower of London.[10] Henry frequently paid the minstrels of others—the queen's, the queen of France's, "my lord of York's" (son Henry), the duchess of York's, the duke of Suffolk's, "the minstrels of Northampton."[11] He bought lutes for his daughters Margaret and Mary[12] and paid 13*s.* 4*d.* for tuning his clavichord.[13]

Vocal music filled Sundays and feast days with devotional singing, while secular celebrations resounded with lyrics of courtly love. *The Fayrfax Book*, which Roger Bowers suggests might have been prepared for Prince Arthur,[14] contains a broad range of lyrics to be sung by unaccompanied voices. Probably compiled by Dr. Robert Fayrfax, organist at St. Albans and gentleman of the Chapel Royal, the 49 surviving songs focus on themes of courtly love, devotional introspection, and satirical treatments of "rustic simplicity."[15] One song, in particular, pays tribute to a queen who finds the white rose to be "most true," a likely reference to Elizabeth of York:

> In a glorious garden green
> Saw I sitting a comely queen
> Among the flowers that fresh been.
> She gathered a flower and sat between;
>> The lily-white rose methought I saw,
>> The lily-white rose methought I sawe,
>>> And ever she sang.
>
> In that garden be flowers of hue:
> The gillyflower gent, that she well knew;
> The fleur-de-lis she did on rue,
> And said, "the white rose is most true
>> This garden to rule by righteous law."
>> The lily-white rose methought I saw
>>> And ever she sang.[16]

The gillyflower "that she well knew" was the device of Elizabeth's mother, Elizabeth Wydeville,[17] and the fleur-de-lis "she did on rue" resonates with memories of being jilted by the dauphin of France. The gentlemen and children of the Chapel Royal sang these songs at secular occasions, including the Twelfth Night drinking of the wassail.[18]

Every summer solstice, Henry sponsored a bonfire around which the Court reveled away Midsummer night, a particularly merry occasion with celebrants dancing through the few hours of darkness to the light of the fires. Bold young men leapt over the bonfires—sometimes receiving a scorched bottom for their courage. Frequently, a man wearing an ass's head added to the frivolity, a motif picked up by Shakespeare's Bottom in *A Midsummer Night's Dream*. During the winter solstice, Henry paid a "lord of misrule," apparently enacted by Abbot Ringley, to entertain far into that long night.[19] Christmas, New Year, and Twelfth Night featured lavish entertainments with performers generously rewarded by John Heron, treasurer of the king's chamber. His Privy Purse expenditures flatly refute Henry Tudor's reputation as a cheerless, stingy, saturnine personality.[20]

The king's fools included "Patch," "Dego the Spaniard," "the Duke of Lancaster," "Scot," "Thomas Blakall," and "Dick" (who was frequently reimbursed for clothing). The fact that Henry

Tudor employed a fool named "the Duke of Lancaster" indicates a sense of humor tolerant of spoofs that may have hit close to home. A "Master Knyvett" and fools of the king and queen of France added to the fun. Both Henry and Elizabeth loved games, with the king frequently losing money at cards, dice, butts, backgammon, and chess. In 1494, tennis cost him 27s 8d, along with £4 paid to a "Spaynyard, the tennis player."[21]

Jewels were Henry's passion: he spent £350 on "household jewels"; £3,800 on cloth-of-gold, precious stones, and pearls to garnish his sallets (visored helmets); £100 for a gold ring; £100 for an "ouche [brooch] set with pearls and stone"; £2,560 for "diverse jewels bought from the Lombards"; £2,000 for jewels of gold; £2,648 9s for "jewels bought in France"; £667 2s 11d for setting and polishing stones; £14,000 for jewels celebrating the marriage of Arthur. Between 1492 and 1507, Henry spent more than £110,000 on jewels and precious stones.[22]

Luxury items provided personal pleasure and enhanced the status of both king and queen, whose regal appearance was meticulously scrutinized by ambassadors, nobles, courtiers, merchants, citizens, and commoners, alike. Magnificent splendor accentuated the majesty of the monarch—and justified exotic purchases such as the king's stomacher made from ostrich skin (purchased for £1 4s in 1494)[23] and a leopard (presumably for the Tower zoo) for which Henry paid £13 6s 8d in 1503.[24]

Presents to Queen Elizabeth—frequent and thoughtful—show affection, indeed love. They range from a small gift of gold wire that cost £2 6s 8d to the payment of her debt of £1,314 11s 6d in 1493.[25] At various times, Henry gave Elizabeth a communion cloth and frontelets, bought plate for her household, lent her £100, exchanged cash (£66 13s 4d) for gold, gave her £27, traded money for jewels, repaid her £10 for garnishing his sallet, gave her £6 13s 4d, and reimbursed her for gowns, furs, and disguisings.[26] Henry paid Elizabeth's physician Master Lewis in 1494 and her surgeon Robert Taylor in 1498.[27] When the queen needed serious money, the king lent it secured by her plate: £2,000 in 1497 and £500 in 1502.[28] Since the queen's Privy Purse records have survived for only the year 1502–3, we do not know whether she repaid the loans. We know only that two years after the queen's death, Henry paid Will Halybrand £120 on May 2, 1505, for "pledging out of certain plate of the Queen's."[29]

The character of the man with whom Elizabeth shared her life is illuminated by his support for scholars at Oxford, gifts to the poor (including "a little fellow of Shaftesbury," "a woman that was with child," a madman in Bedlam, and several children given to the king).[30] Subjects who brought gifts received rewards for simple, everyday offerings—cherries, carps, peascods, a red rose, and even two glasses of water (whose donor received 5s).[31] The "poor man that had his corn eaten with the King's deer" received 3s 4d, "one that was hurt with a chariot" 6s 8d, and "the Jewess towards her marriage" £2.[32]

Henry and Elizabeth shared a love for books. The king not only bought books, but also paid poets, limners (illuminators), binders, balladeers, and rhymers from Scotland and Wales. Even "my Lord Prince" had his own poet whom the king rewarded with £3 6s 8d in 1498. Frequent rewards went to the court poet/historian Bernard André. The education of Prince Arthur and Prince Henry, whose tutor was the poet laureate John Skelton, reveal a father determined to raise knowledgeable, well-rounded sons.

Elizabeth's signatures in manuscripts and incunabula provide rare insights into her interests. Many of the books associated with her are religious, especially "Books of Hours" (devotional collections of prayers and psalms recited during specified hours on days of the ecclesiastical year). Their pages, generally illuminated with paintings of saints and other religious subjects, inspired spiritual contemplation and prayer. A manuscript in the British Library, written and illuminated in England *circa* 1415–20 and known as "The Hours of Elizabeth the Queen" contains her signature at the bottom of folio 22.[33] Signing a manuscript in mid-text is unusual, but folio 22 presents an exquisite miniature of the Crucifixion. Below Christ is the Virgin Mary, supported by four mourning women. To Christ's left, a patriarch unfurls a banner that reads, "This was the son of God." Three armed soldiers stand to the Patriarch's left. Beneath the page's ornate border is the inscription "Elysabeth ye queen," perhaps an expression of private devotion and especial compassion for Christ's sacrifice.

An "Offices of the Virgin" owned by Stonyhurst College contains the signature "Elysabeth Plantaegenet" on folio 198v with "the qwene" added below in darker ink by another hand.[34] The "Plantaegenet" surname suggests Elizabeth's ownership of this volume during Richard III's reign when Parliament had declared her a "bastard" and she adopted the family surname (compare "Elisabet Plantageneta" in the papal dispensation issued on April 6, 1484, for her marriage to Henry Tudor).[35] The signature itself provides tantalizing clues: "Elysabeth" is written by a practiced hand, while "Plantaegenet" sprawls across the page as if its author was laboriously inscribing an unfamiliar word. The first two syllables spread out until the right margin forces "-genet" into the cramped space remaining. The physical signature may reflect the psychological uncertainty of a writer trying to master her new identity.

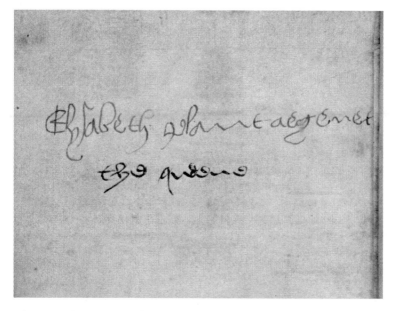

Photo 7 Autograph of "Elysabeth Plantaegenet" with "the queene" written below by another hand and in darker ink. The letters of "Elysabeth," practiced and sure, contrast with those of "Plantaegenet," which sprawl across the page as if they were meticulously formed by an unpracticed hand. Perhaps this signature was written between 1483 and 1485 when Parliament declared the children of Edward IV "bastards," and Elizabeth adopted the surname of illegitimate royal children. When young, Elizabeth usually added "the king's daughter" to her Christian name. As queen, she generally wrote "ye queen" after her signature. "Offices of the Virgin," MS 37, fol. 198v. By permission of the Governors of Stonyhurst College.

A later inscription in a translation of the *Scala perfectionis* by Walter Hylton, printed by Wynkyn de Worde in 1494, reveals a surer hand. This devotional guide to "perfection" belonged to Mary Roos, one of the Queen's ladies to whom Elizabeth wrote:

> I pray you pray for me
> Elysabeth ye quene

The king's mother wrote below:

> Mastres Rosse y [I] truste yn your prayers
> the whyche y pray yow y may be partener
> of. Margaret R the kynges
> modyr[36]

Presentation copies of religious texts were popular in the fifteenth century. A *Book of Hours* with the signatures of Henry and Elizabeth apparently belonged to another lady of the court. Written in the king's hand is the inscription, "Madame I pray you Remembre me your lovyng maister, Henry R." Elizabeth's inscription follows: "Madam I pray you forget not me to pray to God that I may have part of your prayers, Elysabeth ye Queene."[37] Elizabeth cosponsored an English version of the *Fifteen Oes* printed by Caxton in 1491 "by commandments of" Margaret Beaufort and Elizabeth of York. During the late fifteenth century, these prayers to Christ were attributed to St. Bridget of Sweden as prayers offered before the Holy Cross at St. Paul's in Rome.[38] Although St. Bridget's authorship has subsequently been discredited, that contemporary belief may have especially appealed to Queen Elizabeth because of her mother's devotion to St. Bridget, founder of the Order of the Most Holy Savior (the Bridgettines). Elizabeth of York's youngest sister Bridget was named in commemoration of this saint.

Incomplete records limit our knowledge of Elizabeth's larger library. A slip of paper in British Library manuscript Cotton. Vesp. F. xiii. f.. 49, contains the inscription:

> thys boke ys myn
> Elysabeth the kyngys dawghtyr

The slip has become separated from the book it designated, but as with her signature in the *Testament de Amyra Sultan Nichhemedy,*

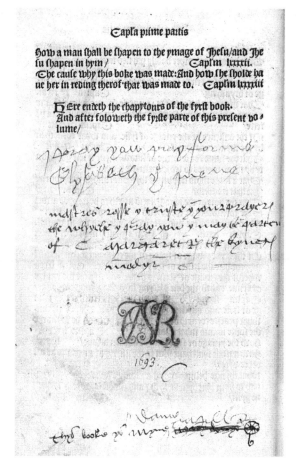

Capla prime partis

How a man shall be shapen to the ymage of Jhesu/and Jhe
su shapen in hym /   Capitn lxxxii.
The cause why this boke was made: And how she sholde ha
ue her in redyng therof that was made to.   Capitn lxxxiii

Here endeth the chapytours of the fyrst book.
And after foloweth the fyrste parte of this present vo
lume/

I pray you pray for me
Elysabeth y̓ quene

Mastres Rosse y [I] truste yn your prayers
the whyche y pray yow y may be partener
of. Margaret R the kynges
modyr

1693.

Photo 8   The Royal Inscriptions of Queen Elizabeth and
           Margaret Beaufort, Countess of Richmond in a copy of
           Walter Hylton's *Scala perfectionis*, a devotional guide to
           "perfection" presented to Mary Roos, one of the
           Queen's ladies:
                   "I pray you pray for me
                   Elysabeth yᵉ quene"
                   "Mastres Rosse y [I] truste yn your prayers
                   the whyche y pray yow y may be partener
                   of. Margaret R the kynges
                   modyr"
           Walter Hylton, *Scala perfectionis* (Westminster:
           Wynkyn de Worde, 1494), leaf A4 verso. Courtesy of
           the Yale Center for British Art, Paul Mellon Collection.

Empereur des Turcs, it was written when her identity as daughter of Edward IV was paramount and before she became queen.

As queen, Elizabeth made several pilgrimages to the Holy House of Nazareth at Walsingham Priory in Norfolk, a shrine featuring a replica of the home where the Virgin received the Annunciation. Contemporaries believed that Mary miraculously appeared at Walsingham in 1051. Laynesmith surmises that Elizabeth's visit in 1495 was "perhaps in response to the recent deaths of her 4-year-old daughter Elizabeth and a son born prematurely."[39] Queen Elizabeth shared her mother's special reverence for the Virgin Mary, their patron saint Elizabeth, and the Feast of the Visitation. In 1492, the queen petitioned the Pope for a special pardon for the Feast of the Annunciation that granted 300 days of pardon to those who recited "the whole salutation of our Lady, *Ave, Maria gratia*" three times after the tolling of each Angelus Bell (at 6:00 a.m., 12:00 noon, and 6:00 p.m.).[40]

The Carthusian charterhouse of Jesus of Bethlehem received regular gifts from Elizabeth of York. Founded at Sheen by Henry V to expiate his father's sin of executing Archbishop Richard Scroope of York, both Queen Elizabeth and her mother Elizabeth Wydeville venerated its strict, ascetic monks who devoted their lives to secluded and scholarly study. The Carthusians frequently wore hair shirts under coarse undyed clothing, ate scanty diets with no meat, lived solitary in cells except for communal worship, and observed vows of silence unless prayers and other devout services required speech. From June 24, 1497, to December 25, 1498, the procurator of the charterhouse at Sheen, Dan Philip Underwood, recorded contributions from the royal family, including alms received from

> the king at Killingworth by the hands of William Tomson £6 13*s* 4*d*; the lady Queen there by the hands of the same William £5, besides smaller contributions at other times; the lady the king's mother at Shene 10*s*."[41]

The queen gave £6 3*s* 4*d* for celebrating the Mass for the year, with another £6 13*s* 4*d* as "alms and rewards for various causes and considerations."[42] A later contribution of £10 provided "for celebration of mass again for a year and a half...also for the horses (*equitatura*) for the lord Duke of York and his sister at divers times."[43] Another £20 funded repairs to the manors and new

buildings for the monastery. Proximity to the royal residence at
Sheen gave the Carthusians unique access to the royal family, but
Elizabeth's frequent contributions signify a special reverence for
their spirituality.

A secular perspective derives from the Spanish ambassadors
who spent much time with the English Court and sent frequent (if
not wholly reliable) descriptions of the queen to Ferdinand and
Isabella. In recording what they observed, the ambassadors added
their interpretations of the royal interpersonal dynamics. On
July 25, 1498, Don Pedro de Ayala informed Ferdinand and Isabella
that the queen is

> beloved because she is powerless. They [the people] love the Prince
> [Arthur] as much as themselves, because he is the grandchild of his
> grandfather [Edward IV]. Those who know him love him also for
> his own virtues. . . . The King is much influenced by his mother and
> his followers in affairs of personal interest and in others. The
> Queen, as is generally the case, does not like it.[44]

Yet Elizabeth was no doormat. Just 10 days earlier, De Puebla
reported a four-hour conversation with the king at which the
queen and his mother were present. During the meeting, De
Puebla gave Queen Elizabeth two letters from Ferdinand and
Isabella and two letters from Princess Katherine:

> The King had a dispute with the Queen because he wanted to have
> one of the said letters to carry continually about him, but the
> Queen did not like to part with hers, having sent the other to the
> Prince of Wales.[45]

The Spanish diplomat does not report the resolution of this royal
tiff.

De Puebla's reports to Ferdinand and Isabella were always com-
plimentary of Elizabeth. On August 25, 1498, he wrote that he

> had given their letter, and the letter of the Princess of Wales
> [Katherine of Aragon], to the Queen of England, and explained
> them. She was overjoyed. "The Queen is the most distinguished
> and the most noble lady in the whole of England." She sent for the
> Latin Secretary, and ordered him to write, in her presence, two
> letters, one of them to the Queen of Spain, and the other to the
> Princess of Wales. The Latin Secretary told him afterwards that

he was obliged to write the said letters three or four times, because the Queen had always found some defects in them. "They are not things of great importance in themselves, but they show great and cordial love."[46]

De Puebla hoped that the Prince of Wales would also write, but Arthur was on progress in his principality.

To reward De Puebla for his good service, Henry wrote to Ferdinand and Isabella on February 3, 1498, offering their ambassador a preferment in a cathedral church. When De Puebla declined, he was next offered "an honorable marriage," which he most decidedly did not welcome.[47] Such kindness and determination on the part of his English hosts taxed the ambassador's diplomatic skills to their limit. After many excuses, De Puebla was "at last...persuaded, principally by the Queen, to accept the marriage, but under the express condition that his King and Queen must first give him their consent."[48] With consummate diplomacy, Ferdinand and Isabella simply did not respond, and on June 16, 1500, De Puebla thanked them for not answering Henry's letter "respecting their consent to the marriage which the Queen of England had offered to him."[49] The ambassador warned them, however, that the king would write again on the same subject and begged them to put off the answer again. De Puebla claimed that he wished to reject the match because it might diminish the confidence of his Spanish monarchs in him "if he were married by the Queen of England to a rich English lady." Thus the Spanish ambassador thwarted the determined benevolence of Elizabeth of York.

During the marriage negotiations for Arthur and Katherine, Queen Elizabeth wrote to Queen Isabella (one of her few extant letters that have survived):

> To the most serene and potent princess the Lady Elizabeth [Isabella], by God's grace queen of Castile, Leon, Aragon, Sicily, Granada, &c., our cousin and dearest relation, Elizabeth, by the same grace queen of England and France, and lady of Ireland, wishes health and the most prosperous increase of her desires.
>
> Although we before entertained singular love and regard to your highness above all other queens in the world, as well for the consanguinity and necessary intercourse which mutually take place between us, as also for the eminent dignity and virtue by which

your said majesty so shines and excels that your most celebrated name is noised abroad and diffused every where; yet much more has this our love increased and accumulated by the accession of the most noble affinity which has recently been celebrated between the most illustrious Lord Arthur prince of Wales, our eldest son, and the most illustrious princess the Lady Katherine, the infanta, your daughter. Hence it is that, amongst our other cares and cogitations, first and foremost we wish and desire from our heart that we may often and speedily hear of the health and safety of your serenity, and of the health and safety of the aforesaid most illustrious Lady Katherine, whom we think of and esteem as our own daughter, than which nothing can be more grateful and acceptable to us. Therefore we request your serenity to certify of your estate, and of that of the aforesaid most illustrious Lady Katherine our common daughter. And if there be any thing in our power which would be grateful or pleasant to your majesty, use us and ours as freely as you would your own; for, with most willing mind, we offer all that we have to you, and wish to have all in common with you. We should have written you the news of our state, and of that of this kingdom, but the most serene lord the king, our husband, will have written at length of these things to your majesties. For the rest may your majesty fare most happily according to your wishes. From our palace of Westminster, 3d day of December 1497.

Elizabeth R.

[Addressed] To the most serene and potent princess the Lady Elizabeth, by God's grace queen of Castile, Leon, Aragon, Sicily, Granada, &c., our cousin and dearest kinswoman.[50]

Even the diplomatic formality and flattery cannot mask the sincerity of Elizabeth of York, who received "our common daughter" warmly after her arrival in England.

Both Queen Elizabeth and the king's mother took an active interest in preparing Princess Katherine for life in England. When Princess Margaret of Austria (sister of Archduke Philip) visited the Spanish court, De Puebla sent Ferdinand and Isabella the following request in July 1498:

The Queen and the mother of the King wish that the Princess of Wales [Katherine] should always speak French with the Princess Margaret, who is now in Spain, in order to learn the language, and to be able to converse in it when she comes to England. This is necessary, because these ladies do not understand Latin, and much less, Spanish. They also wish that the Princess of Wales should accustom herself to drink wine. The water of England is not drinkable, and even if it were, the climate would not allow the drinking of it.[51]

Three years later the queen commends Katherine's progress:

> The King, the Queen, and the Prince of Wales... have great pleasure in hearing that the Princess Katherine is beginning to speak French. The Queen, especially, rejoices at the progress the Princess is making in the French language.[52]

Beyond her interactions with the Spanish ambassadors, very little is known about Elizabeth's political and diplomatic role. Only two letters survive regarding her efforts to intercede for the benefit of others. On August 1, 1499, she wrote to King Ferdinand of Spain to recommend the services of "Henry Stile, who wishes to go and fight against the Infidels," adding her recommendation to that of King Henry, who had already written in the soldier's favor. The queen's letter included a personal observation about Stile: "Though he is a very short man, he has the reputation of being a valiant soldier."[53] Another letter to the Prior of Christ Church, Canterbury, asks permission to nominate one of her chaplains to the vacant living of the parish church of All Saints in Lombard Street, London.[54] After her death, a single record mentions an action relating to Thomas Whytyng and his wife Margaret, who received rent for the lordship of Havering at the Bower, "notwithstanding a fine and recovery made there in the court of Elizabeth late queen of England."[55] As Laynesmith points out in her seminal study of late medieval queens, Elizabeth of York's chambers often hosted important political events and her personal sociability contributed to Henry's success with foreign ambassadors and English nobility.[56] Scanty records, however, limit more precise knowledge of Elizabeth's political role.

Years of marriage and the birth of seven children caused the tall, slim features of the young Elizabeth to mature into a full face and rather portly body. The Portuguese ambassador Joham Farinha Dalmadaa describes Elizabeth in a letter written on May 8, 1501, to Emanuel, king of Portugal, when he was created Knight of the Garter:

> There are no more news to write to your highness, except that the queen was supposed to be with child; but her apothecary told me

that a Genoese physician affirmed that she was pregnant, yet it was not so; she has much *embonpoint* [plumpness] and large breasts.[57]

Henry did not seem to mind Elizabeth's maturing appearance and included her in activities where he could easily have acted alone. When the king arranged a major diplomatic visit to Calais to meet with Philip, archduke of Austria and duke of Burgundy, the queen accompanied him. Henry VII and Elizabeth sailed for Calais on May 8, 1500, arriving that night. Henry was accompanied by the duke of Buckingham, the bishops of Durham and of London, 13 nobles and 2 ambassadors of Spain. Each traveled with their servants—three for the ambassadors, two for the duke and the bishops, one for everyone else. The king's contingent was completed by his secretary, Dean of Chapel, almoner, 35 knights, 9 squires for the Body, 21 gentlemen ushers, 6 chaplains, 6 ushers of the chamber, 3 head officers of the household (assisted by 50 servants), 7 heralds of arms and pursuivants, 1 henchman, 1 sergeant porter, 4 clerks of the signet, 8 sergeants of arms, 15 yeoman, grooms and pages, 4 persons of the jewel house, 80 guards, 10 spears of Calais, plus trumpets, minstrels, and assorted servants and henchmen.[58] The queen had a similar contingent of attendants.

The meeting with archduke Philip took place outside the walls of Calais in St. Peter's Church, richly decorated with arrases and hangings, including an 11-piece tapestry of the "Destruction of Troy" bought by Henry from the Burgundian merchant Pasquel Grenier.[59] Much of the discussion at Calais focused on the proposed marriage of Arthur to Katherine of Aragon. Philip had recently married Joanna of Castile, the elder sister of Katherine, and the meetings provided an opportunity for a member of the Spanish royal family to assess personally the individuals with whom Katherine would spend the rest of her life. The discussions included Queen Elizabeth:

> On Tuesday in Whitsuntide the Archduke had an interview with the King of England at Calais. They met in a church in the fields. The Queen of England also went to see the Archduke. The King and the Archduke had a very long conversation, in which the Queen afterwards joined. The interview was very solemn, and attended with great splendor.[60]

While the king and the archduke were discussing foreign policy, Henry's heralds and knights consulted with their Burgundian counterparts about the festivities that had commemorated the marriage of Philip and Joanna.[61] In planning the wedding of Arthur and Katherine, Henry was determined to match—indeed, surpass—the magnificent ceremonies for Katherine's older sister. Here was an ideal opportunity for England's king to impress his Continental rivals with displays of Tudor dynasty and destiny.

The consultations at Calais resulted in a sharing of aesthetic traditions that produced unsuspected and momentous consequences. England imported themes and theatrical innovations from Burgundy that influenced and enriched the literature of its sixteenth century. The evolution would require another two generations, but the seeds were gathered in Calais and planted in London in 1501.

The resounding success of the Calais expedition caused De Puebla to write Ferdinand and Isabella:

> The internal peace of the kingdom [England] is perfect. It is so great that the King and Queen left England, on Friday the 8th of May, for Calais, and until two days beforehand no one knew of their intended journey. The King and Queen have already stayed thirty-nine days at Calais. It is said that they will return tomorrow to England.[62]

The long-delayed marriage of Arthur and Katherine could proceed.

His trip a triumph, Henry and his Court set sail and arrived at Dover on June 16.[63] The journey from Greenwich to Calais and return lasted nine weeks and cost £1589 12s 10d.[64] Unfortunately, the euphoria was short lived. Just three days after King Henry and Queen Elizabeth landed at Dover, their third son Edmund died at the bishop's "Old Palace" in Hatfield on June 19, 1500. At age 16 months, the child may have succumbed to the plague epidemic in England at the time. The prince received a royal burial with his body transported through Fleet Street, where the mayor and members of all the crafts stood to pay their respects. Prince Edmund was buried next to the shrine of St. Edward in Westminster Abbey on Monday, June 22. The cost of the little boy's burial, exclusive of expenses to the abbot and convent of Westminster, amounted to £242 11s 8d.[65]

Another son named Edward is also buried at Westminster Abbey, having lived so short a time that his dates of birth and death are unknown. Life had taught Queen Elizabeth to bear such tragedies bravely. Perhaps she found consolation in preparing for the wedding of her eldest son, Arthur. Plans were already underway for the arrival of Katherine of Aragon in England and the marriage of England's first-born Tudor heir to the Spanish princess. The occasion would be the most lavish and splendid the country had ever experienced.

CHAPTER 14

A PRINCESS ARRIVES IN ENGLAND

D uring the latter half of 1501, all of England reveled in the marriage of Prince Arthur to Katherine of Aragon. Queen Elizabeth's role in this essentially political event added an important personal touch to the diplomatic formalities that welcomed the Spanish princess, hosted foreign dignitaries, and entertained visitors and subjects with weeks of festivities. The marriage of England and Spain offered unprecedented opportunities for spectacle and pageantry, to which the court and the city of London responded with verve.

The civic authorities taxed themselves a fifteenth-and-a-half to pay for pageants that welcomed the princess to London.[1] Richard Pynson's pamphlet *The traduction & marriage of the Princess*, published perhaps as early as June 1500, publicized the plans of the Privy Council. Men of substance throughout the nation were commanded to attend the princess: 18 months before Katherine landed at Plymouth, Sir John Paston received a letter from King Henry ordering him to prepare for her arrival:

> and so to continue in readiness upon an hour's warning, til that by our other letters we shall advertise you of the day and time of her arrival, and where you shall give your said attendance; and not to fail therein, as you tender our pleasure, the honor of yourself, and this our foresaid Realm.[2]

London had always greeted its queen consorts upon entering the city—the processions of Elizabeth Wydeville and Elizabeth of York were just two recent examples—but the welcome for Katherine of Aragon set a new standard. Henry VII himself spent lavishly—extravagantly—on wedding tournaments, disguisings, banquets, and gifts to his guests. Political symbolism and theatrical gadgetry turned traditional pageants into allegorical drama that exceeded anything the nation had previously known. In displaying his magnificence to the world, Henry was bent on creating Tudor mythology.

From the beginning, Elizabeth of York participated in planning the celebrations. Privy Council orders in 1500 specified that when Katherine entered London on a "rich litter," the Master of the Queen's horses would provide three henchmen in side-saddles and harness "all of one suit" to follow her.[3] A "palfrey with a pillion richly arrayed" for the princess, plus another 19 palfreys "all of one suit" for her lady attendants, would follow next in the procession. Five chariots, one "richly apparelled and garnished" for the princess and four for ladies appointed by the queen's chamberlain, added more magnificence. Between each chariot, five or six palfreys would parade, ridden by ladies selected and assigned their hierarchical order by the queen's chamberlain.

Contemporary documents confirm the interest of the general populace in this historic occasion. Separate accounts appear in the *Great Chronicle* of London, in the *Vitellius A XVI* manuscript (another London civic chronicle), and in *The Receyt of Ladie Kateryne* (the most complete record, likely compiled by a court scribe). Their specificity and detail provide rare insights into the elegance and manners that defined Elizabeth of York's adult life.

The marriage had been in process since negotiations began in March 1488 when Arthur was 18 months old. A treaty of marriage in October 1496 was followed in August 1497 by a formal betrothal at Woodstock, the royal residence near today's Blenheim. Arthur, almost 11 years old, represented himself while the Spanish ambassador De Puebla stood as proxy for Katherine, who was 9 months older than her husband. For the careful, meticulous Henry VII, however, betrothal was insufficient. He took every precaution to assure that this union was legally unassailable—absolutely binding—from betrothal through physical consummation. Papal dispensations and multiple ceremonies rigorously enacted the bond. Thus, on Whitsunday, May 19, 1499, after Katherine reached the marriageable age of 12, another "indissoluble marriage" was sworn at Bewdley in Worcestershire (where King Henry had built Tickenhill Palace for Arthur). Again, De Puebla stood as proxy for Katherine.[4] Those marriage vows were repeated in 1501 after Arthur turned 14. Katherine's journey to England was delayed, however, until Ferdinand and Isabella were satisfied with Katherine's dower and the stability of the English crown.

The sea passage of Princess Katherine, who left La Coruña in Galicia on August 17, 1501, was fraught with peril.[5] Storms tore her ships' masts out of their sockets, destroyed tackling, and forced her fleet to return to Spain for a month's worth of repairs.[6] Reembarking from Laredo on September 27, her ships set sail again and landed unexpectedly at Plymouth on October 2, 1501— far west of her anticipated arrival port of Southampton. The Privy Council scrambled to revise their best-laid plans and dispatched a reception committee to Devonshire. Sir Robert Willoughby, lord Broke and steward of the king's house, met Katherine's party at Plymouth to take charge of her large retinue and supply food, horses, carriages, and all necessities for the journey to London. The earl of Surrey and other lords provided a diplomatic escort. The duchess of Norfolk and a "goodly company of Countesses, Baroness, and many other honorable gentlewomen" attended the princess herself.[7]

Henry VII followed Katherine's carefully choreographed progress, but soon became impatient with proxy attendance and left Richmond on November 4 with his own retinue of dukes, earls, barons, knights, esquires, and gentlemen to greet the 15-year-old princess personally. The next day Prince Arthur joined the king's party at East Hampstead, where father and son spent the night together. On the following day, the Prothonotary of Spain arrived to inform Henry VII that King Ferdinand forbade any meeting or communication with "their Lady and Princess" until the day of her marriage. Henry immediately parleyed with his advisors, both spiritual and temporal, and declared the Spanish prohibition impossible since the princess was "so far entered into his empire and realm" that her "pleasure and commandment" now lay in the "grace and disposition of our noble King of England."[8]

Henry left no doubts about who was in charge. "Leaving the Prince [Arthur] behind upon the plain," the king rode on to greet Princess Katherine where she was lodged at the home of the bishop of Bath in Dogmersfield, Hampshire. Henry found the princess accompanied by an archbishop, a bishop, an "earl," and 60 other Spanish nobles, ladies, and gentlewomen, as well as the English entourage he had sent.[9] When informed by the archbishop and others that Katherine was "in her rest," Henry responded "that if she were in her bed, he would see and commune with her,

Photo 9   Katherine of Aragon (1485–1536). Juan de Flandes
          painted this portrait of the *Infanta* perhaps in the
          context of marriage negotiations that began in 1488 to
          wed her to Prince Arthur. Their marriage in 1501 ended
          with Arthur's death in 1502. Subsequently Katherine
          wed Arthur's younger brother Henry VIII in 1509,
          when he was age seventeen and she twenty-three.
          Sedgwick Collection, University of California, Santa
          Barbara, University Art Museum, 1960.7.

for that was the mind and the intent of his coming." The princess received the king in her "third chamber," where both parties expressed "great joy and gladness."

After changing from his riding garments, the king greeted Prince Arthur, who had just arrived. Arthur joined his father in a second meeting with Katherine, where the bishops interpreted the conversations through Latin. This meeting was significant, since deputies had contracted previous marriage agreements. Now, in the presence of each other, those contracts were "ensured."[10] After supper, the king and Arthur returned to Katherine's chamber to dance to the music of Spanish minstrels.

On November 7, Princess Katherine resumed her journey to London where she was met at Kingston-on-Thames by the duke of Buckingham with "3 or 4 hundred" attendants garbed in Buckingham's livery of black and red. Escorted to Lambeth, the princess lodged there until her formal entrance into London. The king returned to Richmond to inform Queen Elizabeth of "the acts and demeanor between himself, the Prince, and the Princess, and how he liked her person and behavior."[11] On November 10, 1501, Henry departed for Baynard's Castle, where he lodged until the wedding. "The Queen's Grace" followed on her own barge "with her goodly company of ladies."[12]

A year of anticipation now reached its climax. Stages were set, the actors ready, and the citizens agog with excitement. "Every Lord, both spiritual and temporal, was keeping their open households with right great royalty of fare and vitall [necessities]."[13] Anyone entitled to wear livery, badges, and cognizances openly displayed them. The king's Yeomen of the Guard were bedecked in "large jackets of damask white and green, goodly embroidered both on their breasts before and also on their backs behind with round garlands of vine branches beset before richly with spangles of silver and gilt, and in the middle a red rose beaten with goldsmith's work."[14] Three hundred yeomen with halberds lined the passages of the palace, forming two rows between which the king walked as he moved from chamber to chamber.

Henry's magnificent, romantic world of luxury, prodigality, and exuberance impressed both European guests and English subjects with his personal wealth and his nation's sophisticated vitality. Queen Elizabeth, nurtured from birth on stories of medieval romance, perfectly complemented this spectacle of Tudor symbolism. If their son Henry VIII is better known today for lavish excess and indulgent entertainment, the child learned his lessons at the knees of his father and mother, many of them taught during the marriage celebrations for his older brother Arthur.

The pageantry witnessed by the 15-year-old princess upon her entrance to London and during subsequent weeks of tournaments, disguisings, and feasts was flamboyant and transformative. The celebrations, designed to eclipse the wedding spectacles of Archduke Philip and Joanna of Castile, exceeded anything that England had previously experienced. Ideas gathered by English heralds from their Burgundian counterparts in Calais had inspired a new form of dramatic allegory.[15] The wedding pageants embodied coherent narrative plots with themes of religious, political, and philosophical import. Six coordinated pageants led Katherine to the throne of "Honor," where she joined England's next monarch in religious and cosmological triumph. The iconographic presentations aimed "to teach and to delight"—not merely England's new princess, but all visitors and subjects who observed them. Henry VII had always understood symbol better than anyone: he exploited symbol from the moment he planted his standard with Cadwalader's red dragon at St. Paul's. Now Tudor dramatists combined symbol, narrative, and stage machinery to create a new mythology.

Katherine of Aragon made her grand entrance into London on Friday, November 12, 1501, accompanied by her Spanish retinue and the entourage of lords assigned by Henry VII. The princess was escorted by the archbishop of York; Henry, duke of York (Arthur's 10-year-old brother and future Henry VIII); the duke of Buckingham, and countless nobles and attendants. Proceeding through Southwark, the procession stopped for the first pageant at the center of London Bridge where a tabernacle of two floors had been erected. On the lower floor stood Saint Katherine holding her signature wheel and surrounded by virgins. The second floor displayed Saint Ursula, an ancestor of the first King Arthur, also surrounded by virgins. Above both floors was a picture of the Trinity. On either side were smaller tabernacles displaying the Garter with the Lancastrian red rose in the middle and six angels on top perfuming with incense. Introducing the allegory that would unfold during the next six pageants, Saint Katherine welcomed Princess Katherine, advised her to love her first spouse Christ, and, similarly, to love and honor her second, earthly spouse,

Arthur. Saint Ursula welcomed Katherine as a second Ursula who would wed the second Arthur of England.[16]

The procession continued to Gracechurch Street, where another elaborate structure, the Castle of Portcullis, displayed the Tudor badge of a red rose with white middle, surmounted by a crown of gold. Above the first battlement was a great gate with folding leaves and bars of iron, above which was a huge portcullis topped by the king's shield displaying the arms of England supported by a "red dragon, dreadful" on the right and a white greyhound on the left (Henry's heraldic supporters). Here an allegorical character named "Policy" welcomed the princess as "the bright star of Spain, Hesperus" and introduced her to two characters essential in her new role: "Nobleness" and "Virtue." "Nobleness," a knight, commended the noble blood of Katherine and urged her to follow virtue as her guide. "Virtue" explained that virtue is essential to achieving nobleness and paid tribute to Katherine's illustrious ancestor Alfonso X, the Spanish king renowned for wisdom and astronomical knowledge.[17]

A third "pageant of the Moon" staged at the conduit in Cornhill was commended by the *Great Chronicle* as "far exceeding the others in cost and cunning of devise."[18] A wheel representing the 12 signs of the zodiac displayed the moon with its "increase and wane."[19] This enactment featured Raphael, the angel of marriage, who informed the princess that angels of God surpass philosophers in teaching knowledge to mankind:

> ...marriages, by God's providence
> [Are] made for love with virtue and reverence,
> For procreation of children, after God's precept,
> Not for sensual lust and appetite to be kept.[20]

Alfonso X, Katherine's ancestor, next pointed to Prince Arthur's astrological sign of Sagittarius and Katherine's star of Hesperus as fortuitous for their marriage. Job, the holy prophet, then urged Katherine to look above astronomy to "know and behold" the Almighty God who predestined their marriage and who would guide the couple to His cardinal virtue of "Temperance." Boethius, the philosopher, pronounced that astronomy and divinity linked Arthur and Katherine together by a golden chain, "in honor and dignity forever to reign."[21]

The procession moved on to the great conduit in Cheapside where "all the pipes of the conduit ran with good Gascon wine" allowing spectators to drink freely from "noon til night."[22] By the time the princess arrived in late afternoon, the good citizens of Cheapside quite happily welcomed her. This "Sphere of the Sun" pageant was framed by four corner posts—one post in front decorated with a red dragon and the other with a white hart wearing a crown of gold about his neck. The two posts in back featured a red lion rampant and a white greyhound. A great revolving wheel propelled by three armed knights perpetually climbing its inner circumference represented the sun. Above the wheel was the Father of Heaven flanked by two angels with trumpets and arms. In the middle of this sun image stood a prince, symbolizing Arthur and his sun-like regal power. Speeches urged the princess to rejoice in the union that would combine her to the "Prince of all Princes," the source of justice and virtue.[23]

At the fifth pageant staged at the Standard (the conduit) in Cheap, the princess found herself in front of the "Temple of God" decorated with a Lancastrian red rose as tall as a man and framed by a white greyhound and a red dragon. Images of wise prophets stood on posts at each of the four corners. Above, seven gold candlesticks with burning wax tapers surrounded a throne where sat "the Father of Heaven, being all formed of gold," surrounded by hierarchies of Angels singing.[24] From his throne, God spoke to the princess:

> ...my well-beloved daughter Katherine,
> Since I have made you to mine own semblance
> In my Church to be married, and your noble children
> To reign in this land as in their inheritance,
> See that ye have me in special remembrance.
> . . . .
> Blessed be the fruit of your belly.
> Your sustenance & fruits shall increase and multiply.[25]

The Prelate of the Church explained that the king on earth resembles the "King celestial" and that the earthly King Henry VII ordained this marriage between his first begotten son Arthur and Katherine, daughter of the king of Spain.

Henry VII watched this fifth pageant from the private home of William Geoffrey, haberdasher, in company with Prince Arthur, the earl of Oxford, the earl of Derby, the earl of Shrewsbury, the Lord Chamberlain, and several ambassadors from France.[26]

...in another chamber stood the Queen's Good Grace, my Lady
the King's Mother, my Lady Margaret, my Lady her sister [Mary],
with many other ladies of the land, not in very open sight, like as
the King's Grace did in his manner and party.[27]

The royal parties carefully observed not merely the pageant, but

> the persons, their raise, order, and behavings of the whole com-
> pany, both of England and of Spain, as well of their apparel and
> their horses as of their discreet and goodly order, points in features
> of their demeanour.[28]

The royals were as curious about their subjects and visitors as the
latter were about them. The herald who recorded the events of the
day perhaps spoke for all Londoners as he watched Katherine's
procession move toward them:

> And eftsoon they began to approach to the King's sight in the
> most goodly wise that ever was seen in England or in any other
> realm that of quick and recent memory may be known or
> understood.[29]

First the mayor appeared on horseback, dressed in crimson
satin with a collar of gold around his neck, followed by the ranks
of sheriffs and 24 aldermen in scarlet. Next came the heralds,
English nobles (some wearing ostrich feathers and bells) and
attendants, Spanish prelates and nobles. Trumpets, sackbuts, and
shawms sounded their approach:

> After them rode the Princess upon a great mule richly trapped
> after the manner of Spain, the Duke of York [Prince Henry] on
> her right hand and the Legate of Rome on her left hand. She was
> in rich apparel on her body after the manner of her country, and
> upon her head a little hat fashioned like a cardinal's hat of a pretty
> braid with a lace of gold at this hat to stay it, her hair hanging
> down about her shoulders, which is fair auburn, and in manner of
> a coif between her head and her hat of a carnation colour, and that
> was fastened from the middle of her head upwards so as men
> might well see all her hair from the middle part of her head
> downward.[30]

At this moment, Queen Elizabeth saw her daughter-in-law for the
first time.

Although Katherine followed the Spanish tradition of riding a mule, the plans of the queen and Privy Council were evident. Behind the princess rode three English maidens of Honor dressed in cloth-of-gold and mounted on horses led by footmen.[31] Next walked the "spare palfrey with a side saddle and a pillion of Estate after the English manner" led by the Master of the Queen's Horse, himself riding on a richly bedecked horse. Nineteen matched palfreys walked in single file, interspersed between each of five chariots.

At the entrance to St. Paul's courtyard, the procession stopped for the sixth pageant, "The Throne of Honor." This stage, framed by pillars decorated with lions, dragons, and greyhounds, had staircases of seven steps on either side. Each step displayed one of the seven Virtues (three theological—Faith, Hope, Charity—and four cardinal virtues—Justice, Temperance, Prudence, Fortitude). The main stage revealed three seats, the middle one occupied by "Honor" clad in purple. Two empty seats were prepared with cushions, scepters, and crowns of gold for Prince Arthur and Princess Katherine. "Honor" observed that while "folk of every degree" seek honor, most fail through lack of virtue. Honor pointed to the seven Virtues standing on the steps as the means through which Arthur and Katherine "shall reign here with us in prosperity forever." The didactic message is explicit: Arthur and Katherine will reign hand in hand with honor.

How much of the didactic message was absorbed by Princess Katherine—and other observers—is unknown. Excitement and crowds surrounded the 15-year old girl, who spoke little English and who was adjusting to a strange new role in an unknown country. At the entrance to St. Paul's churchyard, the mayor and city officials presented the princess with "much treasure and great plenty of plate of silver and gilt, as basins and pots filled with coin to a great sum" (traditionally 500 marks).[32] Led by the archbishop of Canterbury, the bishop of Durham, and the choir of St. Paul's to the shrine of St. Edward, the princess made an offering before exiting to the Bishop's Palace, her lodging just outside the west door of St. Paul's.

Mentally and physically, the demands were challenging. And two weeks of nonstop obligations and celebrations lay ahead! The next day was especially traumatic. On Saturday, November 13, Henry VII sitting in his "seat regal" and flanked by Prince Arthur on his right and Henry, duke of York, on his left received the representatives of the king of Spain, who certified in a public meeting that Princess Katherine was a virgin. This assurance was "published full wise and perfectly before the King's Highness" in the presence of his lords spiritual and temporal and the king's Council.[33]

Katherine met her mother-in-law for the first time on Saturday, November 13. Around three or four o'clock in the afternoon, the princess left Bishop's Palace with a "right great assembly" of English and Spanish gentlemen and ladies dressed in their best silk and gold. Conducted by the Master of the Queen's Horse, she arrived at Baynard's Castle where Queen Elizabeth received her "with pleasure and goodly communication." Dancing and "disportes" extended late into the evening, after which the princess returned to her lodgings by torchlight.

Her big day would dawn on the morrow.

CHAPTER 15

A ROYAL WEDDING

Henry VII and Queen Elizabeth observed the wedding of Prince Arthur to Katherine of Aragon on Sunday, November 14, 1501, from a latticed closet constructed high in the vault above the consistory of St. Paul's Cathedral. The night before, the king and queen had secretly moved to a private residence adjoining St. Paul's from which they entered the cathedral unseen. The huge interior was splendidly decorated: the altar displayed plate, jewels, and relics, and the choir walls were hung with rich arrases. A walkway covered with red cloth and elevated 6 feet above the ground extended 600 feet from the west door to a specially constructed stage that permitted guests to view the groom and bride from the moment they entered the Cathedral through the sacrament of marriage.

Around 9 or 10 in the morning, Prince Arthur left his lodgings at the King's Wardrobe to go to a secret chamber in the Bishop's Palace, where he changed into his white satin wedding suit. Princess Katherine, escorted by Henry, duke of York, and a Spanish "earl," entered the Cathedral followed by an entourage of English and Spanish attendants. Cecily, sister to Queen Elizabeth, carried the bride's train with 100 ladies and gentlewomen following.[1] Katherine wore a white coif and veil with an inch-and-a-half border of gold, pearls, and precious stones. Her white satin dress with large sleeves displayed a pleated skirt spread over large, rigid hoops. Trumpets, shawms, and sackbuts sounded from the moment the princess departed the Bishop's Palace until she reached the high altar. At the entrance to the choir, the prince and princess, walking hand in hand, turned to the south and to the north so that the "multitude of people might see and behold their persons."[2]

After the two-hour ceremony, Henry, duke of York, and the Spanish "earl" conducted the princess back to Bishop's Palace to

Photo 10   Arthur, Prince of Wales (1486–1502). Painted *circa* the
            time of his marriage to Katherine of Aragon in 1501,
            this portrait shows Arthur holding a white gillyflower,
            a device associated with the Virgin Mary and
            symbolizing purity, virtuous love, and marriage.
            Anglo-Flemish School. Photograph courtesy of Hever
            Castle, Kent. © Hever Castle Ltd.

prepare for the wedding feast. Outside the west door of St. Paul's, they stopped for a seventh pageant displaying a mountain covered with green herbs and rocks of precious stones. On top of the mountain grew three trees displaying heraldic shields in front of which stood images of the kings of France, England, and Spain, symbolizing the realms of which Katherine was now a part.

The political emblems reminded everyone that this was no ordinary wedding. The fully armed King of England standing on a ship in front of the central tree (decorated with red roses and "a red dragon dreadful" emerging at its top) dominated the kings of France and Spain. In marrying Arthur of England, Katherine of Aragon had joined the rich and powerful Tudor dynasty that would be preeminent in Europe. From the base of the fountain ran wine for the commoners to drink while contemplating their political good fortune. The wine ran throughout the marriage ceremony and into the night, providing sustenance from the largess of the king.[3]

The wedding feast continued until four or five o'clock in the afternoon, at which time King Henry directed the earl of Oxford to supervise preparation of the bedchamber for the newly wed couple. The duchess of Norfolk, the countess of Cabra (Katherine's Spanish *dueña*), the Lady Mistress to the prince, and the Lady Mistress to the princess carried out this crucially important task. No marriage was valid unless consummated, and Henry, careful from the first day of negotiations with Spain, rigorously supervised this final aspect of the marital contract. The duchess, countess, and lady mistresses took between two and three hours to prepare the chamber and bed of Estate, which was then examined and certified by the earl of Oxford: "first...the side that the Prince should lie and eftsoons...the side that the Princess also should rest."[4] The contemporary scribe describes what happened next:

> The Lord Prince [Arthur], and His Grace [Henry VII], and nobles after the goodly disports, dancings with pleasure, mirth, and solace before used, departed to his said arrayed chamber and bed, wherein the Princess before his coming was reverently laid and reposed. Then after the congruent usages and custom in marriage of persons of noble blood, their said bed and lodging was blessed with the effusion of certain orisons thereunto limyt [appointed] and appropriate by the bishops and prelates there present.[5]

This blessing of the nuptial bed, the chamber, and the newly married couple in bed was prescribed by the *Sarum Missal*.[6] The prelates and other visitors then left the bedchamber.

> And thus these worthy persons concluded and consummated the effect and complement of the sacrament of matrimony. The day thus with joy, mirth, and gladness deduced to its end.[7]

While all the rituals leading to consummation were rigorously conducted and meticulously recorded, the actual fact of physical union cannot be absolutely verified. The contemporary scribe believed that consummation occurred. Common sense and knowledge of human nature (especially that of two 15 year olds) would lead to the same conclusion. Henry VII's rigor in carrying out every letter of marital law would argue that he included a discussion with his son about the groom's responsibilities on his wedding night. But even the story of Arthur's braggadocio the next morning does not constitute proof:

> ... his familiar servitours, which had then neither cause nor reward to lie or feign, declared openly that in the morning he [Arthur] called for drink, which he before times was not accustomed to do. At which thing one of his chamberlains marveled, required the cause of his drought. To whom he answered merely saying, "I have this night been in the midst of Spain, which is a hot region, and that journey maketh me so dry, and if thou hadst been under that hot climate, thou wouldst have been dryer than I."[8]

Edward Hall reported this story in his *Chronicles*, written 47 years after the fact. Hall may have obtained his information from depositions taken in 1529 as Henry VIII began proceedings to divorce Katherine of Aragon. Sir Antony Willoughby, who had been in service to Prince Arthur, testified that he

> was present when prince Arthur went to bed on his marriage night in the palace of the Bishop of London. In the morning the Prince, in the presence of Mores St. John, Mr. Cromer, Mr. William Woddall, Mr. Griffith Rice, and others, said to him, "Willoughby, bring me a cup of ale, for I have been this night in the midst of Spain"; and afterward said openly, "Masters, it is good pastime to have a wife."[9]

From this eyewitness experience, Lord Willoughby "supposes that the marriage was consummated." Another eyewitness, whose name is missing from the deposition, corroborates this testimony with almost the same, exact words.[10]

If Arthur really told this tale, those who wish to deny consummation can argue that the 15 year old was merely showing off to his gentlemen attendants—indulging in a bit of locker room exaggeration about his sexual exploits. In 1528, Katharine flatly contradicted Arthur's claim in testimony recorded by the Papal Legate Campeggio:

> First, she affirmed on her conscience that from her marriage with Prince Arthur, on the 14th November, until his death on the 2nd of April, she had not slept in the same bed with him more than seven nights, *et che da lui resto intacta et incorrupta come vene dal ventro di sua madre* [and that from him I remain untouched and pure as she came from the belly of her mother].[11] [My thanks to Sebastian Cassarino for translating and clarifying that Campeggio quotes Katherine up to "incorrupta," then changes to the third person in describing her birth from the belly of her mother.]

In testifying for and against Henry VIII's divorce, Henry's witnesses and Queen Katherine were on opposite sides: Henry's nobles wished to prove consummation and Katherine her virginity.

The issue could not be more crucial. The validity of the subsequent marriage of Henry VIII to Katherine of Aragon—and the Reformation in England—hinged on whether Arthur and Katherine completed their marriage contract on their wedding night (or during any of the subsequent 139 nights the couple lived together as man and wife). Canon law prohibited the marriage of a man to his brother's widow as an incestuous union (although a persistent supplicant with proper connections and appropriate contributions could usually obtain a Papal dispensation). When Henry VIII married Katherine, everyone agreed that she was a virgin.

Some believe that Henry VII's delay after Arthur's death in creating Henry Prince of Wales indicates that the king was waiting to see if Katherine gave birth to a male who would inherit that title. But that delay of more than year may be attributed to the dreadful tragedies of 1502 and 1503, which consumed the king's energies and will. When Henry VII subsequently decided to marry Prince Henry to Katherine, he argued that consummation had never occurred. Legal depositions and common gossip about the physical union of Arthur and Katherine dominated the next century of English history. Speculation continues today.

Evidence that contemporaries believed the union was consummated may lie in the scribe's account of what happened on Monday. Attendants were given the day off. Visitors were banned to the princess, who "kept and observed her secret chamber sole with her ladies and gentlewomen."[12] Only the Great Chamberlain of England was allowed access, "sent from the King's Grace unto her with an especial token." The Chamberlain carried the message that his Highness "thought long unto the time that he might see her to his great joy and gladness." That same day, "my lady the king's mother" hosted the Spanish delegation at dinner in her residence of Coldharbour.

On Tuesday the king and queen attended a Solemn Mass at St. Paul's after which Princess Katherine joined the king for dinner.[13] That afternoon, all boarded their individual barges for the journey to Westminster, where 58 Knights of the Bath (an unusually large number) were dubbed to celebrate the grand occasion of the wedding. More than 40 barges "well decked and arrayed" transported the court, the mayor, aldermen, and craftsmen of London up river for another 2 weeks of banquets, disguisings, and pageants. The civic authorities attached such importance to the festivities that the mayor took action when he discovered the barge of the Mercers to be inadequately "garnished and appareled." The mayor, "grievously discontented," sent the Mercers' barge home and held a hearing the next day. When the Mercers failed to explain their deficiency, they were fined £10.[14]

During the next weeks, Queen Elizabeth graciously presided over the huge number of ladies and gentlewomen who attended the royal festivities. On Thursday, the wedding tournaments began on a newly graveled and sanded tilting field between Westminster Hall and the Palace—the field extending from the water gate to King's Street near Westminster Abbey. To the south of the lists, a special stage accommodated the king and the queen, which they entered through a tent connected directly to Westminster Hall. The king and his attendants sat on the right side of the stage, divided by a partition and decorated with hangings and cushions of gold. The queen and her ladies sat on the left.

After dinner, Queen Elizabeth entered the stage in company with "my lady the king's mother," Princess Katherine, the Lady Princesses Margaret and Mary, and "two or three hundred" other ladies and gentlewomen of honor.[15] The king then entered his side with Prince Arthur, the duke of York, English nobles, Spanish guests, and hundreds of attendants. Every space around the tilting field was crammed with spectators. The jousters entered the lists on elaborately decorated pageant cars, the challengers led by the duke of Buckingham (first cousin of the queen) and the defenders by the second marquess of Dorset (nephew of the queen). Both men carried on the great tournament traditions of their Wydeville relatives. Elizabeth of York felt right at home in the midst of the family-dominated "Jousts Royal" of 1501.

Friday featured disguisings and pageants in Westminster Hall, the mood set by a lavish display of the king's wealth: a cupboard extended across the breadth of the Chancery with seven shelves filled with gold plate, flagons, cups, bowls, and other gilt objects. *The Great Chronicle* valued two similar cupboards at the wedding banquet at £12,000 in the hall where the mayor dined and at £20,000 in the chamber next to where the princess dined.[16] Similar displays appeared at every celebratory venue to remind Henry's guests, both Spanish and English, of his magnificence. Flaunting his wealth was not merely a gesture of titillating ostentation: at the conclusion of the celebrations, the king gave away much of the plate to his parting guests.

For now, Henry VII entertained everyone with lavish dining and elaborate pageants. On Friday night, the king and queen took their seats in Westminster Hall beneath cloths of Estate to watch three pageants with their guests. Each pageant entered the hall on a great moveable car—and began two weeks of dramatically innovative court entertainments. Traditional English drama, strictly controlled by the Church, had featured biblical stories (with some added satire about Noah's wife or Mak, the thieving shepherd) and allegorical struggles of man as he sought salvation. On secular occasions, dancers and minstrels performed to satirical, humorous, and sometimes ribald songs. At Court, elaborately masked "disguisers" danced complicated patterns to the music of professional instrumentalists. The pageants of 1501 imported Burgundian motifs and techniques that used plot, symbol, scenery, dancing, and stage machinery to dramatize themes of romantic love. William Cornish, the gentleman of the Royal Chapel who had

sung at the Twelfth Night disguising in 1494, was the chief impre-
sario who created complex allegorical dramas depicting political,
humanistic, and romantic ideals.

The first pageant car to enter Westminster Hall on Friday
night, November 19, was drawn by chains of gold pulled by men
disguised as heraldic beasts (two lions, a hart, and an ibex). The
car bore a huge castle with eight "goodly and fresh ladies" looking
out the windows and children of the Royal Chapel dressed as
maidens singing from each of the castle's four towers. Once the
king, queen, and guests had marveled at this innovative tableau, a
second pageant car appeared, its wheels turned by some unseen
force. Constructed as a ship fully rigged with masts, sails, and
tackling, this pageant featured mariners and a lady dressed as a
princess of Spain. The ship cast anchor, and two individuals representing "Hope" and "Desire" descended to woo the eight ladies in
the castle for the "Knights of the Mount of Love." When the
ladies "utterly refused" their solicitations, Hope and Desire
warned that Knights from the Mount of Love would attack them.
Immediately, a third pageant car entered the hall bearing the
Mount of Love. "Eight goodly knights" emerged, and after being
informed by Hope and Desire that the ladies had disdained their
love, the knights did, indeed, assault the castle. Overcome by the
"power, grace, and will of those noble knights," the eight ladies
ultimately yielded to the forces of Love. All ended happily with
four couples dancing harmoniously together "after the English
fashion" and four "after the manner of Spain."

Prince Arthur next danced with his aunt Cecily, after which he
joined the king's party and Cecily the queen's. Princess Katherine
then danced with one of her ladies before joining the queen's party.
The action picked up speed when the 10-year-old Henry, duke of
York danced with his 12-year-old sister Margaret:

> He, perceiving himself to be encumbered with his clothes, sud-
> denly cast off his gown and danced in his jacket with the said Lady
> Margaret in so goodly and pleasant manner that it was to the King
> and Queen right great and singular pleasure, and so departed ayen,
> the Duke to the King and the Lady to the Queen.[17]

As the night drew to its end, 100 earls, barons, and knights entered
the hall bearing spice plates and cups, followed by yeomen of the
Guard with pots of wine to fill the cups. The scribe marveled that

even with the great number of plates and cups required to serve such a huge crowd, none of the gold and gilt on display in the massive cupboard had been touched.

Rain and bad weather brought relief on Saturday morning. The celebrants had a full day to recover before the next banquet on Sunday. Held in the Parliament Chamber, this banquet featured a raised stage for the cupboard of gold and gilt (*no* silver, recorded the scribe!) that extended in length from the closet door to the chimney. The king sat at a side table with Princess Katherine at his side. Queen Elizabeth sat at a table in the upper part of the Chamber, "the table of most reputation of all the tables in the Chamber."[18] Henry's deference to Elizabeth in permitting her to occupy "the table of most reputation"—sufficiently remarkable for the scribe to note it—was extraordinary in the rank-conscious English Court. With the queen was "my lady the king's mother," the bishop of Spain, and the queen's sisters Cecily and Katherine. Prince Arthur headed a third table with his sister Margaret, the duchess of Norfolk, and his brother Henry. A fourth table included ladies of Spain and England served by 30 barons and knights. Esquires held the torches. The banquet began at 7:00 p.m., lasted two hours, and included five "courses of flesh," each with seven dishes. Dessert featured five dishes of fruits, followed by wafers and hippocras. After two dances by an earl, the party adjourned to Westminster Hall for an interlude and disguisings.

This evening, the first of two pageant cars featured an arbor surrounding 12 lords, knights, and men of honor. The stage set was displayed to the king and queen for their admiration before the disguisers exited through a gate in the arbor to dance "a long space, divers and many dances."[19] Then trumpets sounded the entry of the second pageant car representing a "lantern," a palace-like structure with many windows illuminated from within. Twelve "goodly ladies" silhouetted against the windows emerged and "danced by themselves in right goodly manner divers and many dances a great space." Finally, the 12 lords and 12 ladies joined together in dance, symbolizing the harmonious union of man and woman: the lonely, separate isolation of Arthur and Katherine had ended in harmony, concord, and symmetry. This evening concluded with a void of spices and wine served by 60 or more earls, barons, and knights, after which the king, the queen, and their attendants departed at midnight.

Monday's tournament featured running, jousts, and the breaking of many spears. Tuesday was a day of relaxation with the nobility dining at home and preparing for the next two days of tilting and pageantry. On Wednesday, the tilts began with the breaking of spears between the duke of Buckingham and marquess of Dorset, followed by traditional sword fights. The third act, however, introduced a special feature into the lists. Dorset and his men entered on a pageant car displaying a ship with tackling and mariners (probably the vehicle featured at the banquet five days earlier). Gunshots announced the ship's arrival and continued as Dorset's knights engaged Buckingham's team with spears, resulting in "the strangest feat of arms and goodliest that hath been seen."[20] Special effects had arrived on the English tilt field! Sound and fury now accompanied the challenge of arms traditionally conducted in silence to avoid distracting the jousters.[21] This theatrical extravaganza eclipsed the simple hermitage on which Anthony, lord Rivers, entered the lists in 1478. The English tournament would never be the same. The stage was set for the elaborate spectacles that would be hosted by Henry VIII.

Thursday's tournament began, as usual, after the king, the queen, Prince Arthur, and Princess Katherine took their places on the stage. On this day, the marquess of Dorset and his men entered the field accompanied by a chariot pulled by heraldic beasts: a red lion, a white lion, a white hart, and an ibex (each formed by two men in disguise). The chariot delivered a "fair young lady" (symbolizing Katherine) to the king's stage, where she remained for the competitions. At tournament's end, the chariot returned to gather the lady and return her to the palace. That night the king, the queen, Prince Arthur, Princess Katherine, "my lady the king's mother," and hundreds of guests gathered in Westminster Hall for the disguisings.

The spectacles that night featured two mountains fastened together by a golden chain, the first adorned with trees, herbs, and fruits (representing England) and the second with ores of gold, silver, lead, crystal, sulphur, and amber spilling from its sides (representing the riches of Spain). On the first mountain sat twelve disguised lords and knights playing tabors, lutes, harps, and recorders. Twelve disguised ladies played clavichords and dulcimers on the second mountain. After the pageant cars traveled the length of Westminster Hall to stop before the king, the men descended and danced. Then the ladies descended and danced together with the lords. As the mountains departed, 80–100 earls, barons, and knights entered to serve the void of spices and wine. At this point, the king distributed gifts to the lords and knights who had jousted in the wedding tournaments: a "diamond of great virtue and price" to the duke of Buckingham, a ruby to the marquess of Dorset, precious stones and rings of gold to the other combatants.[22] All departed with "excellent mirth and gladness" to prepare for the next day's move to Richmond Palace for more of the same.

On Friday, as many barges as possible chained themselves to Westminster pier while others "rowing and skimming" in the Thames waited their turn to pick up their illustrious passengers. Separate barges for the king, the queen, Prince Arthur, Princess Katherine, the duke of York, "my lady the king's mother," the duke of Buckingham, the earl of Oxford, the mayor, the sheriffs, the aldermen, every craft, ad infinitum, created a wonderful chaotic scene as the wedding celebrants changed venue. Trumpets, clarions, shawms, tabors, and recorders sounded at the boarding of each barge rowing upstream to Richmond.

On the ashes of Sheen, Henry VII had built a magnificent palace whose brick walls incorporated features of the newly popular Burgundian style. The king named the palace Richmond in honor of his earldom inherited from his father, but his subjects appropriately interpreted the name as "Rich mount."[23] The spectacular edifice dazzled his guests—exactly the impact the king desired. *The Receyt* soberly describes "this earthly and second paradise of our region of England." Windows illuminated the galleries and the Great Hall with its statuary, tapestries, and "pictures of the noble kings of this realm in their harness and robes of gold." Portraits of Brute, Hengist, King William Rufus, King Arthur, King Henry, King Richard, and King Edward decorated the walls—all dominated by a splendid painting of Henry VII in the higher part of the hall.[24]

Richmond's chapel with its pictures of saints and altar set with relics, jewels, and rich plate included a private closet for the king on the right and for the queen, the princes, and the king's mother on the left. Richmond also housed England's first royal library where Henry's Flemish librarian Quentin Poulet developed a collection admired even by the Burgundians.[25] The three-story main structure provided richly decorated living quarters for the royal family and guests, including "pleasant dancing chambers and

Photo 11 Richmond Palace from the River Thames, 1562. Built on the ashes of Sheen Palace, Richmond's brick walls incorporated the newest architectural features imported from Burgundy. Construction finished just in time for the wedding of Prince Arthur and Katherine of Aragon, whose guests were dazzled by "this earthly and second paradise of our region of England." The many windows illuminated interior galleries and the portraits, statuary, and tapestries decorating the Great Hall. Reconstruction model. Courtesy of the Museum of Richmond.

Photo 12   Richmond Palace from the Garden, 1562. Extensive gardens beneath the lodgings of the king and queen displayed topiary in the shapes of animals. Galleries at the far end of the gardens hosted games of chess, cards, bowling, archery, and tennis, as well as plays and "disguisings." Reconstruction model. Courtesy of the Museum of Richmond.

secret closets most richly enhanged, decked, and beseen."²⁶ To the north of the Great Hall were the pantry, buttery, cellar, and kitchen with the coals and fuels safely stored in open yards.

Gardens beneath the windows of the lodgings of the king and queen displayed topiary in the shapes of lions, dragons, and other "marvelous beasts."²⁷ At the lower end of the garden, separate galleries hosted games of chess, dice, cards, bowling, archery, and tennis, as well as plays and disguisings. A large park next to the palace offered hunting with bow and hound.

Elizabeth of York may have played a hitherto unsuspected role in these architectural innovations. Similar renovations already underway at Greenwich Palace were following a "new platt [plan]...devised by the Queen."²⁸ Simon Thurley, the modern authority on Tudor architecture, comments that "the reference to Queen Elizabeth's part in the design is most interesting; it testifies not only to her fondness for Greenwich, but it also suggests that the readily discernible Burgundian influences reflect her personal taste rather than the King's."²⁹ The reference also suggests that Queen Elizabeth worked closely with the king's mason Robert Vertue in designing Tudor architecture that incorporated Burgundian features. Her father Edward IV had first imported Burgundian styles in building St. George's Chapel at Windsor Palace. Her mother had inherited Burgundian sensibilities from Elizabeth's grandmother Jacquetta of Luxembourg. Her uncle Anthony Wydeville translated Burgundian literature and introduced its pageantry to the tilting field. Her Wydeville relatives in the Tudor court transformed martial tournaments with allegorical spectacle imported from Burgundy. Combined with Henry's penchant for employing poets, librarians, chroniclers, historians, portrait painters, illuminators, and tapissiers from the Continent, Burgundian influences became pervasive.³⁰

Because kings always receive credit for achievements during their reigns—and because records are scanty and incomplete—Elizabeth of York's influence on Tudor architecture, art, and drama has been ignored—except for that dependent clause in a mason's payment account for "the new platt of Greenwich which was devised by the Queen." Yet her influence may have been significant. Her presence at disguisings and tournaments, always noted by the scribes, may reflect something more than passive attendance. It may indicate an inspirational, perhaps even generative, force. Certainly after Elizabeth's death, pageantry and spectacle at the Tudor court greatly diminished—until its spirit revived under her son Henry VIII.

At Richmond in 1501, that spirit was at its height. Wedding guests hunted on Saturday and strolled through the extensive gardens after Sunday church services. A Spanish tight-rope walker tumbled, danced, juggled, and leaped on a cable stretched across the lawn: "eftsoon he cast himself suddenly from the rope and hanged by the toes, sometime by the teeth most marvelously, and with greatest sleight and cunning that any man could possibly exercise or do."[31] After supper, guests assembled for the final disguising of the two-week celebrations. Once more, a cupboard filled with "rich and costly plate to great substance and quantity" displayed Tudor wealth and magnificence.

The last pageant on Sunday evening featured a two-story chapel-like structure representing a throne of honor. Drawn into the hall by three wildmen (ancient Britains) accompanied by mermaids and mermen (symbolizing the surrounding sea), the structure displayed a cupboard with costly plate testifying to the richness of the kingdom. The lower story held eight disguised lords, knights, and men of honor; the upper story eight "fresh ladies." As the eight lords descended from the chapel, they released rabbits to run through the hall and make "very great disport." After dances by the men, the ladies descended while releasing doves that flew about the hall, creating "great laughter and disport."[32] The lords and ladies then "coupled together and danced a long season many courtly rounds and pleasant dances." The doves and rabbits combined the emblem of Venus with traditional fertility icons to symbolize love and lust united within the sacrament of marriage. Music and dance similarly joined man and woman in dignified, harmonious motion. (A century later, Shakespeare ended many comedies with music and dance signifying the perfect union of marriage.)

This last disguising concluded two weeks of wedding celebrations. After the void of spices and wine, Henry VII distributed gifts to his Spanish guests, *largess* that was generous and awesome. The Spanish archbishop received a cupboard of the king's plate and treasure worth 600 or 700 marks. The bishop received a cupboard worth 500 marks, the "earl" 500 marks, and the earl's brother 300 marks. Expressions of appreciation for their diligence, labor, and pain in bringing Princess Katherine to her new life in England accompanied the gifts.

The Spanish departed Richmond on Monday further laden with books, pictures, and other presents. Selected attendants remained behind to serve the princess in her new foreign world. Henry VII, quite sensitive to Katherine's feelings and loss, called the princess and her ladies, both Spanish and English, to his library. He showed them his books, then summoned his jeweler who displayed rings with "precious stones and huge diamonds and jewels of most goodly fashion."[33] Henry gave Katherine her choice of the treasures spread before her. Then each lady of Spain selected her preference. The rest was distributed to the ladies of England.

Magnanimous, generous, and sensitive, Henry exceeded all expectations in easing Katherine's transition to married life in a foreign country. As consort to the Prince of Wales, Katherine of Aragon had a vital role to fulfill, royal responsibilities that began immediately. The king assigned the governance of Wales to his eldest son, and before Christmas 1501, Prince Arthur and Princess Katherine departed for Ludlow to begin life together.

CHAPTER 16

EUPHORIA TURNS TRAGIC

The year 1502 began auspiciously for the royal family. The Court had hardly recovered from celebrating the wedding of Arthur and Katherine—and the festivals of Christmas and Twelfth Night—when another marriage took center stage. On January 25, 1502, Lady Princess Margaret, age 12, wed James IV, king of the Scots, age 28. Ambassadors from Scotland had arrived in London on Saturday, November 20, 1501, to conclude the negotiations. Their timing was impeccable. They arrived exactly one week before Margaret's twelfth birthday (her marriageable age) and just a week after the wedding of Arthur and Katherine. They were, therefore, in town for the postwedding celebrations. Met at Bishopsgate by "many noble men and jolly gallants," they were escorted to St. John's, the noble and wealthy Priory headquarters of the Knights Hospitaller in England. On Monday they joined the king at Westminster Palace for the jousts.[1] Imagine how Henry's hospitality and riches, tournaments and banquets impressed the Scots, who joined the celebrations of the marriage of England and Spain.

Henry VII's proposal for Margaret was not his first effort to negotiate peace with Scotland through marriage. In July 1486, a complicated contract wedded queen dowager Elizabeth Wydeville to James III, with James's eldest son having his choice of Elizabeth of York's sisters, except that Katherine was designated for James's second son.[2] That proposal ended when James III died. Henry's next proposal attempted to undercut Perkin Warbeck's influence in Scotland by marrying daughter Margaret to James IV in June 1495.[3] That plan ended when James IV warmly welcomed Perkin Warbeck to Scotland in November 1495. James in turn proposed to wed a daughter of Ferdinand and Isabella in 1496; the Catholic monarchs responded that the king of Scots might marry a daughter of Henry VII.[4] Ferdinand and Isabella hoped to encourage peace between England and Scotland before sending Katherine to England. Two years later, De Ayala wrote to Ferdinand and Isabella that Henry appreciated their suggestion, but had responded:

> I [Henry] am really sorry that I have not a daughter or a sister for him [James IV]: for I have loved him most sincerely since the conclusion of the peace; not to mention that he is my relative. He has behaved very well towards me. I wish to see him as prosperous as myself. But I have already told you, more than once, that a marriage between him and my daughter has many inconveniences. She has not yet completed the ninth year of her age, and is so delicate and weak [*feminina*] that she must be married much later than other young ladies. Thus it would be necessary to wait at least another nine years. Besides my own doubts, the Queen and my mother are very much against this marriage. They say if the marriage were concluded, we should be obliged to send the Princess directly to Scotland, in which case they fear the King of Scots would not wait, but injure her, and endanger her health. Therefore I do not wish you to trouble yourself about this affair.[5]

Henry's response reflects his masterful diplomatic skills. He simply ignored his own 1495 proposal to marry Margaret to James IV. In rejecting the marriage in 1498, he speaks glowingly of the potential husband and cites his daughter's youth as a mere "inconvenience," a deterrent easily overcome by the passage of a few years. And by blaming the queen and his mother for opposing the union, Henry suggests that his own mere "doubts" might be less firm.

"Long and deliberate communication" between the two kings resulted in the gathering at Richmond on St. Paul's Day, January 1502, to marry Margaret Tudor to James IV of Scotland, whose proxy representative was Patrick, earl of Bothwell.[6] Following Mass and a sermon in the Chapel, the wedding party proceeded to the queen's great chamber for the ceremony. If not as elaborate as Prince Arthur's, the assembled group was impressive. In addition to the king and the queen were the duke of York and princess Mary; the archbishops of Glasgow, Canterbury, and York; four bishops; ambassadors from Scotland, Spain, and Venice; a representative from France; and the Pope's Collector. Among the lords temporal were the duke of Buckingham, the marquess of Dorset, 6 earls, and 12 lords and knights. The ladies included the duchess of Norfolk, the queen's sister Katherine, her sister-in-law the lady marquess of Dorset, Lady Katherine Gordon (the Scottish widow of Perkin Warbeck), plus 14 others. Twenty-eight bannerettes and knights completed the wedding party.

The Pope's dispensation for consanguinity, affinity, and nonage was read, and the king, the queen, and Princess Margaret each certified that no impediments existed to the marriage. When the archbishop of Glasgow asked the princess if "she were content without compulsion and of her free will," she responded: "If it please my Lord and Father the King, and my Lady my Mother the Queen."[7] Margaret received blessings from the king and queen, after which the earl of Bothwell, standing for King James IV, contracted matrimony with her. The vows of Margaret included a statement that she had completed 12 years of age and was therefore eligible to marry.

The vows concluded, the trumpeters standing on the leads at the chamber's end blew their horns and the minstrels played. The king went to dinner in his chamber with the archbishop of Glasgow and the earl of Bothwell. John Young, Somerset herald, recorded a touching moment following the nuptials:

> The Queen took her daughter the Queen of Scots by the hand, and dined both at one Mess covered.[8]

Two queens, mother and daughter, the one almost 36 and the other just 12. Queen Elizabeth surely treasured this moment. Her two eldest children, well married, had promising futures. How pleasant to dine with her daughter, the queen of Scots. How bright the Tudor stars were shining!

During the afternoon, two teams of jousters entertained the wedding guests, followed by "a notable banquet" that evening. The City of London celebrated with "competent fires," 12 of which featured a hogshead of Gascon wine for all who wished to imbibe.[9] The next morning in the queen of England's great chamber, the queen of Scots thanked the nobles who had jousted. After consulting the ladies of the Court, she praised those jousters who had distinguished themselves. Among the prizewinners was Charles Brandon, following the knightly tradition of his father, Sir William Brandon, who died while carrying the standard of Henry VII at the battle of Bosworth. Young Brandon would one day marry Margaret's little sister Mary, and their daughter Frances would give birth to Lady Jane Grey.

The evening pageant celebrating Margaret, Queen of Scots, featured a large "lantern" with windows (probably the pageant car from Arthur's celebrations). Morris dancers emerged to entertain the wedding guests, followed by a disguising with six gentlemen and ladies. The evening ended with a "notable banquet or void."[10] During the jousts held on Thursday, Charles Brandon broke more spears than his opponent, although Sir John Peche was noted for "the best broken Spear (both horses standing, and the Knights well sitting) that I have seen."[11] After a "notable supper" that night, Henry VII distributed gifts to his guests: the archbishop of Glasgow received a cupboard of gold containing a cup of gold with cover, 6 great standing pots of silver, 24 great bowls of silver with covers, a basin and a ewer of silver, and a chassoir of silver. The earl of Bothwell received a similar "cupboard of great value"; the Elector of Murray a covered standing cup of gold, plus 1,000 crowns of gold in a bag of crimson velvet; the Scottish Lion King of Arms a purse with 100 crowns of gold, plus a gown of fine satin. Other gentlemen received gowns of velvet. No penurious piker, this king!

Writs sent throughout the kingdom commanded sheriffs to proclaim peace between Henry VII, King of England, and James IV, King of Scotland, concluded on January 24, 1502 and "for evermore," and to announce the marriage between King James and Princess Margaret. The town and castle of Berwick, long fought over because of its strategic location on the Tweed, now stood under perpetual peace.[12] Despite the ceremony, the celebrations, and the resultant rapprochement between nations, however, the departure of Margaret to Scotland was delayed 18 months until June 27, 1503, undoubtedly due to the strong feelings of Queen Elizabeth and the king's mother, who remembered giving birth at age 13.

England's future and the Tudor dynasty seemed secure. Peace reigned throughout the island of Great Britain. Centuries of conflict between Scotland and England had ended. The Prince's Council in Wales, established by Edward IV in 1473, had quelled local quarrels and civic unrest. Prince Arthur at Ludlow Castle resided in the center of a peaceful and prosperous region.

But if Henry VII had achieved peace within his nation, his personal tranquility was about to shatter. Between Christmas and Easter, Prince Arthur contracted a fatal disease:

From the Feast of the Nativity of Christ in the year beforesaid unto the solemn Feast of the Resurrection, at the which season grew and increased upon his body, whether it were by surfeit or by cause natural, a lamentable and…most pitiful disease and sickness, that with so sore and great violence had battled and driven in the singular parts of him inward; that cruel and fervent enemy of nature, the deadly corruption, did utterly vanquish and overcome the pure and friendful blood, without all manner of physical help and remedy.[13]

"The deadly corruption" that caused the death of an apparently healthy young man cannot be diagnosed from this scanty narrative (the only contemporary description of his illness). Speculation has ranged from the "sweating sickness" to a malady caught when the prince washed the feet of 12 poor men on Maundy Tuesday.

Arthur died on April 2, 1502, less than four months after his splendid wedding in St. Paul's Cathedral. If the political consequences were significant, they were nothing compared to the cataclysmic devastation wrecked on King Henry and Queen Elizabeth. A contemporary scribe describes how they received the news delivered to them at Greenwich:

Immediately after his [Arthur's] death, Sir Richard Pole, his Chamberlain, with other of his Council, wrote and sent letters to the King and Council to Greenwich, where his Grace and the Queen's lay, and certified them of the Prince's departure. The which Council discreetly sent for the King's ghostly Father, a friar observant, to whom they showed this most sorrowful and heavy tidings, and desired him in his best manner to show it to the King.

He in the morning of the Tuesday following, somewhat before the time accustomed, knocked at King's Chamber door; and when the King understood it was his confessor, he commanded to let him in. The Confessor then commanded all those present to avoid, and after due salutation began to say, *Si bona de manu dei suscipimus, mala autem quare non sustineamus?* [If we receive good from the hand of God, should we not also tolerate the bad?] and so showed his Grace that his dearest son was departed to God.

When his Grace understood that sorrowful heavy tidings, he sent for the Queen, saying that he and his Queen would take the painful sorrows together. After that she was come and saw the King her Lord, and that natural and painful sorrow, as I have heard say, she with full great and constant comfortable words besought his Grace that he would first after God remember the weal of his own noble person, the comfort of his realm and of her. She then said that my Lady his mother had never no more children but him only, and that God by his Grace had ever preserved him, and brought him where he was. Over that, how that God had left him yet a fair Prince, two fair Princesses; and that God is where he was, and we are both young enough. And that the prudence and wisdom of his Grace sprung over all Christendom, so that it should please him to take this accordingly thereunto. Then the King thanked her of her good comfort.

But Elizabeth of York was suffering more than she let her husband know:

After she was departed and come to her own Chamber, natural and motherly remembrance of that great loss smote her so sorrowful to the heart that those that were about her were fain to send for the King to comfort her. Then his Grace of true gentle and faithful love, in good haste came and relieved her, and showed her how wise counsel she had given him before, and he for his part would thank God for his son, and would she should do in like wise.[14]

The love between Henry and Elizabeth, elegantly and eloquently recorded by an unknown scribe, cannot be doubted.

Arthur's body lay in state in the Great Hall at Ludlow Castle until April 23, when it was transferred to the parish church in Ludlow. From there, the cortege went on to Bewdley, the first of several stops on its way to burial in Worcester Cathedral under the banners of the king of England, the queen of England, the king of Spain, and the queen of Spain. The earl of Surrey was chief mourner. Neither the king nor queen attended the services. Also absent was Katherine, princess of Wales, who may herself have been ill.

More sadness would soon be visited upon this kingdom. Queen Elizabeth of York would follow her beloved son within the year.

CHAPTER 17

THE QUEEN'S LAST YEAR

Q ueen Elizabeth lived a peripatetic existence during her final year of life. The frequent moves between her London residences were typical, indeed essential, to permit the resident staff and facilities to recover from serving the hundreds of individuals in the royal household. Servants had to restock the pantry, wash the bedding, clean the floors, repair the furniture, dust the tapestries—and prepare for the next visit. In August 1502, the queen began a two-month progress through Wales, a strenuous journey on rutted roads with broken carts, diverted wagons, and inadequate bedsteads.[1] That Elizabeth was pregnant throughout the trip only added to the difficulties and her discomfort. (See chart of timelines, page 188)

Even ordinary transfers of the queen and her household by barge on the Thames demanded elaborate arrangements. The trip from Greenwich to Richmond on May 19 required 21 rowers and a master for her personal barge, followed by another "great boat" for her ladies and gentlewomen propelled by 9 rowers and master. The royal barges, fitted with "soft furnishings," burnt "sweet herbs" to mask the river's noxious smells.[2]

When the Queen arrived at her destination, some essential item always seemed to be left behind—or was stored at a different palace. Couriers sailed up and down the Thames fetching stools, gowns, and jewels. Elizabeth seemed to have a favorite stool, which she sent Richard Justice, Page of the Robes, to bring to Greenwich from London at the cost of 6d;[3] another trip retrieved a "stool covered with scarlet" from the Tower that was needed at Greenwich, along with a gown of russet velvet, a gown of purple velvet, and white fustian for making socks for the queen.[4] At one point a boat was hired from Westminster to London to fetch the queen of Scots' "sleeves of orange color sarcenet."[5] Corpus Christi Day at Richmond required the queen's cloth-of-gold gown that was in London—and a special trip by boat to get it.[6] Another

ITINERARY OF ELIZABETH OF YORK
March 24, 1502–February 11, 1503

March 24	Westminster
25	Richmond
April 2	Greenwich
27	Tower of London
May 2	Greenwich
19	Richmond
June 6	Westminster
11	Richmond
17	Windsor
July 12	Colnbrook, near Windsor
	Wycombe, Buckinghamshire
13	Notley Priory
	Bostall, Buckinghamshire
14	Woodstock [Queen is ill]
August 4	Begins progress to Wales
5–6	Langley, Oxfordshire
	Flaxley Abbey, Gloucestershire
	Northleache
	Coberley Manor
	Vineyard (County seat of an Abbot of Gloucester)
	Flaxley Abbey
14	Mitchell Troy (Monmouth)
19	Raglan (Herbert estate)
28	Chepstow (crossed Severn)
	Wollaston, Gloucesterhire
29	Berkeley
	Beverston Castle
September 12	Coates (near Cirencester)
	Fairford
	Langley
October 6	Minster Lovell
9	Abington
13	Ewelme, Oxfordshire (Suffolk estate)
	Henley-upon-Thames
16	Easthampstead
	Windsor
25	Richmond
27	Westminster
November 14	Greenwich
19	Baynard's Castle
26	Westminster
December 12	Tower of London
21	Mortlake (Richmond)
January 14	Hampton Court to Richmond
26	Tower of London
February 2	Katherine born
11	Elizabeth of York died at Tower of London

urgent request sent the Page of the Robes "from Westminster to London in the night for a gown of blue velvet for the Queen."[7]

Normally, gowns traveled in a wardrobe from palace to palace: from the Tower to Richmond cost 18*d*, from Greenwich to the Tower 4*d*, from Richmond to Westminster and return 2*s*.[8] The wardrobe of the beds was sent by water from Richmond to Baynard's Castle,[9] as was a boatload of "stuff" from Baynard's Castle to Westminster.[10] The queen's progress through Wales included "carts of stuff,"[11] attended by a "Yeoman of the Stuff" to manage silk points, pins, brushes, and other small items.[12]

The queen's jewels required special care: Thomas Woodnote and John Feld, grooms of the queen's chamber, each earned 6*d* per day for waiting upon her jewels as they moved from palace to palace—as from Richmond to Greenwich (and return) or from Richmond to Windsor.[13] Sometimes the only way to track the queen's whereabouts is to follow the jewels. In June and July 1502, the jewels went from Richmond to Windsor to Wycombe (Buckinghamshire) to Notley Priory (Bucks.) to Bostall (Bucks.) to Woodstock Manor (Oxfordshire) to Langley Manor (Oxon.).[14] Unfortunately, payment to the grooms weeks later did not specify dates of travel, making it impossible to determine exactly when the queen visited each site.

Elizabeth's activities during 1502 contrast starkly with the grandiose pageants, tournaments, and disguisings of the preceding year. The Court was in deep mourning for Arthur, and even ordinary entertainments were inappropriate. Her journey to Wales seems to be unique, although scanty records preclude certainty about Elizabeth's earlier travels. When the queen accompanied the king (to Calais, for instance), court heralds and ambassadors recorded her presence. The chronicles sometimes note pilgrimages to the shrine at Walsingham. Otherwise, almost no records document Elizabeth's daily life and activities. Her 1502 excursion to Wales is known only because her Privy Purse accounts survived for the year beginning on March 24, 1502. This record of money spent—essentially Elizabeth's personal checkbook—provides an intimate glimpse into the life, character, and personality of this queen. Thanks to its fortuitous survival, Elizabeth of York's last year on earth is the best documented of her life.

The first entry for 1502 records Queen Elizabeth's traditional giving of alms: on Maundy Thursday, each of 37 poor women (the number reflecting the age of the queen) received 3*s* 1*d*.[15] Another

15s 5d bought shoes for the women, with a rather lavish £14 16s providing each with 3 yards of cloth.[16] Charitable and religious donations were typically small, but frequent and consistent: on feast days she generally gave 5s, while local shrines received 3–6s during her various journeys. On a trip from Windsor to Woodstock in July, she gave 7s;[17] during other journeys her chaplain Christopher Plomer dispensed 23s,[18] her cleric Mr. Harding 2s 8d,[19] and her Confessor Dr. Underwood 20s.[20] Special days such as New Year's Eve elicited 60s[21] and Good Friday 66s 8d, but on Easter Sunday the queen offered 5s at each Mass.[22] Saints usually received 2s 6d on their feast days. As a comparative value, it should be noted that the queen's personal spending money was quite small: regular deposits to her purse amounted to only 20s until late in the year when they increased to 40s.[23]

Larger contributions indicate the queen's special interest in the recipients. The Friars Observant at Greenwich and at Canterbury each received alms of £6 18s 8d to purchase 52 barrels of beer for the "whole year."[24] The Friars Observant, a fundamentalist branch of the Franciscans, vowed to reestablish the ideals of humility, simplicity, and poverty practiced by St. Francis. They believed that over the centuries the Franciscan Order had strayed from those ideals as wealth flowed into its coffers. Elizabeth's father, Edward IV, sponsored the first English house of the Friars Observant at Greenwich in 1482,[25] patronage continued by Henry VII. The Observants now served the royal family as confessors, counselors, and preachers.

Queen Elizabeth seemed especially attracted to individuals who devoted their lives to the strict, ascetic worship of God. On May 1, for instance, she gave 11s to three nuns of the Minories (Dame Katherine, Dame Elizabeth, and "a daughter of William Cromer") and to the "old woman servant to the Abbess." On the same day she gave only 5s to the Fraternity of Corpus Christi at Saint Sepulcher in London.[26] The "Minoresses" or "Poor Clares" were women followers of St. Francis, who, like the Friars Observant, dedicated their lives to silence, prayer, and complete poverty. On November 6, the same three nuns, the "poor woman servant," and the Abbess herself received another 15s 8d.[27]

Similarly, the Anchoress of St. Peter at St. Albans received 3s 4d on March 28, and the Anchoress at St. Michael near St. Albans 26s 8d in the accounts settled after Elizabeth's death.[28] These anchoresses had retreated from the world to a solitary life of prayer and contemplation, "anchored" to God in a small cell that they never left. Anchorite cells were usually attached to a parish church with a small window allowing the anchoress to receive communion and hear the Mass. Another small opening allowed the passage of food and access to devout visitors who sought spiritual advice and prayers. Such frugal, ascetic, and total devotion to God—similar to that of the Carthusians at Sheen, the Bridgettines at Syon, the Friars Observant, and the Poor Clares—touched Elizabeth of York's heart.

The queen also paid men to make pilgrimages for her. During the 11 months covered by these Privy Purse accounts, William Burton received 22s 6d for a pilgrimage of 23 days, Richard Milner 10s 10d for a pilgrimage of 13 days, and "a man that went on pilgrimage to our Lady of Willesdon" 3s 4d.[29]

Much of the queen's charity went to anonymous individuals. In many ways, the shoes and yards of cloth given to the poor women on Maundy Thursday symbolize Elizabeth of York's benevolence, perhaps revealing a preference for individuals over institutions. Most touching is the "poor man who guided the Queen's Grace" or "a poor woman that brought a present of butter and chickens to the Queen."[30] The queen always tipped the many poor subjects who brought gifts from their homes and gardens—apples, pears, roses, puddings, cheeses, peascods, cakes. Servants delivering gifts from their masters received quite generous amounts: 13s 4d for two vessels of Rhenish wine,[31] 10s for a wild boar,[32] 3s 4d for tripe.[33] Patch, the Fool, knew a good mistress when he had one and picked up tips for gifts of pomegranates, apples, and oranges.[34] No fool, this Patch!

Perhaps Queen Elizabeth was a soft touch. On December 9, 1502, she gave 12d to a "man of Pontefract" who claimed that he had lodged in his home the queen's uncle Anthony Wydeville, earl Rivers, during the year of his execution—19 years earlier in 1483![35] She paid expenses for several children given her as gifts.[36] She provided a new lawn shirt to "a child of Grace at Reading."[37] The diet, clothing, schooling, and books of Edward Pallet, son of an otherwise unknown Lady Jane Bangham, cost the queen a fairly substantial 50s 3d for the year.[38] John Pertriche, "one of the sons of mad Beale" received his diet, a gown, a coat, four shirts, six pairs of shoes, four pairs of hose, "his learning," a primer, a psalter, and services of a "surgeon which healed him of the French pox," courtesy of Elizabeth of York.[39] Seven shillings paid for "the burying of the men that were hanged at Wapping Mill."[40]

The queen was equally generous to those associated with her Court. William Paston, page of the queen's beds, received 40s toward his wedding clothes.[41] William was a member of the Paston family from Norfolk whose sons had attended the court since the time of her father, Edward IV. William's father, Sir John Paston the younger, knighted at the battle of Stoke, was a favorite of Henry VII and served as knight of the King's Body in 1501. Son William apparently left Cambridge, where he was a student in 1495, to serve the queen. When he married Bridget, daughter of Sir Henry Heydon of Baconsthorp in Norfolk, the queen contributed his wedding suit. Another member of the queen's staff, Nicholas Grey, a clerk at Richmond, received 60s when his house burned.[42] Nicholas Mathew, yeoman of the queen's chambers, was given 26s 8d toward his expenses when "hurt by the servants of Sir William Sands."[43] Ministers of the King's Chapel received 20s "to drink at a tavern with a buck."[44] The queen bought "horse meat," provender for the horse of the laundress who accompanied her to Wales, at the rate of 4d a day.[45]

The queen provided clothes for many court attendants: doublets, gowns, shirts, hose, and shoes for her footman;[46] kirtles and gowns for her ladies;[47] white and green coats of sarcenet for the king's four minstrels and four trumpeters;[48] sarcenet coats for the minstrels of Prince Arthur, the duke of York, and the duke of Buckingham.[49] William, the queen's Fool, not only received a coat, shirts, hose, socks, and shoes, but additional pay for his board, wages, and "necessaries" when ill for four weeks.[50]

The queen's greatest generosity went to her family and those connected even peripherally with family—expenditures revealing the importance of personal ties to this queen who had lost so many loved ones to wars, executions, and natural death. One poignant expense in her Privy Purse is tiny: 3½ yards of cloth to "a woman that was nurse to the Prince, brother to the Queen's grace."[51] Nineteen years after the young prince disappeared, his older sister remembered the nurse who took care of him. Similarly, she regularly sent alms to "a poor man" who was a former servant of Edward IV.[52] In 1501 Elizabeth welcomed to her household Arthur Plantagenet, illegitimate son of Edward IV by his mistress Elizabeth Wayte: the queen's half-brother was about 39 years old when he joined her court.[53] Elizabeth paid the expenses of her youngest sister Bridget, a nun at the Dominican Convent in Dartford: 66s 8d in July 1502 and again in March 1503.[54] In

September the queen paid John Weredon for a two-day trip to visit the Lady Bridget.[55]

Elizabeth was even more generous to her sister Anne, who had carried the christening robes of both Arthur and Margaret. The marriage of Anne to Thomas, lord Howard, in 1495 was politically advantageous to Henry VII, but unfortunately Lord Howard would receive his inheritance only after the death of his father, the duke of Norfolk (in 1524, long after the death of Anne in 1511). The queen accordingly paid an annual stipend of £120 for Anne's "diet."[56] Other gifts to Anne included a kirtle, 10 marks "due unto her for a year ended at Michaelmas," and £6 13s 4d spending money.[57]

The queen's sister Katherine received an annual pension of £50, along with frequent gifts to herself and her husband, William, lord Courtenay, whose father, the earl of Devon, controlled the family's wealth. Courtenay was sent to prison in 1502 for supporting the rebellion of his friend Edmund de la Pole, earl of Suffolk, against Henry VII. Katherine had no means of support until Queen Elizabeth began paying the bills for her sister and the Courtenay children. Lady Katherine received black satin and velvet for covering her saddle, and her husband William was given shirts, gown, and a night bonnet. The queen also paid expenses of the three Courtenay children living under the governance of Margaret Cotton, including clothes, medicine, "diet," two servants, a groom, and three rockers.[58] When little Edward died, the queen was the one consulted about his burial, for which she paid the costs.[59]

Cecily, the queen's sister, was repaid 73s 4d for money she had lent Elizabeth. In 1502 Cecily lost favor with the king when she remarried without his permission. Viscount Welles had died in 1499, and Cecily subsequently married a lowly esquire, Thomas Kyme of Friskney.[60] Henry VII, enraged, banished Cecily from the Court. Not only had Cecily defied the king's authority, but she also denied him the rewards he could have demanded for marriage to the queen's sister. Fortunately, this most beautiful of Edward IV's daughters was much loved by the king's mother (half-sister to Viscount Welles), who provided a refuge for the newly wed Kyme couple at her Collyweston estate in Northamptonshire. Margaret Beaufort also interceded with the king to assure that Cecily retained a life interest in some of the property disputed by the heirs of Viscount Welles.[61] In later years, the king's mother reserved a chamber for Cecily at Croydon Manor, her residence ten miles south of London (owned by the archbishop of Canterbury but made available to the king's mother). When Cecily died in 1507, the king's mother paid part of her funeral expenses.[62] The record is silent on Queen Elizabeth's reaction to Cecily's banishment. Whether the sisters ever saw each other after Cecily married Thomas Kyme is unknown.

Queen Elizabeth was especially kind to the young, widowed Katherine, princess of Wales, after the death of Arthur. In addition to settling past due bills accrued from the wedding, the queen paid to cover with black velvet the litter that brought Katherine from Ludlow to London.[63] Messengers went back and forth between the queen and the princess who lived part of the time at Croydon.[64] On September 27, the queen sent five bucks for the princess's table in London and later gave her four yards of flannel.[65] In November, the queen's barge transported the princess from the bishop of Durham's palace to Westminster for a visit.[66] A litter of blue velvet with cushions of blue damask was provided to an unidentified "lady of Spain," probably one of Katherine's attendants.[67] Had Queen Elizabeth lived, the poverty endured by Katherine during her later widowhood may have been mitigated.

Among her own children, Margaret, queen of Scots, received the most frequent gifts: a black velvet gown, several sets of sleeves, furs for her gowns, strings for her lute.[68] Early in the year, Margaret received from her mother accoutrements essential for the boudoir of a married women: three basins of pewter, a chafer of brass, two washing bowls, a fire pan, a great trussing basket, and a pair of bellows.[69] Small sums for spending money were provided—12*d* in May and 20*s* when the queen departed for Wales.[70] Mary, age six, received a black satin gown, necessary for mourning her brother Arthur.[71]

A few entries allow a glimpse into the relationship shared between Elizabeth and Henry. A sum of 3*s* 6*d* spent for "eggs, butter, and milk for the King and Queen" implies a special treat, but gives no clue about when, where, and how the ingredients were used—or why they were purchased from the queen's Privy Purse rather than from the kitchen accounts.[72] Her purchase of a pound-and-a-half of gold of Venice, 8 ounces of gold of Damascus, and an ounce of Venetian silk for making the "lace and buttons for the King's mantle of the Garter" suggests that Elizabeth made the Garter with her own hands, a distinct act of affection in a

17-year-old marriage that had the Great Wardrobe *couture* at its disposal.[73] On December 3, she assigned £333 6s 8d from her land "for the use of the King's Grace," the largest single sum of the year's budget.[74] Considering that at year's end £500 had to be borrowed against the queen's plate to balance her Privy Purse, this sum is significant—and unexplained.[75]

Elizabeth's two-month progress through Wales during the summer also had a family focus. Her destination was the Raglan estate of Sir Walter Herbert, son of the man who had raised Henry Tudor when he was a boy. King Henry and Sir Walter grew up together at Raglan after William Herbert, earl of Pembroke, bought Henry's custody from Edward IV in 1462.[76] Perhaps Elizabeth wished to see her husband's childhood home, but most certainly she wanted to visit Sir Walter's wife Anne, her first cousin (and sister of the queen's principal Lady-in-Waiting Elizabeth Stafford). Anne and Elizabeth were daughters of Henry Stafford, duke of Buckingham, and Katherine Wydeville, the queen's aunt. Nostalgia perhaps drew the queen to Raglan to reminisce about shared memories of the court of Edward IV and Elizabeth Wydeville where Elizabeth of York, as a child of six, had danced with the 17-year-old duke of Buckingham in her mother's chambers at Windsor.[77] The trip to Wales culminated in a family reunion of the queen and her Stafford cousins.

The journey was challenging, especially since Elizabeth was pregnant with her eighth child. Just before starting out, she was ill at Woodstock in late July, but she recovered well enough to depart in early August 1502.[78] Her progress entailed a massive logistical effort: grooms rode ahead to prepare the queen's lodging, two grooms tended her jewels, a laundress washed clothes, grooms drove the carts, and ostlers tended the horses. Food for her many attendants required bucks delivered to Monmouth, Berkeley, Fairford, Langley—with the queen tipping the providers.[79] The "carts of stuff" took six days to reach Raglan from Langley.[80] The queen's stool followed her from London to Oxford to Langley—and presumably onward.[81] A local guide showed the queen the way from Flaxley Abbey to Mitchel Troy (about three miles south of Monmouth). Another helped retrieve the cart with the wardrobe of the robes that broke down somewhere between Flaxley Abbey and Monmouth.[82] On the way home, a closed cart and "load of stuff" apparently too heavy to cross the Severn at Chepstow traveled overland from Raglan to Berkeley via Gloucester before it rejoined the entourage at Woolaston.[83] From Berkeley, John Bolton rode to Bristol to obtain wine for the queen.[84] By the time she was back at Minster Lovell in October, the queen needed a new bedstead.[85]

At Raglan Castle (seven miles southwest of Monmouth), the queen relaxed in great comfort. A "palace fortress of splendor and strength,"[86] the castle enclosed two courtyards—the "Pitched Stone Court" surrounded by the office wing, kitchen, pantry, buttery, and Great Hall, and the "Fountain Court" with central marble fountain and grass lawn bounded by the chapel, blocks of apartments, and a "Grand Stair." Four garderobes (toilets) were located on the ground floor and five on the first.[87] A bridge over a moat connected this public section of the castle with the Keep, a great tower with separate quarters for the lord and his family. The Keep had its own well, and each floor housed a single room with garderobe. Built by Lord Herbert in the decade after Edward IV became king, Raglan Castle's high quality stonework, large windows, oriels, and fireplaces provided luxurious living in a setting of "pomp and display."[88] Surrounded by the green fields of the Welsh countryside, its vista added unmatched splendor to the amenities and aesthetics of the castle itself. If Elizabeth's journey to Raglan was long and difficult, it ended in comfort, luxury, and the warm hospitality of her cousins.

A medieval vestment, currently preserved by the parish church of St. Bridget in Skenfrith (six miles north of Monmouth) may have an interesting association with the queen's journey to Wales. Kirstie Buckland's research suggests that "the Skenfrith Cope," a red velvet ecclesiastical garment depicting the Assumption of the Virgin Mary as its central image, may have been a gift from Queen Elizabeth during her 1502 visit.[89] Analysis by Reverend Rupert Morris dates the embroidery of "the Skenfrith Cope" to the late fifteenth century.[90] On the back of the Cope, radiating outward from the Blessed Virgin Mary, are traditional figures of double-headed eagles, fleurs-de-lis, flowers, and angels standing on wheels. The figures are stitched on fine linen, which is appliquéd to the velvet.

Elizabeth of York arrived at Mitchell Troy in Monmouthshire on August 14, the eve of the Feast of the Assumption. The timing of the visit, the motifs of the embroidery, and the Cope's contemporary date all suggest a connection between this vestment and Queen Elizabeth. Her host Sir Walter Herbert was steward of

Photo 13   The Skenfrith Cope dates from the late fifteenth
century. Its dating, rich fabric, and image of the
Assumption of the Virgin Mary associate the cope with
Queen Elizabeth's visit to Monmouth Priory on the
Feast of the Assumption in 1502. Courtesy of
St. Bridget's Church, Skenfrith.

Monmouth Priory, and the queen may possibly have given this
cope to the local religious establishment. On May 5, 1502, Elizabeth
had paid her mercer £40 13s 5d for "velvets and other stuff of their
occupation,"[91] the disposition of which is unknown (unlike other
purchases of velvet specifically designated for gowns, cloaks, or
her bed).[92] Her royal embroiderer Robynet (who received 16d
weekly wages and £2 annually for rent)[93] could have constructed
the cope, a task requiring considerable skill. On the other hand, as
Buckland points out, speculation that this particular cope was a
gift from Elizabeth of York may be nothing more than "insub-
stantial fantasy." In the absence of evidence tying it directly to the
queen, the origin of the magnificent Skenfrith Cope must remain
a mystery,[94] but its date suggests that it was at least worn during
services on the Feast of the Assumption 1502 when Elizabeth of
York visited Monmouth.

Throughout the queen's peregrinations through Wales and elsewhere, her receiver of revenues and keeper of the Privy Purse,
Mr. Richard Decouns, carefully recorded each expenditure.

Elizabeth reviewed the accounts and signed each individual page through September 21, 1502. Laynesmith suggests that the absence of signatures after that date can be explained by the Christmas holiday, Elizabeth's advancing pregnancy, and her subsequent death.[95]

The accounts reveal that the queen was perpetually short of funds and made frequent partial payments against large outstanding bills. In June Henry Bryan received £10 in payment on his bill of £107 10s for silks and "other stuff of his occupation."[96] That pattern was typical: £13 6s 8d paid on a bill of £32 16s 1d for robes, gowns, and kirtles; £32 6s on a bill of £107 10s for silks; £46 on a bill of £129 16s 6d from her mercer; £60 on £210 19s 8d due her goldsmith; £40 against £140 6d owed for more silks; £20 against £60 6s 5d to her silkwoman for frontlets and bonnets; £20 against 100 marks worth of plate burned at Richmond; £82 2s on £114 5s 5d owed to her skinner; £20 17s 6d on her goldsmith's bill of £144.[97] In addition, Elizabeth borrowed money from lenders, some of which was repaid in May: £100 to Sir William Capell, £100 to William Stafford, and £206 13s 4d to William Bulstrode against plate she had pledged.[98]

The lifestyle of a queen of England cost money. Magnificence required the queen's wardrobe to display the stature and honor of the nation, especially when meeting with foreign ambassadors such as the Hungarians who arrived in May.[99] Elizabeth of York accordingly wore rich gowns of silk and velvet, accessorized with expensive jewelry. But if she spent lavishly on gowns and jewels, she also thriftily hemmed kirtles, lined gowns, and mended worn clothing.[100]

The queen also paid for repairing furniture, restoring castles, and securing royal possessions. Locks required frequent repair—for a wardrobe door at Westminster, the chest that held the wardrobe of the robes, the ewry door at Baynard's Castle (storage of basins, table linens, and towels).[101] She paid for bricks, lime, sand, and nails for repairing Baynard's Castle and for building an arbor at Windsor.[102] She bought wax for candles and grease for "liquoring of the Queen's barehides" (hides for covering packages and clothes).[103] Her stables required huge expenditures: £56 5s 3d on June 1, £56 3s on July 8, £86 22d on September 10, £138 13s 9d on November 14, £143 6s 8d on March 3, 1503.[104]

Loving the outdoors, Elizabeth of York bought horses, kept greyhounds, and rewarded a servant for a goshawk at Chepstow.[105]

She tipped the gardener at Windsor and paid the gardener's wages at Baynard's Castle.[106] The arbor built in the "little park of Windsor" was apparently used for an outdoor banquet.[107] She paid grooms and pages for bonfires on the eves of St. John the Baptist and St. Peter.[108]

Indoors, the queen played games of "tables" (backgammon), dice, and cards for which she gambled 100*s* at her Christmas "disport."[109] Court minstrels and Children of the King's Chapel provided music for spiritual and secular occasions. Her own children played lutes and clavichords. Her fools William and Patch told humorous stories and tales. In October, a *disare* (storyteller) "played the Shepherd before the Queen."[110]

As 1502 drew to its end, there was no indication that the queen had any unusual health problems. Indeed, she was involved in renovating the palace at Greenwich with the king's mason, Robert Vertue.[111] On September 17, Elizabeth's apothecary received money "for certain stuff of his occupation by him delivered to the use of the Queen,"[112] but whether this medicine was related to her illness at Woodstock in July or was associated with her advancing pregnancy is unclear. Nothing alarming appears in any record. When the queen returned to the Thames valley in mid-October, she resumed her usual court activities and all seemed well in the royal household. Elizabeth shared the excitement of everyone in England when Sebastian Cabot presented to the king "3 men taken in the New found Isle land...clothed in beasts skins."[113]

Nothing predicted the catastrophe that would strike in February 1503.

CHAPTER 18

DEATH OF A QUEEN

Queen Elizabeth's eighth child may have been born prematurely. The queen was visited by two nurses in November—Mistress Harcourt at Westminster on the 14 and "a French woman" at Baynard's Castle on the 26—but nothing seemed out of the ordinary, and her life continued in all its usual routine.[1] In late autumn her subjects brought her presents—a wild boar, tripes, puddings, and chine of pork—and received their usual rewards. The queen ordered new bedding and curtains in late November,[2] and black satin for a new riding gown on November 26.[3] The "Yeoman Cook for the Queen's Mouth" purchased chickens and larks for her December dining.[4] Ten shillings was paid to a man who had spent five weeks breaking a horse for the queen.[5]

On December 13, a monk delivered the girdle of Our Lady the Virgin to the queen, a garment guarded by the monks at Westminster and worn by royal women as they prepared to give birth.[6] On December 19, Christopher Askew received 160s 6d for 149 ells of linen cloth for bearing sheets, trussing sheets, sheets for the stool, a press sheet, and foot sheets, perhaps in preparation for the impending birth. On the same day William Fowler was paid for 272 yards of wardemole (coarse cloth) in blue and murrey for the queen's barge.[7]

Elizabeth spent Christmas and New Year's at Richmond, where she rewarded William Cornish one mark for composing a carol and gave another mark to the Children of the King's Chapel.[8] The queen lost 100s playing cards and paid George Colbronde for 2 gallons of Rhenish wine.[9] King Henry gave Elizabeth 10s for the disguising and £20 for "furs bought."[10] On January 14, the queen traveled by boat from Hampton Court to Richmond and on January 20 rewarded "a maid that came out of Spain" with a mark for dancing before her.[11] On January 26—just seven days before she gave birth—the queen traveled by barge from Richmond to London.[12]

Unless Elizabeth was deliberately ignoring the ritual of taking to her chambers a month before the birthing date, these activities indicate a premature arrival of the baby on February 2. The queen could, of course, have miscalculated the period of pregnancy, but after seven prior births, that seems unlikely. An individual of lesser stature might have become complacent after seven births and casually ignored the traditional period of seclusion, but the death of Arthur and her promise to Henry of more children—as well as the strictness of Margaret's *Ordinances*—would argue otherwise.

The contemporary chronicles also indicate that something was amiss:

> Upon Candlemas Day in the night following the day, the King and the Queen then being lodged in the Tower of London, the Queen that night was delivered of a daughter, where she intended to have been delivered at Richmond.[13]

> Candlemas Day in the night, the King and Queen being then at the Tower, the Queen travailed of child suddenly and was delivered of a daughter, the which was christened in the parish church of the said Tower & named Katherine. And upon the 11th day of the said month being Saturday in the morning, died the most gracious and virtuous princess the Queen, where within the parish church of the foresaid Tower her corpse lay 11 days after.[14]

The Privy Purse expenses indicate an urgent situation:

> Item: to James Nattres for his costs going into Kent for Doctor Hallysworth, physician, to come to the Queen by the King's commandment. First, for his boat hire from the Tower to Gravesend and again, 3*s* 4*d*. Item: to two watermen abiding at Gravesend unto such time the said James came again, for their expenses, 8*d*. Item: for horse hire and two guides by night and day, 2*s* 4*d*. and for his own expenses 16*d*.[15]

Such a tiny sum—7*s* 8*d*—for such a cataclysmic event. Elizabeth of York, the gracious queen of England, died on Saturday, February 11, 1503, the date of her thirty-seventh birthday.

The records do not indicate exactly when King Henry summoned Doctor Hallysworth or what caused Elizabeth's death. The nine-day interval between the birth of the baby and the death of the mother suggests that puerperal fever, that systemic infection that rages through a mother's body, caused her death. But hemorrhaging or other anatomical trauma could equally have caused death in an era of limited medical knowledge. The child, named Katherine, lived just 16 days and died on February 18. Ironies abound in contemplating the death of this queen. Elizabeth of York died in the same Tower of London where her brothers had disappeared not quite 20 years earlier. On the day after her death, her Privy Purse accounts dispassionately continue as if nothing had happened—as financial records must:

> Item: the 12th day of February to Robert Adington for lining and hemming of a kirtle of black satin for the Queen's grace 12*d*. Item: for making of three doublets of satin of Bruges for the Queen's footmen at 20*d* the piece 5*s*.... Item... for mending of 8 gowns of divers colors belonging to the Queen's grace from Midsummer to Christmas....[16]

Richard Decouns, Keeper of the Privy Purse, closed out the last year of Queen Elizabeth's life by paying bills and wages. Her expenses for not quite a full year amounted to £3,411 5*s* 9*d*. Her receipts from dower manors, towns, fee farms, wardships, fines, and loans totaled £3,585 19*s* 10 1/2*d*. The surplus was obtained only by pledging the queen's plate in return for £500 lent by Sir Thomas Lovell.[17] The loan allowed her attendants to be paid— her ladies and gentlewomen, her minstrels, the keeper of her goshawk, her midwife (£10), her attorneys, auditors, scribes, the rockers of the Courtenay children. Elizabeth of York would have approved.

Henry VII was devastated by Elizabeth's death. He ordered his Council to prepare the queen's funeral and placed Thomas Howard, earl of Surrey and treasurer of England, and Sir Richard Guilford, comptroller of his household, in charge. Then Henry went into seclusion:

> [He] took with him certain of his secretest, and privately departed to a solitary place to pass his sorrows and would no man should resort to him but such his Grace appointed, until such time it should please him to show his pleasure.... And in his departing ordained...the next day following for 636 whole masses said in London. And by Sir Charles Somerset and Sir Richard Guilford sent the best comfort to all the Queen's servants that hath been seen of a sovereign Lord with as good words.

> Also then were rung the bells of London every one, and after that
> throughout the Realm with solemn dirges and Masses of Requiems
> and every Religious place, colleges, and Churches.[18]

Within 10 months Henry Tudor had lost his first-born son—a personal and dynastic cataclysm—and his beloved wife whose quiet
words had steadied him through the traumas of Arthur's death
and 15 years of rebellions. With rebels quelled, the king was reasonably secure. The man, however, had lost the gracious presence
who had sustained him emotionally. Elizabeth's "departing was as
heavy and dolorous to the King's Highness as hath been seen or
heard of."[19]

Henry spared no expense in providing Elizabeth with a State
funeral worthy of a queen beloved of husband and nation. Her
embalmed body was wrapped in 40 ells of Holland linen, enclosed
in a lead coffin, and placed in a wooden chest covered with "a rich
cloth of black velvet with a Cross of cloth-of-gold."[20] On Sunday,
her coffin was removed from her chamber and placed within a
hearse in the Tower's chapel where it rested for 10 days. On that
first day after the queen's death, Lady Elizabeth Stafford was the
principal mourner, leading the queen's ladies walking two by two.
Until mourning garments could be prepared, all wore the "most
sad and simplest clothing." Kerchiefs hung to their shoulders and
closed under their chins. Mourning mantels (long gowns with
trains) and hoods were ordered for the queen's attendants and the
household of Prince Henry, her only surviving son and heir to the
throne. The cost was £1,483 15*s* 10*d*.[21]

For the next nine nights, four gentlewomen, two officers of
Arms, and seven yeomen and grooms watched over the queen's
body. Six ladies knelt continually around the corpse. The king's
chaplain supervised the daily masses sung by abbots and bishops.
Lady Katherine, the queen's sister, served as chief mourner,
accompanied by the earl of Surrey, the earl of Essex, and Lady
Elizabeth Stafford who carried her train. During the Mass sung
by the abbot of Westminster, Lady Katherine knelt alone at the
head of the coffin until the offering; then "two of the greatest
Estates there present" led her to present her offering. The six
ladies, the Estates, ladies and gentlewomen, knights, squires, and
gentlemen next presented offerings. On the seventh day, three
solemn masses were offered.

After mass on the tenth day, the queen's coffin was placed on a bier for the slow, sad journey to Westminster Abbey. Six matched horses trapped in black velvet drew the bier, which was covered with black velvet and a cross of white cloth-of-gold. White banners at each corner signaled that its occupant died in childbirth. An effigy of the queen lay on top of the coffin clothed in robes of Estate, made of nine yards of crimson satin bordered with black velvet.[22] A "very rich crown on her head, her hair about her shoulders, her scepter in her right hand, and her fingers well garnished with gold and precious stones" completed the effigy.[23] A gentlemen usher knelt on each end of the bier all the way to Westminster, while "two chariot men" and four henchmen wearing black gowns with mourning hoods rode the horses. Each horse displayed four lozenges of the queen's arms "beaten in oil rolled upon sarcenet with fine gold." A man of honor wearing a mourning hood walked beside each horse.

Following the bier were eight palfreys, saddled and trapped with black velvet, for the eight Ladies of Honor: Lady Katherine, Lady Elizabeth Stafford, the countess of Essex, Lady Herbert, Lady Lucey of Mountaigne, Lady Anne Percy, Lady Lisle, and Lady Scrope of Upsall. A man wearing a short black gown without hood led each horse. Next came a chariot carrying Lady Anne, the Lady Marquess of Dorset, Lady Daubeny, and Lady Clifford. In a third chariot rode Lady Gordon, widow of Perkin Warbeck. Then followed the citizens of London on horseback, the king's servants, and the lords' servants—a procession of hundreds.

Immediately in front of the queen's chariot rode Thomas Stanley, earl of Derby, Constable of England, and husband of the king's mother. In descending order of rank from the chariot toward the front of the procession were the Garter King, the mayor of London, the queen's chamberlain, the queen's confessor, and her almoner. Walking in front of the confessor and almoner on the left side were the children of the King's Chapel, the choir of St. Paul's, the Augustine and Dominican friars, and 200 poor men carrying torches and dressed in mourning habit. On the right side walked the lords of the Estates, the Chief Judges, the Master of the Rolls, the knights of the Garter, chaplains, deans, aldermen of London, knights, squires for the Body, gentlemen, and other squires. Near the front of the procession were representatives of foreign governments, including "the Easterlings" (the Hanseatic League), the

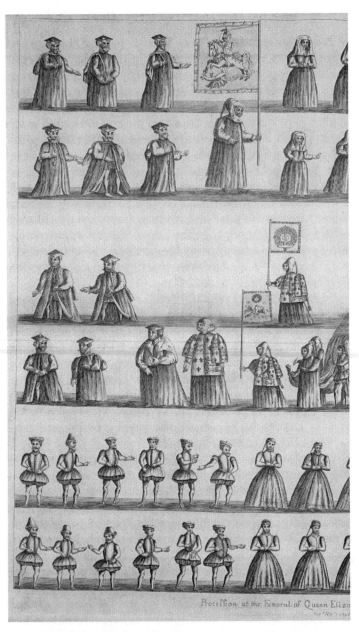

Photo 14 *Procession of the Funeral of Queen Elizabeth, 1502.* The aldermen, prelates, friars, judges, noblemen, and the of England, immediately preceded the queen's bier citizens, and servants followed the bier. Engraving, Special Collections, Stanford University Libraries.

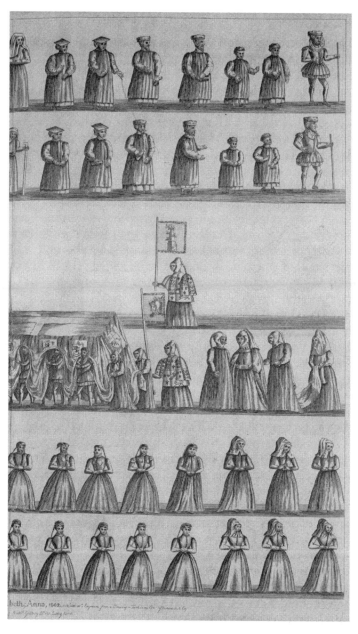

procession included foreign representatives, squires, knights,
mayor of London. Thomas Stanley, earl of Derby and Constable
with its effigy. The queen's ladies-in-waiting, attendants,
Antiquarian Repertory, 4: 655. Courtesy of Department of

French, the Portuguese, and Venetians. Minstrels and trumpeters on horseback (without their instruments) and messengers led the procession through the streets to Westminster.

Four to five thousand torches burned along one side of the street to Temple Bar. Members of the fellowships dressed in liveries lined the other side.²⁴ Thirty-seven virgins in white linen and wearing wreaths of green and white (the Tudor colors) held burning candles.²⁵ The citizens of London lined Cheap Street, where the mayor's wife had stationed 37 virgins holding burning candles. As the queen's bier passed, churches rang their bells, curates censed the corpse, and parishioners sang and prayed. Spain and Venice were each represented by 24 torchbearers with escutcheons bearing their country's arms. France displayed 12 torches with arms. Near Charing Cross, torchbearers representing the crafts of London stood in gowns and hoods of white woolen cloth. At the bridge next to Charing Cross, the abbot of Westminster and the abbot of Bermondsey censed the queen's body and accompanied it into the churchyard of St. Margaret's, where the procession disbanded.

The queen's coffin with effigy was removed from the bier and carried on the shoulders of nobles to the hearse in Westminster Abbey located between the high altar and the choir. More than 1,000 lights burned on the hearse, which displayed banners and a cloth of Majesty. The vaults and Cross of the church were hung with black cloth and lighted with 273 tapers weighing two pounds each. That evening the abbot of St. Albans and nine bishops conducted the dirge with Lady Katherine serving as chief mourner. After dirge, Lady Katherine was led by the marquess of Dorset and the earl of Derby to sup in the queen's great chamber at Westminster with the lords of the Estates and the officers of Arms. Twenty-four torchbearers, plus ladies, gentlewomen, knights, esquires, officers of Arms, and yeomen watched over the queen's body during the night.

After midnight matins, the prior and members of Westminster Convent departed the choir to gather around the queen's hearse and say psalms. They then visited St. Edward's shrine before returning to the convent. At six o'clock in the morning, the King's Chapel said the Lauds; at seven o'clock the bishop of Lincoln sang Our Lady's Mass. Lady Katherine as chief mourner was led by the marquess of Dorset and earl of Derby with her train carried by Lady Marquess the Elder (widow of Thomas Grey, the queen's half-brother). At this mass, only the chief mourner offered a gold piece of 3*s* 4*d*. At the second mass of the Trinity sung by the bishop of Salisbury, Lady Katherine offered a gold piece of 5*s*. At the third mass of Requiem sung by the bishop of Lincoln, all the ladies and nobles offered, including the queen's sisters Katherine and Anne, Lady Marquis of Dorset, and Lady Elizabeth Stafford. Cecily, the queen's sister, is not mentioned and presumably did not attend the services. Bridget, Elizabeth's youngest sister, likely remained secluded at Dartford Convent.

The nobles, the Chief Justice, knights of the Garter, aldermen of London, knights, esquires, and gentlemen next made offerings, followed by the ladies of the queen's court who laid 37 palls (rich cloths symbolizing burial) across the queen's effigy. The Great Wardrobe supplied 15 of the palls, made of red and green cloth-of-gold.[26] Each lady presented one pall, except for Viscountess Lisle who gave two, the countess of Essex and Lady Elizabeth Stafford who each presented three, and the queen's sisters five. Following the sermon by the bishop of Rochester, the ladies departed, the palls were removed, and the queen's effigy with its crown and rich robes taken "to a secret place to St. Edward's shrine."[27]

After the grave was opened and hallowed by the bishop of London, the coffin was placed inside. Following tradition, the queen's chamberlain and the ushers broke their staffs of office and cast them into the grave, weeping as they ended their service to Queen Elizabeth of York. Alms were distributed to "bed-rid folks, lazars, blind folks," to the friars of London, to parish churches in London and the suburbs, and to colleges and hospitals throughout the country. Also distributed was "the greatest livery of black gowns that ever was given in our days."[28]

The interment of Elizabeth of York cost £2389 7*d* delivered to the Undertreasurer of England, plus another £433 6*s* 8*d* to Sir Robert Hatton.[29] Those sums were munificent when compared to the £1,496 17*s* 2*d* cost of the 1483 funeral of her father Edward IV.[30] The private, truncated, scantily attended burial services for her mother, Queen Elizabeth Wydeville, 10 years earlier bears no comparison at all.[31]

Following her death, Henry settled several of Elizabeth's outstanding obligations. In April 1503, the king paid wages to several of the queen's attendants: £68 to her ladies and gentlewomen, £47 12*s* 4*d* to the servants of her staple, and £3 6*s* 8*d* to her dry nurse (perhaps the woman who attended her during her last illness).[32]

He also paid some of her debts: £100 to Steven Jenyns for pledged jewels, £30 to James Jentille, and £120 to William Halybrand for pledging out certain plate.[33] Until the end of his life in 1509, Henry paid the queen's minstrels 40*s* annually. It may be overly sentimental to surmise that King Henry began each New Year by remembering the holidays—and life—he had shared with his Elizabeth, but it is indisputable that he could have dismissed her minstrels without incurring any criticism whatsoever. Instead, every January 1 John Heron, treasurer of the king's chamber, paid 40*s* "to the Queen's minstrels in reward."[34] It seems safe to conclude that Henry Tudor celebrated Elizabeth of York each New Year by rewarding the musicians she had so loved.

Similarly, the requiem mass Henry endowed on November 20, 1504, at the church of St. Mary the Great in Cambridge was held during his lifetime on February 11, the anniversary of Elizabeth's birth and death. The service prayed for the king's "good and prosperous estate during his life" and after his death.[35] In the year of Henry's death, the requiem was sung twice: on February 11 and in April. In subsequent years the mass commemorated the king on April 21, the date of his death, but during the five years remaining in Henry's life, his requiem remembered Elizabeth.

Henry was not alone in his love and admiration for Elizabeth of York. Perhaps the scribe who recorded her funeral ceremonies best summarized the tributes to this queen: "she was one of the most gracious and best beloved princesses in the world in her time being."[36] The *Annals* of Ulster described her as "a woman that was of the greatest charity and humanity from Italy to Ireland."[37] Alvise Mocenigo, the Venetian ambassador, wrote that she was "a very handsome woman and of great ability...and in conduct very able (*di gran governo*)."[38] The *Vitellius* chronicler describes her simply as "noble and virtuous."[39] Polydore Vergil found her "intelligent above all others, and equally beautiful.... She was a woman of such a character that it would be hard to judge whether she displayed more of majesty and dignity in her life than wisdom and moderation."[40] For once, the hyperbolic encomium of Bernard André may have been spot on:

Inerat illi ab unguiculus Dei timor et servitium admirabile, in parentes vero mira observantia, erga fraters et sorores amor ferme incredibilis, in paupers Christique ministros reverenda ac singularis affectio.[41]

[There dwelt in her from earliest infancy a fear of God and admirable devotion, to her parents a truly amazing obedience, towards her brothers and sisters an almost incredible love, to the poor and the servants of Christ a reverent and extraordinary affection.]

CHAPTER 19

LEGACY

When Elizabeth of York died, her three surviving children were Margaret, age 13; Henry, age 11; and Mary, age 6. The king took on the task of preparing the children for the lives conferred by their royal births. Since Margaret was already married to James IV, king of Scotland, Henry had little to do except to send his daughter north to her husband. In June 1503, he bought £16,000 worth of jewels and plate, some for the queen of Scots,[1] and on June 27, the king and Margaret departed Richmond for the Collyweston residence of his mother, Margaret Beaufort. Margaret Tudor left Collyweston in Northamptonshire for her journey north to Scotland on July 8. Henry VII could hardly have suspected the role his daughter would play in subsequent English history.

In Edinburgh, Margaret was crowned queen consort at Holyrood Abbey on August 3, 1503. Of the six children born to James IV and Margaret, only one survived the second year of childhood. When James IV was killed at the battle of Flodden Field on September 9, 1513, his one-year-old son succeeded him as King James V. Queen Dowager Margaret, née Tudor, subsequently married Archibald Douglas, sixth earl of Angus, whom she divorced in 1528 to marry Henry Stewart, lord Methven. Stability in marriage was fast becoming an elusive quality for Tudor descendants.

In adulthood James V married Madeleine of France, who died within the year, and second, Mary of Guise, who gave birth to two sons who died within their first year of life. A daughter, Mary, was born on December 8, 1542. At the death of James V on December 14, 1542, his 6-day old daughter inherited his throne. She was crowned Mary, Queen of Scots, at the age of 9 months on September 9, 1543. Raised by her mother Mary of Guise, this queen of Scots married Francis, son of Henry II, king of France, on April 24, 1558. Francis II succeeded to the throne of France on July 6, 1559, and Mary, queen of

Scots, thus became queen of France until the early death of her husband on December 5, 1560. Mary returned to Scotland where she married Henry Stuart, lord Darnley (her first cousin of the half-blood) on July 29, 1565 and gave birth to son James on June 19, 1566, at Edinburgh Castle. Lord Darnley was murdered on February 10, 1567.

Three months later, Mary, queen of Scots, married James Hepburn, fourth earl of Bothwell. Having run afoul of other Scottish lords determined to control her son, Mary, queen of Scots, was forced to abdicate on July 24,1567, and to flee south across the Tweed to the protection of her first-cousin-once-removed Elizabeth I, queen of England. Held prisoner for 18 years, Mary was accused of plotting to seize the throne of England and was executed on February 8, 1587 at Fotheringhay Castle—barely 10 miles from the Collyweston estate from which her grandmother Margaret Tudor departed 84 years earlier on her journey to Scotland. At the death in 1603 of Queen Elizabeth I—the last Tudor monarch—Mary's son, James VI of Scotland, became King James I of England. The Stuart dynasty thus began with James I, great-great-grandson of Henry VII and Elizabeth of York.

* * *

Elizabeth of York's only surviving son, 11-year-old Henry, duke of York, had a lot to learn after the death of his older brother. Arthur had received the princely education destined for the future king—accompanying his father on forays through the countryside, observing Perkin Warbeck's capture at Taunton, greeting the Venetian ambassador at Woodstock. His younger brother Henry—though well educated in grammar, languages (especially Latin), literature, philosophy, music, and military skills[2]—had to catch up in learning about regal responsibilities. Soon after Arthur's death, negotiations between England and Spain began to discuss marriage between Henry and Katherine of Aragon, his brother's widow. Canon law forbid marriage between a man and his brother's wife as an incestuous union, but the political advantages of aligning England with Spain caused the Pope ultimately to grant a dispensation. Everyone was pleased. Henry VII kept Katherine's marriage portion paid for the liaison with Arthur. The Spanish monarchs forestalled a marriage between Prince Henry and the King of France's daughter.[3] The fact that Katherine at age 17 was 6 years older than her proposed husband bothered no one. Years later when Queen Katherine was too old to bear children and Henry VIII lacked a male heir, her age became a significant factor in Henry's quest for a divorce.

Henry VII initially showed great kindness to Princess Katherine, who was often ill. In August 1504, the king took Katherine to Richmond, then on to Windsor:

> There they stayed twelve or thirteen days, going almost every day into the park and the forest to hunt deer and other game. From Windsor they returned to Richmond, where they passed a week.
>
> The Princess had been unwell for three days, suffering from ague and derangement of the stomach. She soon got better. From Richmond the King proceeded to Westminster, leaving the Prince of Wales [Henry] behind, but taking the Princess of Wales [Katherine], the Princess Mary, and all the English ladies with him. A few days later they all went together to Greenwich. After staying six or seven days in Greenwich, the Princess fell ill again, and much more seriously than before.[4]

For four weeks, Katherine suffered ague and bouts of colds and coughing, her illness undoubtedly exacerbated by the stress of her uncertain position in England. Her physicians treated her with purgings and attempted bleedings that failed to draw blood. The Spanish ambassador informed Queen Isabella that King Henry was quite solicitous to Katherine, sending messages and offering physicians. At the same time, Henry VII was also introducing Prince Henry to his new responsibilities as royal heir:

> The Prince of Wales is with the King. Formerly the King did not like to take the Prince of Wales with him, in order not to interrupt his studies. It is quite wonderful how much the King likes the Prince of Wales. He has good reason to do so, for the Prince deserves all love. But it is not only from love that the King takes the Prince with him; he wishes to improve him. Certainly there could be no better school in the world than the society of such a father as Henry VII. He is so wise and so attentive to everything; nothing escapes his attention. There is no doubt the Prince has an excellent governor and steward in his father. If he lives ten years longer, he will leave the Prince furnished with good habits, and with immense riches, and in as happy circumstances as man can be.[5]

Clearly the Duke de Estrada, who penned these sentiments to Queen Isabella on October 10, 1504, was trying to allay any doubts Ferdinand and Isabella might have about their daughter's future in England.

Unfortunately, negotiations for the marriage of Prince Henry and Katherine became entangled in Continental politics. Even more unfortunately, Queen Isabella died on November 26, 1504, leaving Katherine devoid of support from any woman with power to intercede on her behalf. The young widow became trapped between the pincers of kings Ferdinand and Henry VII as each tried to out-flank the other. When Ferdinand demanded that Katherine be given possession of her dower lands in England, due upon her marriage to Arthur, Henry responded that her English dower would not be conferred until Ferdinand paid the final 100,000 scudi required by that marriage contract. Ferdinand answered that he would send the marriage portion only after Katherine received her English dower. This roundabout lasted for years, while Ferdinand went off to Naples to fight the French in Italy.

Katherine's financial situation steadily deteriorated. On April 22, 1506, the young widow wrote to her father begging him

> to consider how she is in debt, not for extravagant things, but for food, and how the King of England will not pay anything, though she has asked him with tears. He had said that the promise made him about the marriage portion had not been kept. [She] is in the greatest anguish, her people ready to ask alms, and herself all but naked.[6]

She also begs her father to send her a confessor, since she cannot understand English and has been near death for six months.

Henry VII has reaped much blame for allowing Katherine to live in poverty, but Ferdinand—a father both unscrupulous and venal—was equally culpable. His letters cavil with craven and specious excuses explaining that her marriage portion was delayed because of the death of Isabella or because he was absent from Castile (excuses sent from Naples, from Valencia, from whereever). In one letter to Katherine, Ferdinand blames her brother-in-law Archduke Philip, who "caused all her misery" by preventing the money from being sent.[7] How much the two deceased queens Elizabeth and Isabella might have ameliorated the suffering of

Katherine is difficult to say, but Elizabeth of York had certainly provided both emotional and financial support during her unfortunate daughter-in-law's widowhood.

Almost immediately after Henry VII died on April 21, 1509, his son Henry married the woman he had escorted from Bishop's Palace to St. Paul's Cathedral when he was 10 years old. Still dazzled by the beauty he witnessed on that splendid November Sunday in 1501, Henry VIII married Katherine of Aragon on June 11, 1509, seven weeks after his father's death. The king was age 17, his consort 23. The couple was crowned together as king and queen of England on June 24, 1509. For 18 splendid years, they celebrated life and reign with love and gusto. But after six births (and perhaps unknown miscarriages), only one daughter, Mary, survived to carry on the Tudor dynasty. Henry VIII wanted—needed—a son. He therefore sought a divorce, now insisting that his marriage to Katherine of Aragon, widow of his brother, was incestuous. The Pope who depended on Katherine's nephew Charles V, Holy Roman Emperor, for financial, political, and military protection refused. The consequences were cataclysmic.

Henry VIII broke with the Church in Rome, institutionalized the Reformation in England, and embarked on marathon marriages in his quest after a male heir for the Tudor throne. His second wife, Anne Boleyn, failed when she produced only another daughter, Elizabeth. His third wife, Jane Seymour, gave birth to the son who became Edward VI, then died. Desperately seeking additional sons, Henry married Anne of Cleves (whom he rejected on sight and annulled the marriage six months later), then Katherine Howard, then Katherine Parr. The last three wives produced no heirs for the aging monarch. After Henry VIII died on January 28, 1547, the Tudor dynasty struggled through the six-year reign of his son Edward VI, the nine-day reign of his grandniece Lady Jane Grey, and the five-year reign of his daughter Mary I. Finally, the Tudors triumphed with the long, glorious 44 years of Elizabeth I, daughter of Anne Boleyn. When Elizabeth, the "Virgin Queen," died on March 24, 1603, the 117-year Tudor dynasty ended.

*　*　*

Even little Mary, age six when Elizabeth of York died, played a significant role in the turbulent times of the Tudor dynasty. Her

Photo 15   Henry VIII (1491–1547, reigned 1509–47). Painted *circa*
1509 when he became king and married Katherine of
Aragon, Henry wears a gown edged with fur and
accented by a heavy chain of rubies surrounded by pearls.
His black cap covers short, straight auburn hair. Henry
holds a red rose with white center, symbol of the Tudor
dynasty. *English School.* Berger Collection at the Denver
Art Museum. Photograph courtesy of the Denver Art
Museum.

father raised Mary to become an accomplished royal consort. Along with the lute purchased for her in August 1505,[8] Henry VII provided an education that produced a charming, lovely, accomplished woman. Briefly tutored by Thomas Linacre, the humanist scholar who taught her brother Arthur, Mary was betrothed at age 11 to the future Charles V, Holy Roman Emperor, a contract soon broken to achieve a closer political liaison with France.

On October 9, 1514, the beautiful 18-year-old Mary was married to the wizened, battle-worn 52-year-old king of France, Louis XII. When the princess moved to Paris, her physician and tutor Linacre accompanied her. Mary Tudor was crowned Queen of France on November 5, 1514. Within two months, she found herself a widow when Louis XII died in Paris on January 1, 1515. Mary was then free to wed the man she had loved from the beginning, Charles Brandon, duke of Suffolk—the same Charles Brandon who had jousted at sister Margaret's wedding in 1502. A good friend of Henry VIII, Suffolk headed the English delegation sent to France to congratulate the new king, and Mary persuaded him to marry her secretly in Paris on March 3, 1515. Friend or not, the marriage infuriated Henry VIII, who had extracted a promise from Suffolk that he would not wed until his return to England. Suffolk was forced to pay a huge fine and Mary to forfeit her jewels and plate, but the couple retook their vows openly in the Church of the Observant Friars at Greenwich on May 13, 1515. Mary gave birth to a son, Henry, and two daughters, Frances and Eleanor.

It was Mary's daughter Frances who would contribute to the disruptions following Edward VI's early death in 1553. Frances Brandon had married Henry Grey, third marquess of Dorset (grandson of Elizabeth of York's half-brother, Thomas Grey). The oldest of their children was the quiet, intelligent, and very Protestant Lady Jane Grey. With the reformation in England still new and unstable at the death of Edward VI, many Protestants feared that Mary Tudor, the heir designated by Henry VIII to succeed his son, would restore Catholicism as the official religion of the nation. The abortive coup that attempted to replace Mary Tudor, daughter of Henry VIII and Katherine of Aragon, with Lady Jane Grey lasted just nine sad days.

Fortunately, Elizabeth of York, long deceased, could not witness the religious conflagrations ignited by her son Henry VIII, the beheading of her great-granddaughter Lady Jane Grey, the religious executions ordered by her granddaughter Queen Mary I, or the beheading of her great-granddaughter Mary, queen of Scots. Elizabeth of York would have been proud, however, of her namesake Elizabeth I, granddaughter and last of the Tudors.

* * *

Many historians have observed that Henry VII was a changed man after the death of Elizabeth of York. His reputation for penury and parsimony grew during the last years of his reign when he showed little sympathy for his subjects who lived with frequent and harsher taxes, assessments, and bonds. The king no longer was influenced by the ameliorating presence of the gracious queen who stood by his side for 15 years. Perhaps Henry's catastrophic losses would have changed any human being. The death of his eldest son, Arthur, followed within months by the death of his beloved Elizabeth irrevocably affected Henry and contributed to his increasingly acquisitive nature. Having suffered irreplaceable human losses, he clung to things—money, jewels, land.

When it suited his purposes, Henry dispensed huge sums in the service of self and nation. The insistent hospitality lavished on Archduke Philip and Joanna of Castile when a storm forced their unexpected landing in England in 1506 recall the days of Elizabeth and their elaborate Court entertainments. Perhaps Henry was indulging in a moment of nostalgia, filling his loneliness with memories of happier times. Negotiations for political marriages began, but none achieved fruition. While Henry continued to pursue dynastic ambitions—lending £226,000 to Maximilian, Archduke Philip, and the infant Charles of Castile between 1505 and 1509 to enhance his Continental influence[9]—his royal family was irrevocably diminished in both size and spirit.

* * *

Elizabeth of York, the first Tudor queen, gave birth to descendants who changed the world, who brought about the Protestant Reformation in England, and who encouraged the English Renaissance. Equally important, however, were Queen Elizabeth's personal contributions during her lifetime—her quiet presence that steadied private lives and stabilized a nation torn apart by decades of civil conflict and family feuds. In the early days of

Henry's reign, Elizabeth of York's lineage secured the loyalty of nobles otherwise alien to Henry's cause—perhaps even hostile to his claim to the throne of England. Throughout their marriage, her quiet presence provided Henry a comforting sense of personal security. Her love of the arts—music, dancing, pageantry, architecture—stimulated the creativity so important to the emerging aesthetics of the English Renaissance. She was beloved by everyone—from the mightiest of diplomats to the lowliest of subjects. During her 17 years as queen, Elizabeth of York was exactly the consort needed by England to help end the ugly, internecine Wars of the Roses.

Sometimes, a gracious personality far outweighs the power of the potentate. Elizabeth of York was such a queen.

NOTES

Chapter 1. The Gracious Queen: Beginnings

1. Robert Fabyan, *The New Chronicles of England and France*, ed. Henry Ellis (London: Rivington, 1811), 654.
2. Fabyan, 655.
3. Fabyan, 655.
4. *The Travels of Leo of Rozmital through Germany, Flanders, England, France, Spain, Portugal and Italy 1465–1467*, ed. Malcolm Letts (Cambridge: Cambridge University Press, 1957), 45–46.
5. Antonio Cornazzano, "La Regina d'ingliterra" quoted from Conor Fahy's "The Marriage of Edward IV and Elizabeth Woodville: A New Italian Source," *English Historical Review* 76 (1961): 660–72; Anne Sutton and Livia Visser-Fuchs, "A 'Most Benevolent Queen': Queen Elizabeth Woodville's Reputation, Her Piety and Her Books," *Ricardian* 10 (June 1995): 232–35, and "The Device of Queen Elizabeth Woodville: A Gillyflower or Pink," *Ricardian* 11 (1997): 17–24.
6. *The Great Chronicle of London*, ed. A. H. Thomas and I. D. Thornley (London: George Jones, 1938), 203.
7. *The Coventry Leet Book: Or Mayor's Register*, ed. Mary Dormer Harris (London: Early English Text Society, 1907–13), 346.
8. *Calendar of State Papers and manuscripts, existing in the Archives and Collections of Milan. Vol. 1*, ed. Allen B. Hinds (London: His Majesty's Stationery Office, 1912), 132.
9. Christ Church, Canterbury, *The Chronicle of John Stone, Monk of Christ Church 1415–1471* (Cambridge: Antiquarian Society, 1902), 113.
10. Gervase Rosser, *Medieval Westminster 1200–1540* (Oxford: Clarendon Press, 1989), 68–74.
11. Charles Lethbridge Kingsford, *English Historical Literature in the Fifteenth Century* (New York: Burt Franklin, 1963; Reprint Oxford, 1913), 386.
12. Kingsford, *English Historical Literature*, 387.

13. See Gordon Kipling, *The Triumph of Honour: Burgundian Origins of the Elizabethan Renaissance* (Leiden: University Press for the Sir Thomas Browne Institute, 1977) for the definitive study of Burgundian influences on the early Tudor court; also Sydney Anglo, *Spectacle, Pageantry, and Early Tudor Policy* (Oxford: Clarendon Press, 1969), 52–108.

Chapter 2. Youth and Tragedy

1. Nicholas Orme, *From Childhood to Chivalry: The Education of the English Kings and Aristocracy 1066–1530* (London: Methuen, 1984), 26, n. 127.
2. *The Complete Peerage of England, Scotland, Ireland, Great Britain and the United Kingdom*, ed. George Edward Cokayne (New York: St. Martin's Press, 1984), 1: 153.
3. *Letters of the Kings of England*, ed. James Orchard Halliwell (London: Henry Colburn, 1846), 136–44; Arlene Okerlund, *Elizabeth Wydeville: The Slandered Queen* (Stroud: Tempus, 2005), 152–54.
4. British Library, MS Royal 14 E.iii.
5. Garrett MS.168. Manuscripts Division, Department of Rare Books and Special Collections, Princeton University Library.
6. Bernard Quaritch, *Catalogue of Illuminated and Other Manuscripts* (London: Bernard Quaritch, 1931), 95.
7. *Calendar of Letters, Despatches, and State Papers, relating to the negotiations between England and Spain, preserved in the Archives at Simancas and elsewhere: Henry VII. 1485–1509*, ed. G. A. Bergenroth (London: Longman, 1862), 156.
8. Orme, 12–59.
9. Quoted from John W. Hales and Frederick J. Furnivall, eds. *Bishop Percy's Folio Manuscript: Ballads and Romances* (London, N. Trübner:, 1868) 3: 329.
10. Hales, 3: 330–31.
11. *The Household of Edward IV: The Black Book and the Ordinance of 1478*, ed. A. R. Myers (Manchester: University Press, 1959), 131–32.
12. *Privy Purse Expenses of Elizabeth of York: Wardrobe Accounts of Edward IV*, ed. Nicholas Harris Nicolas, Esq. (London: William Pickering, 1830; New York: Barnes & Noble Facsimile edition, 1972), 29; *Excerpta Historica, or Illustrations of English History* (London: Samuel Bentley, 1831), 125, 133.
13. *PP*, 41.
14. *PP*, 58.

15. Oxford Dictionary of National Biography (Oxford and New York: Oxford University Press, 2004–), online: http://www.oxforddnb.com.
16. *PP*, 8.
17. Curt. F. Bühler, "The Dictes and Sayings of the Philosophers," *Library* 15 (1934), 316; Okerlund, 380–88.
18. Bodleian Library, University of Oxford, MS 264.
19. Janet Backhouse, "Illuminated Manuscripts Associated with Henry VII and Members of His Immediate Family," *The Reign of Henry VII: Proceedings of the 1993 Harlaxton Symposium,* ed. Benjamin Thompson (Stamford: Paul Watkins, 1995), 180.
20. Charles Ross, *Edward IV* (Berkeley: University of California Press, 1974), 264–67.
21. Kipling, *Triumph*, 15 passim; Okerlund, 177–89.
22. British Library: *Acts of Sovereigns and other Supreme Authorities. Louis XI, King* (William Machlinia: London, 1483).
23. Cora Scofield, *The Life and Reign of Edward the Fourth* (London: Longmans, Green, 1923), 2: 142.
24. Philippe de Commines, *The Memoires of Philip de Commines, Lord of Argeton,* ed. Andrew R. Scoble (London: Henry G. Bohn, 1855). An online edition is available at http://www.r3.org, Book 5, Ch. 20.
25. Sutton and Vischer-Fuchs, *The Reburial of Richard Duke of York 21–30 July 1476* (London: Richard III Society, 1996), 19.
26. John Anstis, ed. *The Register of the Most Noble Order of the Garter, from its Cover in Black Velvet Usually Called the Black Book* (London: John Barber, 1724), 197.
27. *PP*, 159.
28. *Illustrations of ancient state and chivalry from manuscripts preserved in the Ashmolean museum,* ed. William Henry (London: W. Nicol, 1840), 30.
29. *Excerpta*, 171–212; Okerlund, 36–37, 88–95.
30. *Excerpta*, 228–38.
31. *Illustrations*, 33.
32. Okerlund, 179–89.
33. Kipling, *Triumph*, 117.
34. *Illustrations*, 39.
35. *Illustrations*, 40.
36. Scofield, 2: 237–38; *Foedera*, ed. Thomas Rymer (London: J. Tonson, 1728–35), 12: 89.
37. Scofield, 2: 242.
38. *Calendar of the Patent Rolls: Edward IV. Henry VI A.D. 1467–1477* (London: Her Majesty's Stationery Office, 1900), 110.
39. *The Crowland Chronicle Continuations: 1459–1486,* ed. Nicholas Pronay and John Cox (London: Alan Sutton, 1986), 149.

Chapter 3. The Lady Princess Deposed

1. Crowland, 151.
2. *Letters and Papers Illustrative of the Reigns of Richard III and Henry VII*, ed. James Gairdner (London: Longman, Green, Longman, and Roberts, 1861), 1: 2–10.
3. *L & P*, 1: 9.
4. Crowland, 155.
5. *Registrum Thome Bourgchier, Cantuariensis Archiepiscopi, AD 1454–1486*, ed. F. R. H. DuBoulay (Canterbury and York Soc., Liv, 1957), 52; *Excerpta*, 378–79.
6. Commines, Book 5, Ch. 20.
7. Ross, 320.
8. W. E. Hampton, "A Further Account of Robert Stillington," *Ricardian* 4 (1976), 27.
9. A. J. Mowat, "Robert Stillington," *Ricardian* 4 (1976), 23–24; *CPR 1452–61*, 631; *CPR 1467–77*, 234 and 310.
10. Mowat, 24; *CPR 1476–85*, 102.
11. *Rotuli Parliamentorium* (London, 1832), 6: 234.
12. *Coventry Leet*, 393.
13. J. L. Laynesmith, "The Kings' Mother," *History Today* 56 (March 2006), 38.
14. Commines, Book 4, Ch. 8.
15. Michael K. Jones, *Bosworth 1485: Psychology of a Battle* (Stroud, Tempus, 2002), 67.
16. Laynesmith, "King's Mother," 38–45.
17. *Wills from Doctors' Commons: A Selection from the Wills of Eminent Persons proved in the Prerogative Court of Canterbury, 1495–1695*, ed. John Nichols and John Bruce (Westminster: Camden Society O.S., 1863), 1 (Emphasis mine.)
18. Laynesmith, "King's mother," discusses Cecily's public display and private practice of religion, 38–45.
19. Crowland, 161.
20. Dominic Mancini, *The Usurpation of Richard the Third*, trans. C. A. J. Armstrong. 2nd ed. (Oxford: Clarendon Press, 1969), 93.
21. Crowland, 163.
22. Crowland, 163.
23. Crowland, 163.
24. Polydore Vergil, *Three Books of Polydore Vergil's English History, comprising the Reigns of Henry VI, Edward IV, and Richard III*, ed. Henry Ellis (London: John Bowyer Nichols, 1844), 196.
25. Fabyan, 670; *GC*, 235, 436.
26. Mancini, 93.
27. Crowland, 163.

28. *Chronicles of London*, ed. Charles Lethbridge Kingsford (Oxford: Clarendon Press, 1905), 191.
29. Livia Visser-Fuchs, "English Events in Caspar Weinreich's Danzig *Chronicle*, 1461–1495," *Ricardian* 7 (1989), 316.
30. Christine Weightman, *Margaret of York, Duchess of Burgundy, 1446–1503* (New York: St. Martin's Press, 1989), 145.
31. Commines, Book 5, Ch. 20.
32. Peter D. Clarke, "English Royal Marriages and the Papal Penitentiary in the Fifteenth Century," *English Historical Review* 120. 488 (2005), 1014–1029. http://ehr.oxfordjournals.org/cgi/content/full/120/488/1014.
33. *Titulus Regius*, http://www.r3.org/bookcase/texts/tit_reg.html.

Chapter 4. Restored to Court

1. Crowland, 171.
2. Ellis, Henry. *Original Letters, Illustrative of English History*, Second Series (New York: AMS Press, 1970), 4: 149–50.
3. Crowland, 171.
4. Crowland, 175.
5. Crowland, 175.
6. Crowland, 175.
7. Crowland, 177.
8. Crowland, 175.
9. Vergil, *The Anglica Historia of Polydore Vergil A.D. 1485–1537*, ed. Denys Hay (London: Royal Historical Society, 1950), 3.
10. George Buck, *The History of King Richard the Third (1619)*, ed. Arthur Noel Kincaid (Gloucester: Alan Sutton, 1979), 191.
11. Alison Hanham, "Sir George Buck and Princess Elizabeth's Letter: A Problem in Detection," *Ricardian* 7 (June 1987), 399.
12. Quoted from Arthur Kincaid, "Buck and the Elizabeth of York Letter," *Ricardian* 8 (March 1988): 48.
13. Kincaid, 47.
14. Visser-Fuchs, "Elizabeth of York's Letter," 18.
15. Kincaid, 48.
16. ODNB: http://www.oxforddnb.com.
17. British Library, MS Royal 20 A xix, f.195.
18. Visser-Fuchs, "Where Did Elizabeth Find Consolation?" 470.
19. British Library, MS Harley 49.
20. Visser-Fuchs, "Where Did Elizabeth Find Consolation?" 469–70.
21. Michael Jones and Malcolm Underwood, *The King's Mother: Lady Margaret Beaufort, Countess of Richmond and Derby* (Cambridge: Cambridge University Press, 1992), 42.

22. Ralph A. Griffiths and Roger S. Thomas. *The Making of the Tudor Dynasty* (Stroud: Sutton, 2005), 143.

Chapter 5. Marriage to a King

1. S. B. Chrimes, *Henry VII* (Berkeley: University of California Press, 1972), 52.
2. *Excerpta*, 152–54.
3. Alison Weir, *Britain's Royal Families: The Complete Genealogy* (London: Pimlico, 2002), 131–32.
4. Chrimes, 8.
5. Chrimes, 12.
6. Jones and Underwood, 25.
7. *Calendar Spain*, 176.
8. *Letters of Kings*, 169–70.
9. Vergil, *Anglica*, 3; Michael Bennett, *Lambert Simnel and the Battle of Stoke* (New York: St. Martin's Press, 1987), 31.
10. *Materials for a History of the Reign of Henry VII From Original Documents preserved in the Public Record Office*, ed. William Campbell (London: Longman and Turbner, 1873), 1: 6.
11. Anne F. Sutton, and P. W. Hammond, *The Coronation of Richard III: The Extant Documents* (Gloucester: Alan Sutton, 1983), 204–27.
12. L. G. W. Legg, *English Coronation Records* (London, 1901), 198.
13. Legg, 201–2.
14. Legg, 200–201.
15. Legg, 204–6, 211.
16. Legg, 212.
17. Anglo, 7; *Materials*, 2: 3–29.
18. *RP*, 6: 270b.
19. *RP*, 6: 288.
20. *Materials*, 1: 122–23.
21. *RP*, 6: 278.
22. I am grateful to Marianina Olcott for her expert assistance in translating Latin.
23. Chrimes, 111.
24. Crowland, 195.
25. Jones and Underwood, 67.
26. Clarke, http://ehr.oxfordjournals.org/cki/content/full/120/488/1014.
27. Archivio Segreto Vaticano, Penitenzieria Apostilica, Reg. 33, f. 40v, quoted from Clarke, note 45 http://ehr.oxfordjournals.org/cki/content/full/120/488/1014.
28. *Calendar of Papal Letters* (London: Her Majesty's Stationery Office, 1960), 11, Part 1: 18.

29. *Calendar Papal*, 11, Part 1: 18.
30. *Calendar Papal*, 11, Part 1: 20.
31. *Materials*, 1: 264.
32. Crowland, 191.
33. Bernard André, *De Vita Atque Gestis Henrici Septimi Historia*. ed. James Gairdner in *Memorials of King Henry VII*. (London, 1858), 38.
34. British Library, MS Harleian 336.
35. *Materials*, 1: 228.
36. *Materials*, 1: 407.
37. Clarke, http://ehr.oxfordjournals.org/cki/content/full/120/488/1014.
38. *Calendar Papal*, 14: 14.
39. William Shakespeare, *I Henry VI*, Act 2, scene 4.

Chapter 6. Birth of a Prince

1. Henrietta Leyser, *Medieval Women: A Social History of Women in England 450–1500* (London: Phoenix Press, 1996), 106–7.
2. Anglo, "The British History in Early Tudor Propaganda," *Bulletin of the John Rylands Library* 44 (1960–61): 28–29.
3. *GC*, 238–39.
4. Anglo, "British History," 37.
5. André, 9–11.
6. Sheila Gray, Winchester Cathedral Voluntary Guide, by personal correspondence; *The Antiquarian Repertory: A Miscellaneous Assemblage of Topography, History, Biography, Customs and Manners*, ed. Francis Grose and Thomas Astle (London: Edward Jeffery, 1807), 1: 355.
7. *Materials*, 1: 338, 347–50; *CPR Henry VII 1485–1494*, 75.
8. Crowland, 195.
9. Vergil, *Anglica*, 11.
10. *Lease Book Number 1, 1486–1595*, Westminster Abbey, folio 9.
11. John Leland, *De rebus Brittanicus Collectanea*, ed. T. Hearne (London: Benjamin White, 1774). 4: 179–80.
12. Leland, 4: 204; *Antiquarian Repertory* 1: 353–57.
13. Leland, 4: 181, 204; "Stowe's Memoranda," *Three Fifteenth Century Chronicles*, ed. James Gardner (Camden Society, 1880), 104–5.
14. Leland, 4: 180, 204–7.
15. Leland, 4: 206.
16. Leland, 4: 207; "Stowes Memoranda," 105.
17. Leland, 4: 207.
18. Leland, 4; 183.
19. Leland, 4: 183–84.
20. Leland, 4: 189.
21. *Antiquarian Repertory* 1: 356.

22. Leland, 4: 207.
23. *Materials*, 2: 58.
24. *Materials*, 2: 103.
25. Elias Ashmole, *The Institution, Laws & Ceremonies of the Most Noble Order of the Garter* (London, 1672; Reprint, Baltimore: Genealogical Publishing, 1971), 712.
26. *Materials*, 2: 115.
27. *Materials*, 2: 115.
28. *Materials*, 2: 116.
29. *Materials*, 2: 221.
30. *Materials*, 2: 142.
31. *CPR Henry VII 1485–1494*, 172.
32. *Materials*, 2: 148–49.
33. *Materials*, 2: 149.

Chapter 7. Rebellion in the Realm

1. *ODNB*, http://www.oxforddnb.com.libaccess.sjlibrary.org/view/article/17058.
2. Vergil, *Anglica*, 13.
3. Bennett, 44; Vergil, *Anglica*, 13.
4. Bennett, 121.
5. André, 49; Bennett, 132.
6. *Letters of the Kings*, 172.
7. Bennett, 53.
8. Chrimes, 76.
9. Paul Murray Kendall, *Richard the Third* (New York: W. W. Norton, 1956), 349–50.
10. Kendall, 377–78.
11. Leland, 4: 207.
12. Bennett, 51.
13. Chrimes, 76; Bennett, 66.
14. Vergil, *Anglica*, 19.
15. Vergil, *Anglica*, 19.
16. *Foedera*, 12: 328–29.
17. *Materials*, 2: 225.
18. *Materials*, 2: 319.
19. Francis Bacon, *The History of the Reign of King Henry the Seventh*, ed. F. J. Levy (New York: Bobbs-Merrill, 1972), 88.
20. Bacon, 84.
21. Bacon, 83.
22. David Baldwin, *Elizabeth Woodville: Mother of the Princes in the Tower* (Stroud: Sutton, 2002), 124–25.
23. Sutton and Visser-Fuchs, "A 'Most Benevolent Queen'," 214–45.

24. Bennett, 58.
25. *Materials*, 2: 322.
26. *CPR Henry VII 1485–1494*, 154.
27. Bennett, 59.
28. Bennett, 59.
29. *Letters of the Kings*, 171.
30. R. Allen Brown, *The History of the King's Works: Vol. II The Middle Ages* (London: Her Majesty's Stationery Office, 1963), 685; Simon Thurley, *The Royal Palaces of Tudor England: Architecture and Court Life 1460–1547* (New Haven and London: Yale University Press for the Paul Mellon Centre for Studies in British Art, 1993), 9–10.
31. *Household*, 104.
32. *CP*, 4: 131–32.
33. Bennet, 71.
34. *Materials*, 2: 157.
35. *Materials*, 2: 179.
36. *Materials*, 2: 170, 175.
37. Bennett, 75.
38. Bennett, 101.
39. Bennett, 101.
40. Vergil, *Anglica* 25.
41. Chrimes, 78.

Chapter 8. The Crowning of a Queen

1. *GC*, 203.
2. Lionel Butler and Chris Given-Wilson, *Medieval Monasteries of Great Britain* (London: Michael Joseph, 1979), 331.
3. Leland, 4: 217.
4. Leland, 4: 218.
5. *GC*, 438.
6. Leland, 4: 216.
7. Leland, 4: 218.
8. Leland, 4: 218.
9. *Three Fifteenth-Century Chronicles*, ed. James Gairdner (Camden Society, 1880), 106–13.
10. Leland, 4: 219–20.
11. Leland, 4: 222.
12. Leland, 4: 223.
13. Leland, 4: 226.
14. Leland, 4: 216.
15. Madeleine Pelner Cosman, *Fabulous Feasts: Medieval Cookery and Ceremony* (New York: George Braziller, 1976), 33.
16. Leland, 4: 227–28.

17. Leland, 4: 228.
18. Leland, 4: 228.
19. Leland, 4: 228.

Chapter 9. "My Lady the King's Mother"

1. Jones and Underwood, 148.
2. *CPR Henry VII, 1485–1494,* 128.
3. Jones and Underwood, 28.
4. Jones and Underwood, 29.
5. Jones and Underwood, 47.
6. Jones and Underwood, 47.
7. Vergil, *Three Books,* 135.
8. Jones and Underwood, 52.
9. André, *Memorials,* 15–16.
10. Jones and Underwood, 58–59.
11. Jones and Underwood, 60.
12. Jones and Underwood, 60–61.
13. Jones and Underwood, 60.
14. *London Topographical Record* (London: London Topographical Society, 1916), 10: 97; Jones and Underwood, 100.
15. Jones and Underwood, 67.
16. *CPR Henry VII 1485–1492,* 113.
17. Jones and Underwood, 164.
18. *Dictionary of National Biography,* ed. Leslie Stephen and Sidney Lee (New York: Macmillan, 1908–9), 8: 647.
19. Jones and Underwood, 126.
20. Jones and Underwood, 134, 162.
21. Jones and Underwood, 134.
22. Jones and Underwood, 162.
23. *Calendar Spain,* 164.
24. *Calendar Spain,* 178.
25. *Records of the Borough of Nottingham, being a series of extracts from the archives of the Corporation of Nottingham* (1485–1547), 3: 301.
26. Jones and Underwood, 161.
27. *Excerpta,* 285.

Chapter 10. Life with Henry

1. Brown, 949.
2. Leland, 4: 234.
3. Leland, 4: 234.
4. Leland, 4: 235.
5. Leland, 4: 235.

6. Thurley, 19.
7. Brown, 886.
8. Leland, 4: 242.
9. Leland, 4: 239.
10. *CCR Henry VII 1485–1500*, 68.
11. *Materials*, 2: 349.
12. Orme, 13.
13. *Materials*, 2: 349, 459.
14. Leland, 4: 243.
15. Leland, 4: 244.
16. *Materials*, 2: 392.
17. Thurley, 9.
18. Brown, 2: 680.
19. *Materials*, 2: 497.
20. *Materials*, 2: 498–99.
21. *Materials*, 2: 498–99.

Chapter 11. The Royal Family

1. Leland, 4: 249.
2. Leland, 4: 255.
3. Leland, 4: 250.
4. Leland, 4: 253.
5. Leland, 4: 254.
6. Leland, 4: 254.
7. Leland, 4: 256.
8. *CPR Henry VII 1485–1494*, 220.
9. *Materials*, 2: 319; *CPR Henry VII 1485–1494*, 236.
10. *CPR Henry VII 1485–1494*, 257, 296, 305.
11. *CPR Henry VII 1485–1494*, 311–12.
12. *CPR Henry VII 1485–1494*, 312.
13. *Materials*, 2: 522.
14. *Materials*, 2: 157.
15. *Materials*, 2: 296.
16. *Materials*, 2: 349.
17. *Materials*, 2: 459.
18. *CPR Henry VII 1485–1494*, 306.
19. Orme, 23.
20. *ODNB,* http://www.oxforddnb.com.libaccess.sjlibrary.org/view/article/16667.
21. André, 43.
22. Kipling, *Triumph,* 18.
23. *Calendar Spain,* 3.
24. *Calendar Spain,* 4 ff.

25. *Materials*, 2: 376.
26. *Materials*, 2: 499.
27. *CPR Henry VII 1485–1494*, 314.
28. *Materials*, 2: 544–46.
29. *CPR Henry VII 1485–1494*, 407.
30. *CPR Henry VII 1485–1494*, 438, 441.
31. *CPR Henry VII 1485–1494*, 453.
32. *Calendar Spain*, 24.
33. *Calendar Spain*, 33.
34. *Calendar Spain*, 39.
35. Sutton and Visser-Fuchs, "Royal Burials," 451–57; Okerlund, 257–59.
36. Sutton and Visser-Fuchs, "Royal Burials," 457.
37. Hayward, 62.
38. *CPR Henry VII 1485–92*, 369–70.
39. *GC* 246–47; *Vitellius*, 197; A. F. Pollard, ed. *The Reign of Henry VII from Contemporary Sources* (New York: London, 1913. Reprint AMS Press, 1967), 1: 91.

Chapter 12. Festivals and Challenges

1. Pollard, 1: *lii*, 91–92.
2. *GC*, 245.
3. *Chronicles of London*, ed. Charles Lethbridge Kingsford (Oxford: Clarendon Press, 1905), 323.
4. *GC*, 251.
5. *GC*, 251–52.
6. *GC*, 252.
7. Ann Wroe, *The Perfect Prince* (New York: Random House, 2003), 116.
8. Wroe, 125 ff.
9. Wroe, 163–65.
10. *Letters of the Kings*, 172.
11. Wroe, 107 ff.
12. Wroe, 126–29.
13. Wroe, 152.
14. *L & P*, 1: 388.
15. *Vitellius*, 201.
16. *L & P*, 1: 389.
17. *L & P*, 1: 392.
18. *The Paston Letters 1422–1509*, ed. James Gairdner (London: Chatto and Windus, 1904), 6: 152.
19. *L & P*, 1: 394.
20. *Vitellius*, 202.
21. *L & P*, 1: 398.

22. *GC*, 255.
23. *Vitellius*, 202.
24. *CPR Henry VII A.D. 1494–1509*, 14.
25. *GC*, 260; *Vitellius*, 207.
26. *Vitellius*, 206.
27. *Vitellius*, 210.
28. James Gairdner, *History of the Life and Reign of Richard the Third to which is added the Story of Perkin Warbeck* (Cambridge: Cambridge University Press, 1898; Reprint New York: Kraus, 1968), 306.
29. *Vitellius*, 213–16.
30. *Vitellius*, 213.
31. Pollard, 2: 331.
32. Pollard, 2: 331–48.
33. *Vitellius*, 217.
34. Wroe, 369.
35. Wendy Moorhen, "Four Weddings and a Conspiracy: the Life, Times and Loves of Lady Katherine Gordon. Part I," *The Ricardian* 12 (2002), 409, 422, n. 70.
36. Wroe, 375.
37. *GC*, 262.
38. *L & P*, 2: 73–74.
39. *Vitellius*, 218.
40. Gairdner, *Richard III*, 329.
41. Wroe, 387.
42. *Calendar Venice*, 1: 266.
43. Kipling, *Triumph*, 3.
44. *Vitellius*, 222.
45. Wroe, 440–41.
46. *Calendar Venice*, 267.
47. *Calendar Milan*, 341.
48. Vergil, *Anglica*, 119.
49. *L & P*, 1: 113–14.
50. *Calendar Spain*, 205.

Chapter 13. The Person Behind the Persona

1. *Calendar Spain*, 11.
2. *Calendar Spain*, 160.
3. *Calendar Venice*, 264.
4. Malcolm Underwood, "The Pope, the Queen and the King's Mother: or, the Rise and Fall of Adriano Castellesi," *The Reign of Henry VII: Proceedings of the 1993 Harlaxton Symposium* ed. Benjamin Thompson (Stamford: Paul Watkins, 1995), 73.
5. *Excerpta*, 85–133.

6. Bacon, 80.
7. Thurley, 19–21.
8. Francis Morgan Nichols, *The Epistles of Erasmus from His Earliest Letters to His Fifty-First Year* (New York: Russell & Russell, 1962), 201.
9. *Excerpta,* III, 94.
10. *Excerpta,* 125.
11. *Excerpta,* 88; Anglo, "Court Festivals," 29, 31.
12. *Excerpta,* 125, 133.
13. *Excerpta,* 126.
14. Roger Bowers, "Early Tudor Courtly Song: An Evaluation of the Fayrfax Book (BL, Additional MS 5465)," *The Reign of Henry VII: Proceedings of the 1993 Harlaxton Symposium,* ed. Benjamin Thompson (Stamford: Paul Watkins, 1995), 195.
15. John Stevens, *Music & Poetry in the Early Tudor Court* (London: Methuen and Co, 1961), 3 ff.
16. Quoted from Stevens, 382.
17. Sutton and Visser-Fuchs, "Device," 17 ff.
18. Fiona Kisby, "Courtiers in the Community: The Musicians of the Royal Household Chapel in Early Tudor Westminster," *The Reign of Henry VII: Proceedings of the 1993 Harlaxton Symposium,* ed. Benjamin Thompson (Stamford: Paul Watkins, 1995), 240.
19. Anglo, "Court Festivals," 21 ff.
20. Anglo, "Court Festivals," 12–45.
21. Anglo, "Court Festivals," 14.
22. *Excerpta,* 88, 90, 90, 98, 103, 118, 119, 120, 125.
23. *Excerpta,* 95.
24. *Excerpta,* 129.
25. *Excerpta,* 89, 95.
26. *Excerpta,* 91, 96, 97, 97, 106, 107, 112, 112, 117, 124, 129.
27. *Excerpta,* 96, 117.
28. *Excerpta,* III, 127.
29. *Excerpta,* 132.
30. *Excerpta,* 88, 93, 103, 106, 89, 121.
31. *Excerpta,* 94, 98, 108, 122, 99.
32. *Excerpta,* 133, 95, 106.
33. British Library, Additional MS 50001.
34. "Offices of the Virgin" (Stonyhurst College), MS 37.
35. Clark, n. 45.
36. Yale Center for British Art, Paul Mellon Collection, a_4v.
37. British Library, Additional MS 17012, f. 21.
38. Charity Meier-Ewert, "A Middle English Version of the Fifteen Oes," *Modern Philology* 68 (1971), 355.
39. Laynesmith, III.

40. *Antiquarian Repertory,* 1: 175.
41. Margaret E. Thompson, *The Carthusian Order in England* (London: Society for Promoting Christian Knowledge, 1930), 195.
42. Thompson, 195.
43. Thompson, 196.
44. *Calendar Spain,* 178.
45. *Calendar Spain,* 154.
46. *Calendar Spain,* 191–92.
47. *Calendar Spain,* 146.
48. *Calendar Spain,* 146.
49. *Calendar Spain,* 228.
50. *Letters of Royal and Illustrious Ladies of Great Britain from the Commencement of the Twelfth Century to the Close of the Reign of Queen Mary,* ed. Mary Anne Everett Wood (London: Henry Colburn, 1846), 114–16.
51. *Calendar Spain,* 156.
52. *Calendar Spain,* 255.
53. *Calendar Spain,* 212.
54. Anne Crawford, *Letters of the Queens of England 1100–1547* (Stroud: Alan Sutton, 1994), 158.
55. *Calendar of the Close Rolls Preserved in the Public Record Office: Edward IV, Edward V, and Richard III A.D. 1476–1485* (London: Her Majesty's Stationery Office, 1954), 2: 119.
56. Laynesmith, 249 passim.
57. *L & P,* 2: 102.
58. *L & P,* 2: 87–92; Pollard, 1: 214–15.
59. Kipling, *Triumph,* 41, n. 2.
60. *Calendar Spain,* 226–27.
61. Kipling, *Triumph,* 9 ff.
62. *Calendar Spain,* 227.
63. Pollard, 1: 215.
64. *Excerpta,* 124.
65. *Excerpta,* 124.

Chapter 14. A Princess Arrives in England

1. *Vitellius,* 229.
2. *Paston* 6: 161.
3. *L & P,* 1: 409.
4. *Calendar Spain,* 209.
5. *Antiquarian Repertory,* 2: 252; *The Receyt of the Ladie Kateryne,* ed. Gordon Kipling (Oxford: University Press for the Early English Text Society, 1990), 114, n. 16.

6. *Calendar Spanish*, 1: 256, 261; *Antiquarian Repertory*, 2: 252.
7. *Antiquarian Repertory*, 2: 253; *Receyt*, 5.
8. *Receyt*, 7.
9. *Receyt*, 7.
10. *Receyt*, 7.
11. *Receyt*, 9.
12. *Receyt*, 9.
13. *Receyt*, 9.
14. *Receyt*, 10.
15. Kipling, *Triumph*, 118–19 ff.
16. *Receyt*, 12–15. See Kipling, *Triumph*, 80–95, and Anglo, *Spectacle*, 56–97, for extended descriptions and analyses of the pageants.
17. *Receyt*, 15–21.
18. *GC*, 301.
19. *GC*, 301.
20. *Receyt*, 22.
21. *Receyt*, 26.
22. *GC*, 304–5.
23. *Antiquarian Repertory*, 2: 274; *Receyt*, 26–27.
24. *GC*, 306.
25. *Receyt*, 29.
26. *GC*, 306; *Antiquarian Repertory*, 2: 277; *Receyt, 30.*
27. *Receyt*, 31.
28. *Receyt*, 31.
29. *Receyt*, 31.
30. *Receyt*, 32.
31. *Receyt*, 32.
32. *Receyt*, 35; 141, n. 813.
33. *Receyt*, 37.

Chapter 15. A Royal Wedding

1. *GC*, 311.
2. *Receyt*, 44.
3. *Receyt*, 44; 148, n. 241.
4. *Receyt*, 46.
5. *Receyt*, 46–47.
6. *Receyt*, 149, n. 304.
7. *Receyt*, 46–47.
8. Edward Hall, *Hall's Chronicle; Containing the History of England, during the Reign of Henry the Fourth, and the Succeeding Monarchs, to the End of the Reign of Henry the Eight.* (1548. Reprint, New York: AMS Press, 1965), 494.

9. *Letters and Papers, Foreign and Domestic, of the Reign of Henry VIII,* ed. J. S. Brewer, J. Gairdner, and R. H. Brodie (London: Her Majesty's Stationery Office, 1876), 4: Part 3, 2577.
10. *L & P Henry VIII,* 4: Part 3, 2580.
11. *L & P Henry VIII,* 4: ccccxvii.
12. *Receyt,* 47.
13. *GC,* 312.
14. *GC,* 312.
15. *Receyt,* 53.
16. *GC,* 311–12.
17. *Receyt,* 58.
18. *Receyt,* 59.
19. *Receyt,* 60.
20. *Receyt,* 63.
21. *Excerpta,* 208; Okerlund, 93.
22. *Receyt,* 68.
23. Pollard, 1: 220.
24. *Receyt,* 71–72.
25. Kipling, *Triumph,* 31–40.
26. *Receyt,* 73,
27. *Receyt,* 73.
28. Thurley, 35.
29. Thurley, 35–36.
30. Kipling, *Triumph,* 15–40 passim.
31. *Receyt,* 75.
32. *Receyt,* 76.
33. *Receyt,* 77.

Chapter 16. Euphoria Turns Tragic

1. *GC,* 314–15.
2. *Foedera,* 12, 328–29.
3. Chrimes, 89, 284; *Foedera,* 12, 572–73, 635–36.
4. *Calendar Spain,* 105.
5. *Calendar Spain,* 176.
6. Leland, 4: 258–65.
7. Leland, 4: 261.
8. Leland, 4: 262.
9. *GC,* 317.
10. Leland, 4: 263.
11. Leland, 4: 264.
12. *CPR Henry VII 1494–1509,* 2: 289.
13. *Receyt,* 79.
14. Leland, 5: 373–74; *Receyt,* 80–81.

Chapter 17. The Queen's Last Year

1. *PP*, 46, 51.
2. Thurley, 75.
3. *PP*, 7.
4. *PP*, 16.
5. *PP*, 34.
6. *PP*, 33.
7. *PP*, 68.
8. *PP*, 17, 34.
9. *PP*, 54.
10. *PP*, 98.
11. *PP*, 40.
12. *PP*, 45.
13. *PP*, 28–29.
14. *PP*, 40.
15. *PP*, 1.
16. *PP*, 85, 74.
17. *PP*, 33.
18. *PP*, 37.
19. *PP*, 50.
20. *PP*, 59.
21. *PP*, 85.
22. *PP*, 1.
23. *PP*, 5, 31, 33, 57, 80 ff.
24. *PP*, 56, 57.
25. Bryan Little, *Abbeys and Priories in England and Wales* (New York: Holmes and Meier, 1979), 49.
26. *PP*, 8–9.
27. *PP*, 57
28. *PP*, 1, 102.
29. *PP*, 3, 4, 96.
30. *PP*, 32, 5.
31. *PP*, 52.
32. *PP*, 64.
33. *PP*, 64.
34. *PP*, 74, 93.
35. *PP*, 78,
36. *PP*, 11, 40, 63.
37. *PP*, 50.
38. *PP*, 76, 96–97.
39. *PP*, 105,
40. *PP*, 14.
41. *PP*, 4.
42. *PP*, 18.

43. *PP*, 70.
44. *PP*, 23.
45. *PP*, 46, 64.
46. *PP*, 34, 46, 69, 75, 81, 85, 96.
47. *PP*, 23, 38.
48. *PP*, 78.
49. *PP*, 78.
50. *PP*, 6, 24, 26, 61.
51. *PP*, 74–75.
52. *PP*, 23, 30, 67, 77.
53. Muriel St. Clare Byrne and Bridget Boland, *The Lisle Letters: An Abridgement* (Chicago: University of Chicago Press, 1983), 13.
54. *PP*, 29, 99.
55. *PP*, 49–50.
56. *PP*, 99.
57. *PP*, 9, 79, 94.
58. *PP*, 20, 25, 32, 62, 63, 70, 75, 77, 88, 100, 103, 104.
59. *PP*, 32, 103.
60. Jones and Underwood, 134.
61. Jones and Underwood, 134–35.
62. Jones and Underwood, 162.
63. *PP*, 10, 103.
64. *PP*, 14, 54.
65. *PP*, 48, 94.
66. *PP*, 61.
67. *PP*, 69.
68. *PP*, 22, 29, 88–89, 93.
69. *PP*, 19.
70. *PP*, 38.
71. *PP*, 22.
72. *PP*, 14.
73. *PP*, 8.
74. *PP*, 76.
75. *PP*, 110.
76. Chrimes, 15, 16 n. 4.
77. Kingsford, *English Historical Literature*, 387.
78. *PP*, 37.
79. *PP*, 38, 45 ff.
80. *PP*, 40.
81. *PP*, 45.
82. *PP*, 46, 47.
83. *PP*, 46.
84. *PP*, 45–47.
85. *PP*, 51.

86. Anthony Emery, "The Development of Raglan Castle and Keeps in Late Medieval England," *Archaeological Journal* 132 (1975), 167.
87. Emery, 160–61.
88. Emery, 180, n. 117.
89. Kirstie Buckland, "The Skenfrith Cope and Its Companions," *Textile History* 14 (1983), 136–38.
90. Rupert H. Morris, "The Skenfrith Cope," *Archaeologia Cambrensis: A Record of the Antiquities of Wales and Its Marches and the Journal of the Cambrian Archaeological Association* 64 (1909), 39.
91. *PP*, 10.
92. *PP*, 17, 19, 22, 65.
93. *PP*, 194.
94. Buckland, 138.
95. Laynesmith, *Last Medieval Queens*, 233.
96. *PP*, 19.
97. *PP*, 40, 55, 60, 64, 67, 92, 92, 97, 98.
98. *PP*, 12.
99. *PP*, 11.
100. *PP*, 7, 35.
101. *PP*, 34. 68, 80.
102. *PP*, 80, 31.
103. *PP*, 16, 56, 103, 37.
104. *PP*, 18, 30, 45, 62, 97.
105. *PP*, 43.
106. *PP*, 7, 102.
107. *PP*, 31.
108. *PP*, 26.
109. *PP*, 43, 52, 84.
110. *PP*, 53.
111. British Library Additional MS 59899; Thurley, 35.
112. *PP*, 48.
113. *GC*, 320, 450; *Vitellius*, 258.

Chapter 18. Death of a Queen

1. *PP*, 62, 69.
2. *PP*, 65.
3. *PP*, 68.
4. *PP*, 78.
5. *PP*, 79.
6. *PP*, 78; Leyser, 129.
7. *PP*, 80–81.
8. *PP*, 81, 83.

9. *PP*, 84.
10. *Excerpta*, 120.
11. *PP*, 95, 89.
12. *PP*, 95.
13. *Vitellius*, 258.
14. *GC*, 321.
15. *PP*, 97.
16. *PP*, 93.
17. *PP*, 110.
18. *Antiquarian Repertory*, 4: 655.
19. *Antiquarian Repertory*, 4: 655.
20. *Antiquarian Repertory*, 4: 656.
21. Hayward, 65.
22. Hayward, 65.
23. *Antiquarian Repertory*, 4: 658.
24. *Antiquarian Repertory*, 4: 659, *GC*, 322.
25. *Antiquarian Repertory*, 4: 659.
26. Hayward, 65.
27. *Antiquarian Repertory*, 4: 662–63.
28. *Antiquarian Repertory*, 4: 663.
29. *Excerpta*, 130.
30. Chrimes, 416.
31. Sutton and Visser-Fuchs, "Royal Burials," 451–57; Okerlund, 257–59.
32. *Excerpta*, 130.
33. *Excerpta*, 130, 132.
34. The treasurer's records are extant for the years 1506–9. Between October 1502 and April 1505, the records have been lost, and supplementary extracts recorded by Craven Orde are incomplete. Anglo, "Court Festivals," 12–13, 40, 41, 43, 44.
35. Hugh Tait, "The Hearse-Cloth of Henry VII Belonging to the University of Cambridge," *Journal of the Warburg and Courtauld Institutes* 19 (1956), 294.
36. *Antiquarian Repertory*, 4: 655.
37. Pollard, 3: 289.
38. *Calendar Venice*, 1, No. 833.
39. *Vitellius*, 258.
40. Vergil, *Anglica*, 7, 113.
41. André, 37.

Chapter 19. Legacy

1. *Excerpta*, 130.
2. Orme, 23–41, 155, passim.

3. *Calendar Spain,* 272.
4. *Calendar Spain,* 329.
5. *Calendar Spain,* 329–30.
6. *Calendar Spain,* 386.
7. *Calendar Spanish,* 404 ff.
8. *Excerpta,* 133.
9. B. P. Wolffe, "Henry VII's Land Revenues and Chamber Finance," *English Historical Review* 79 (1964), 253–54.

BIBLIOGRAPHY

Biographies

Harvey, Nancy Lenz. *Elizabeth of York: The Mother of Henry VIII.* New York: Macmillan, 1973.

Nicolas, Nicholas Harris. "Memoir of Elizabeth of York," *Privy Purse Expenses of Elizabeth of York: Wardrobe Accounts of Edward IV.* London: William Pickering, 1830; facsimile New York: Barnes & Noble, 1972.

Strickland, Agnes. *Lives of the Queens of England.* Vol. 1. Chicago: Belford, Clarke, 1843.

Primary Sources

André, Bernard. *De Vita Atque Gestis Henrici Septimi Historia.* Ed. James Gairdner in *Memorials of King Henry VII.* London, 1858.

The Antiquarian Repertory: A Miscellaneous Assemblage of Topography, History, Biography, Customs and Manners. Ed. Francis Grose and Thomas Astle. 4 vols. London: Edward Jeffery, 1807.

Bodleian Library, University of Oxford, MS 264, *The Romance of Alexander.*

British library Harleian manuscript 433. Ed. Rosemary Horrax and P.W. Hammond. 4 vols. Gloucester: Alan Sutton for The Richard III Society, 1979–83.

British Library. *Acts of Sovereigns and other Supreme Authorities.* Louis XI, King. William Machlinia: London, 1483.

———. Additional MS 17012: *Horae B. Mariae.*

———. Additional MS 19398, Original Letters: Vol. 1, f. 35.

———. Additional MS 50001: *The Hours of Elizabeth the Queen.*

———. Additional MS 59899: *Chamber Issue and Memoranda Book of Henry VII, 1502–1505.*

———. Cotton Tiberius E. X. f. 238v. Buc, Sir George, "*A history of King Richard III.*"

British Library. Harley 49, f. 155: *Tristan.*

——. Royal 14 E iii. *Romance of the Saint Graal.*

——. Royal 20 A xix, f. 195: Boethius, *De consolatione Philosophiae.*

——. Cotton Vespasian F. xiii, f. 49.

Calendar of the Close Rolls Preserved in the Public Record Office: Edward IV, Edward V, and Richard III A.D. 1476–1485. London: Her Majesty's Stationery Office, 1954.

Calendar of Letters, Despatches, and State Papers, relating to the negotiations between England and Spain, preserved in the Archives at Simancas and elsewhere: Henry VII. 1485–1509. Vol. 1. Ed. G. A. Bergenroth. London: Longman, 1862.

Calendar of Papal Letters. Vols. 11 and 14. London: Her Majesty's Stationery Office, 1960.

Calendar of the Patent Rolls: Edward IV. Henry VI A .D. 1467–1477. London: Her Majesty's Stationery Office, 1900.

——. *Henry VII A. D. 1485–1494. Vol. 1.* London: His Majesty's Stationery Office, 1914.

——. *Henry VII A. D. 1494–1509. Vol. 2.* London: His Majesty's Stationery Office, 1916.

Calendar of State Papers and manuscripts, existing in the Archives and Collections of Milan. Vol. 1. Ed. Allen B. Hinds. London: His Majesty's Stationery Office, 1912.

Calendar of State Papers and Manuscripts, relating to English Affairs, existing in the Archives and Collections of Venice, and in other Libraries of Northern Italy. Vol. 1: 1202–1509. Ed Rawdon Brown. London: Longman, Green, 1864.

Christ Church, Canterbury: The Chronicle of John Stone, Monk of Christ Church 1415–1471. Cambridge: Antiquarian Society, 1902.

Chronicles of London. Ed. Charles Lethbridge Kingsford. Oxford: Clarendon Press, 1905.

Commines, Philippe de. *The Memoires of Philip de Commines, Lord of Argeton.* Ed. Andrew R. Scoble. London: Henry G. Bohn, 1855. An online edition is available at http://www.r3.org.

Cornazzano, Antonio. "La Regina d'ingliterra" quoted from Conor Fahy's "The Marriage of Edward IV and Elizabeth Woodville: A New Italian source," *English Historical Review* 76 (1961), 660–72.

The Coronation of Elizabeth Wydeville: Queen Consort of Edward IV on May 26th, 1465. Ed George Smith. London: 1935; reprint Gloucester, 1975.

The Coventry Leet Book: Or Mayor's Register. Ed. Mary Dormer Harris. London: Early English Text Society. 1907–13.

"The Cristenynge of Prince Arthure, sonne to Kynge Henrie ye VII. at Sent Swithins in Winchester," *Three Fifteenth-Century Chronicles, with Historical Memoranda by John Stowe, the Antiquary.* Ed. James Gairdner. Westminster: Printed for the Camden Society, 1880.

The Crowland Chronicle Continuations: 1459–1486. Ed. Nicholas Pronay and John Cox. London: Alan Sutton,, 1986. An online edition is available at http://www.r3.org.

Ellis, Henry. *Original Letters, Illustrative of English History.* New York: AMS Press, 1970.

Excerpta Historica, or Illustrations of English History. London: Samuel Bentley, 1831.

Fabyan, Robert. *The New Chronicles of England and France.* Ed. Henry Ellis. London: F. C. & J. Rivington, 1811.

Foedera. Ed. Thomas Rymer. Vols. 10, 11, 12. London: J. Tonson, 1728–35.

The Great Chronicle of London. Ed. A. H. Thomas and I. D. Thornley. London: George Jones, 1938.

Hall, Edward. *Hall's Chronicle; Containing the History of England, during the Reign of Henry the Fourth, and the Suceeding Monarchs, to the End of the Reign of Henry the Eight.* 1548; reprint New York: AMS Press, 1965.

The Household of Edward IV: The Black Book and the Ordinance of 1478. Ed. A. R. Myers. Manchester: University Press, 1959.

Hylton, Walter. *Scala perfectionis.* Westminster: Wynkyn de Worde, 1494.

Illustrations of ancient state and chivalry from manuscripts preserved in the Ashmolean museum. Ed. William Henry. London: W. Nicol, 1840.

Lease Book Number 1, 1486–1595, Westminster Abbey, f. 9.

Leland, John. *De rebus Brittanicus Collectanea.* Ed. T. Hearne. 6 vols. London: Benjamin White, 1774.

Letters and Papers, Foreign and Domestic, of the Reign of Henry VIII. Ed. J. S. Brewer, J. Gairdner, and R.H. Brodie. 21 vols. London: Her Majesty's Stationery Office, 1876.

Letters and Papers Illustrative of the Reigns of Richard III and Henry VII. Ed. James Gairdner. 2 vols. London: Longman, Green, Longman, and Roberts, 1861.

Letters of Royal and Illustrious Ladies of Great Britain from the Commencement of the Twelfth Century to the Close of the Reign of Queen Mary. Ed. Mary Anne Everett Wood. Vol. 1. London: Henry Colburn, 1846.

Letters of the Kings of England. Ed. James Orchard Halliwell. London: Henry Colburn, 1846.

Mancinus, Dominicus. *The Usurpation of Richard the Third.* Translated C. A. J. Armstrong. 2nd ed. Oxford: Clarendon Press, 1969.

Materials for a History of the Reign of Henry VII From Original Documents preserved in the Public Record Office. Ed. William Campbell. 2 vols. London: Longman and Turbner, 1873

Memorials of King Henry VII. Ed. James Gairdner. London: Longman, Brown, Green, Langmans, and Roberts, 1858.

"Offices of the Virgin." MS 37. Stonyhurst College.

The Paston Letters 1422–1509. Ed. James Gairdner. London: Chatto and Windus, 1904.

Pollard, A.F., ed. *The Reign of Henry VII from Contemporary Sources.* 3 vols. London: 1913; reprint AMS Press, 1967.

Privy Purse Expenses of Elizabeth of York: Wardrobe Accounts of Edward IV. Ed. Nicholas Harris Nicolas, Esq. London: William Pickering, 1830; facsimile New York: Barnes & Noble, 1972. An online edition is available at http://www.r3.org.

The Receyt of the Ladie Kateryne. Ed. Gordon Kipling. Oxford: University Press for the Early English Text Society, 1990.

Records of the Borough of Nottingham, being a series of extracts from the archives of the Corporation of Nottingham. Vol. 3 (1485–1547).

Registrum Thome Bourgchier, Cantuariensis Archiepiscopi, AD 1454–1486. Ed. F. R. H. DuBoulay. Canterbury and York Society, Liv, 1957.

Rotuli Parliamentorum. Vol. 6. London, 1832.

"Stowe's Memoranda," *Three Fifteenth Century Chronicles.* Ed. James Gardner. Camden Society, 1880.

Testament de Amyra Sultan Nichemedy, Empereur des Turcs. Constantinople: 12 Sept. 1481; facsimile Istanbul University, 1952. (Edition signed by Elizabeth is Garrett MS. 168, Collection of Medieval and Renaissance Manuscripts, Princeton University Library.)

The Travels of Leo of Rozmital through Germany, Flanders, England, France, Spain, Portugal and Italy 1465–1467, Ed. Malcolm Letts. Cambridge: University Press, 1957.

Titulus Regius. http://www.r3.org/bookcase/texts/tit_reg.html

Two Fifteenth-Century Cookery-Books. Ed. Thomas Austin. London: Oxford University Press, 1888; reprint 1964.

Vergil, Polydore. *Three Books of Polydore Vergil's English History, comprising the Reigns of Henry VI., Edward IV., and Richard III.* Ed. Henry Ellis. London: John Bowyer Nichols 1844.

———. *The Anglica Historia of Polydore Vergil A.D. 1485–1537.* Ed. Denys Hay. *Camden Series* 74 (1950) © Royal Historical Society, 1950.

Vitellius A XVI in *Chronicles of London.* Ed. Charles Lethbridge Kingsford. Oxford: Clarendon Press, 1905.

"Wardrobe Accounts of Edward the Fourth" in *Privy Purse Expenses of Elizabeth of York.* Ed. Nicholas Harris Nicolas, Esq. London: William Pickering, 1830; facsimile New York: Barnes & Noble, 1972.

Wills from Doctors' Commons: A Selection from the Wills of Eminent Persons proved in the Prerogative Court of Canterbury, 1495–1695. Ed. John Nichols and John Bruce. Westminster: Camden Society O.S., 1863.

Secondary Sources

Anglo, Sydney. "The British History in Early Tudor Propaganda," *Bulletin of the John Rylands Library* 44 (1960–61): 12–48.

———. "The Court Festivals of Henry VII: A Study Based Upon the Account Books of John Heron, Treasurer of the Chamber," *Bulletin of the John Rylands Library* 44 (1960): 12–45.

———. "The Foundation of the Tudor Dynasty: The Coronation and Marriage of Henry VII," *Guildhall Miscellany* 2 (1960): 3–11.

———. *Spectacle, Pageantry, and Early Tudor Policy.* Oxford: Clarendon Press, 1969.

Anstis, John, ed. *The Register of the Most Noble Order of the Garter, from Its Cover in Black Velvet Usually Called the Black Book.* London: John Barber, 1724.

Ashdown-Hill, John. "Edward IV's Uncrowned Queen: The Lady Eleanor Talbot, Lady Butler," *Ricardian* 11 (1997): 166–90.

Ashmole, Elias. *The Institution, Laws & Ceremonies of the Most Noble Order of the Garter.* London, 1672; reprint Baltimore: Genealogical Publishing, 1971.

Backhouse, Janet. "Illuminated Manuscripts Associated with Henry VII and Members of His Immediate Family," *The Reign of Henry VII: Proceedings of the 1993 Harlaxton Symposium.* Ed. Benjamin Thompson. Stamford: Paul Watkins, 1995, 175–87.

Bacon, Francis. *The History of the Reign of King Henry the Seventh.* Ed. F. J. Levy. New York: Bobbs-Merrill, 1972.

Baldwin, David. *Elizabeth Woodville: Mother of the Princes in the Tower.* Stroud: Sutton, 2002.

Bennett, Michael. *Lambert Simnel and the Battle of Stoke.* New York: St. Martin's Press, 1987.

Bober, Phyllis Pray. *Art, Culture, & Cuisine: Ancient and Medieval Gastronomy.* Chicago: University of Chicago Press, 1999.

Bowers, Roger. "Early Tudor Courtly Song: An Evaluation of the Fayrfax Book (BL, Additional MS 5465," *The Reign of Henry VII: Proceedings of the 1993 Harlaxton Symposium.* Ed. Benjamin Thompson. Stamford: Paul Watkins, 1995, 188–212.

Brown, R. Allen, H. M. Colvin, and A. J. Taylor. *The History of the King's Works: Vol. II The Middle Ages.* London: Her Majesty's Stationery Office, 1963.

Buck, George. *The History of King Richard the Third (1619).* Ed. Arthur Noel Kincaid. Gloucester: Alan Sutton, 1979.

Buckland, Kirstie. "The Skenfrith Cope and Its Companions," *Textile History* 14 (1983): 125–39.

Bühler, Curt. F. "The Dictes and Sayings of the Philosophers," *Library* 15 (1934): 316–29.

Butler, Lionel and Chris Given-Wilson. *Medieval Monasteries of Great Britain*. London: Michael Joseph, 1979.

Byrne, Muriel St. Claire and Bridget Boland. *The Lisle Letters: An Abridgement*. Chicago: University of Chicago, 1983.

"Caxton's Patrons," http://www.bl.uk/treasures/caxton/patrons.html#two.

Clarke, Peter D. "English Royal Marriages and the Papal Penitentiary in the Fifteenth Century," *English Historical Review* 120. 488 (2005): 1014–1029. http://ehr.oxfordjournals.org/cgi/content/full/120/488/1014.

Chrimes, S. B. *Henry VII*. Berkeley: University of California, 1972.

Collins, Hugh E. L. *The Order of the Garter 1348–1461: Chivalry and Politics in Late Medieval England*. Oxford: Clarendon Press, 2000.

The Complete Peerage of England, Scotland, Ireland, Great Britain and the United Kingdom. Ed. George Edward Cokayne. New York: St. Martin's Press, 1984.

Cosman, Madeleine Pelner. *Fabulous Feasts: Medieval Cookery and Ceremony*. New York: George Braziller, 1976.

Crawford, Anne. "The King's Burden?—The Consequences of Royal Marriage in Fifteenth-Century England," *Patronage, the Crown, and the Provinces in Later Medieval England*. Ed. Ralph A. Griffiths. Gloucester: Alan Sutton, 1981.

———. *Letters of the Queens of England 1100–1547*. Stroud: Alan Sutton, 1994.

———. *The Yorkists: The History of a Dynasty*. London: Hambledon Continuum, 2007.

Croft, P. J. *Lady Margaret Beaufort, Countess of Richmond: Descriptions of Two Unique Volumes Associated with One of the First Patrons of Printing in England*. London, Bernard Quaritch, 1958.

Cunningham, Sean. *Henry VII*. London: Routledge, 2007.

Dictionary of National Biography. Ed. Leslie Stephen and Sidney Lee. 22 vols. New York: Macmillan, 1908–9.

Emery, Anthony. "The Development of Raglan Castle and Keeps in Late Medieval England," *Archaeological Journal* 132 (1975): 151–86.

Gairdner, James. *History of the Life and Reign of Richard the Third to Which Is Added the Story of Perkin Warbeck*. Cambridge: Cambridge University Press, 1898; reprint New York: Kraus, 1968.

Gray, Sheila, Winchester Cathedral Voluntary Guide. Personal correspondence.

Griffiths, Ralph A. and Roger S. Thomas. *The Making of the Tudor Dynasty*. Stroud: Sutton, 2005.

Hales, John W. and Frederick J. Furnivall, eds. *Bishop Percy's Folio Manuscript: Ballads and Romances*. Vol. 3. London: N. Trübner, 1868.

Hammond, P. W. "The Coronation of Elizabeth of York," *Ricardian* 83 (1983): 270–72.

———. *Food and Feast in Medieval England*. Stroud: Alan Sutton, 1993.

Hampton, W. E. "A Further Account of Robert Stillington," *Ricardian* 4 (1976): 24–27.

Hanham, Alison "Sir George Buck and Princess Elizabeth's Letter: A Problem in Detection," *Ricardian* 7 (June 1987): 398–400.

Harrod, Henry. "Queen Elizabeth Woodville's Visit to Norwich in 1469," *Norfolk Archaeology* 5 (1859): 32–37.

Hayward, Maria. *Dress at the Court of King Henry VIII.* Leeds: Maney, 2007.

Henisch, Bridget Ann. *Fast and Feast: Food in Medieval Society.* University Park: Pennsylvania State University, 1976.

Horrox, Rosemary. *Richard III: A Study of Service.* Cambridge: Cambridge University Press, 1989.

Horrox, Rosemary and P. W. Hammond. *British Library Harleian Manuscript 433.* Gloucester: Alan Sutton for the Richard III Society, 1979.

Jones, Michael K. *Bosworth 1485: Psychology of a Battle.* Stroud: Tempus, 2002.

Jones, Michael K. and Malcolm Underwood. *The King's Mother: Lady Margaret Beaufort, Countess of Richmond and Derby.* Cambridge: Cambridge University Press, 1992.

Kendall, Paul Murray. *Richard the Third.* New York: W. W. Norton, 1956.

Kincaid, Arthur. "Buck and the Elizabeth of York Letter: A Reply to Dr. Hanham," *Ricardian* 8 (March 1988): 46–49.

Kingsford, Charles Lethbridge. *English Historical Literature in the Fifteenth Century.* New York: Burt Franklin, 1963; reprint Oxford, 1913.

———. "Historical Notes on Mediaeval London Houses," *London Topographical Record* Vol. 10. London: London Topographical Society, 1916, 44–144.

Kipling, Gordon. *Enter the King: Theatre, Liturgy, and Ritual in the Medieval Civic Triumph.* Oxford: Clarendon Press, 1998.

———. *The Triumph of Honour: Burgundian Origins of the Elizabethan Renaissance.* Leiden: University Press (for the Sir Thomas Browne Institute), 1977.

Kisby, Fiona. "Courtiers in the Community: The Musicians of the Royal Household Chapel in Early Tudor Westminster," *The Reign of Henry VII: Proceedings of the 1993 Harlaxton Symposium.* Ed. Benjamin Thompson. Stamford: Paul Watkins, 1995, 229–60.

Knowles, Dom David. *The Religious Orders of England.* 3 vols. Cambridge: Cambridge University Press, 1971.

Laynesmith, J. L. "The Kings' Mother," *History Today* 56 (March 2006): 38–45.

———. *The Last Medieval Queens: English Queenship 1445–1503.* Oxford: Oxford University Press, 2004.

Laynesmith, J. L. "The People's Other Princess," *BBC History* (February 2003): 30–33.

Legg, Leopold George Wickham. *English Coronation Records.* London, 1901.

Leyser, Henrietta. *Medieval Women: A Social History of Women in England 450–1500.* London: Phoenix Press, 1996.

Little, Bryan. *Abbeys and Priories in England and Wales.* New York: Holmes and Meier, 1979.

London Topographical Record. Vol. 10. London: London Topographical Society, 1916.

Mattingly, Garrett. *Catherine of Aragon.* Boston: Little, Brown, 1941.

Meier-Ewert, Charity. "A Middle English Version of the Fifteen Oes," *Modern Philology* 68 (1971): 355–61.

Moorhen, Wendy. "Four Weddings and a Conspiracy: The Life, Times and Loves of Lady Katherine Gordon. Part I," *Ricardian* 12 (2002): 394–424.

———. "Part II," *Ricardian* 12 (2002): 446–78.

Morris, Rupert H. "The Skenfrith Cope," *Archaeologia Cambrensis: A Record of the Antiquities of Wales and Its Marches and the Journal of the Cambrian Archaeological Association* 64 (1909): 35–42.

Mowat, A. J. "Robert Stillington," *Ricardian* 4 (1976): 23–28.

Nichols, Francis Morgan. *The Epistles of Erasmus from His Earliest Letters to His Fifty-First Year.* 3 vols. New York: Russell & Russell, 1962.

Nichols, John Gough. *Autographs of Royal, Noble, Learned, and Remarkable Personages Conspicuous in English History, from the Reign of Richard the Second to That of Charles the Second.* London: J. B. Nichols and Son, 1829

Okerlund, Arlene. *Elizabeth Wydeville: The Slandered Queen.* Stroud: Tempus, 2005.

Orme, Nicholas. *From Childhood to Chivalry: The Education of the English Kings and Aristocracy 1066–1530.* London: Methuen, 1984.

Oxford Dictionary of National Biography. Oxford and New York: Oxford University Press, 2004–. Available online at http://www.oxforddnb.com.

Quaritch, Bernard. *Catalogue of Illuminated and Other Manuscripts.* London: Bernard Quaritch, 1931.

Renfrow, Cindy. *Take a Thousand Eggs or More.* 2nd ed. 1998.

Ross, Charles. *Edward IV.* Berkeley: University of California, 1974.

Rosser, Gervase. *Medieval Westminster 1200–1540.* Oxford: Clarendon Press, 1989.

Scharf, G. "On a Votive Painting of St. George and the Dragon, with Kneeling Figures of Henry VII, His Queen and Children," *Archaeologia* 49 (1886): 243–300.

Scofield, Cora. *The Life and Reign of Edward the Fourth.* 2 vols. London: Longmans, Green, 1923.

Stevens, John. *Music & Poetry in the Early Tudor Court*. London: Methuen, 1961.

Sutton, Anne F. and Livia Visser-Fuchs. "A 'Most Benevolent Queen': Queen Elizabeth Woodville's Reputation, her Piety and her Books," *Ricardian* 10 (June 1995): 214–45.

——. "The Device of Queen Elizabeth Woodville: A Gillyflower or Pink," *Ricardian* 11 (1997): 17–24.

——. *The Reburial of Richard Duke of York 21–30 July 1476*. London: The Richard III Society, 1996.

——. "Richard III's Books: X. The *Prose Tristan*," *Ricardian* 9 (1911): 23–37.

——. "The Royal Burials of the House of York at Windsor: II. Princess Mary, May 1482, and Queen Elizabeth Woodville, June 1492," *Ricardian* 11 (1999): 446–62.

Sutton, Anne F. and P. W. Hammond. *The Coronation of Richard III: The Extant Documents*. Gloucester: Alan Sutton, 1983.

Tait, Hugh. "The Hearse-Cloth of Henry VII Belonging to the University of Cambridge," *Journal of the Warburg and Courtauld Institutes* 19 (1956): 294–98.

Thompson, E. Margaret. *The Carthusian Order in England*. London: Society for Promoting Christian Knowledge, 1930.

Thurley, Simon. *The Royal Palaces of Tudor England: Architecture and Court Life 1460–1547*. New Haven and London: Yale University Press for the Paul Mellon Centre for Studies in British Art, 1993.

Underwood, Malcolm. "The Pope, the Queen and the King's Mother: Or, the Rise and Fall of Adriano Castellesi," *The Reign of Henry VII: Proceedings of the 1993 Harlaxton Symposium*. Ed. Benjamin Thompson. Stamford: Paul Watkins, 1995, 65–81.

Visser-Fuchs, Livia. "Elizabeth of York's Letter," *Ricardian Bulletin* (Winter 2004): 18–20.

——. "English Events in Caspar Weinreich's Danzig *Chronicle*, 1461–1495," *Ricardian* 7 (1989): 310–20.

——. "Where Did Elizabeth of York Find Consolation?" *Ricardian* (1991–93): 469–74.

Weightman, Christine. *Margaret of York, Duchess of Burgundy, 1446–1503*. New York: St. Martin's Press, 1989.

Weir, Alison. *Britain's Royal Families: The Complete Genealogy*. London: Pimlico, 2002.

Williams, Barrie. "Elizabeth of York's Last Journey," *Ricardian* 8 (1988): 18–19.

Wolffe, B. P. "Henry VII's Land Revenues and Chamber Finance," *English Historical Review* 79 (1964): 225–54.

Wroe, Ann. *The Perfect Prince*. New York: Random House, 2003.

INDEX

Lightning Source UK Ltd.
Milton Keynes UK
UKOW050736150312

189015UK00001B/5/P